EXPLORE THE FASCINATING WORLD OF YOUR DREAMS

☆ ☆ ☆

When you dream of:

Using a rake . . . . . Expect a happy family celebration.

Children at play . . . . . Expect success in love and personal relationships.

A barbecue . . . . . Expect friends and relatives to impose on you.

A circle . . . . . Expect joy beyond your greatest expectations.

Hearing footsteps . . . . . Expect to learn something that will be to your advantage.

Your office . . . . . Expect a change in your love life.

☆ ☆ ☆

From dreams of abandonment and danger to the serene symbol of the zither, 3,000 symbols and situations are alphabetically arranged for instant bedside reference. Including obvious symbols, symbols that have meanings contrary to what one might expect, and symbols with subtle emotional nuances, here is the key that opens the door to understanding your inner world of dreams.

About the authors

Born and educated in Ohio, Stearn Robinson worked as a journalist and then radio script writer. While living in Los Angeles at the peak of the glamorous Hollywood era, she wrote and produced a half-hour daily radio program for a West Coast network in which she originated the concept of integrated commercials.

She resigned the Vice-Presidency of a New York advertising agency at the time of her marriage to Sir Robert Robinson, world-renowned scientist and Nobel Laureate. Lady Robinson takes a lively interest in scientific matters, which she finds fascinating, and it was this which led to her creation of the first space-oriented animated cartoon series for children.

Lady Robinson has had a life-long interest in the interpretation of dreams prior to the writing of this book.

The well-known British psychic Tom Corbett has been linked by the press with leading figures in London society and royalty. His knowledge of ghosts was demonstrated in Diana Norman's *Tom Corbett's Stately Ghosts of England*; which *Publishers Weekly* called "very well written and fun to read."

THE
DREAMER'S
DICTIONARY

From A to Z . . .
3,000 Magical Mirrors
to Reveal the Meaning
of Your Dreams

LADY STEARN ROBINSON
& TOM CORBETT

GRAND CENTRAL
PUBLISHING

NEW YORK   BOSTON

This Hachette Book Group Edition is published by arrangement with Taplinger Publishing Company, Inc.

Cover design by Rachel McClain
Cover illustration by Stephanie Garcia

Grand Central Publishing
Hachette Book Group
1290 Avenue of the Americas
New York, NY 10104
Visit our website at www.HachetteBookGroup.com

Grand Central Publishing is a division of Hachette Book Group, Inc. The Grand Central Publishing name and logo is a trademark of Hachette Book Group, Inc.

The Hachette Speakers Bureau provides a wide range of authors for speaking events. To find out more, go to www.hachettespeakersbureau.com or call (866) 376-6591.

The publisher is not responsible for websites (or their content) that are not owned by the publisher.

Printed in the United States of America

First Hachette Book Group Paperback Printing, May 1975
Reissued, May 1994

63 62 61 60 59 58 57 56 55

*This book is dedicated to the memory of
Richard Taplinger,
without whose help and encouragement
it would not have been written.*

Introduction

From time immemorial dreams have been regarded with an interest transcending mere superstition. Their cause and their meaning have been the subject of study and investigation by learned men throughout the ages. The many references to records concerning dreams which turned out to be "events casting their shadows before them" can leave little doubt as to the importance of dreams in history.

What are dreams? Well, through the past centuries, dreams were defined as "states of consciousness occurring during sleep." We inherited this nebulous and paradoxical definition before the rise of physics; but since the mid-nineteenth century a great deal of scientific research has been done to try to establish more clearly the nature of dreams.

Dreaming certainly belongs to our most intimate experiences. Generally, during waking hours, our reaction to our experiences is mainly emotional. In our dreams it is even more emotional because dreams are a concentrating agent for our various subjective motives. They also constitute an interrelation between the now, the past, and the future of human experience. In our dreams we create a world where space and time have no limiting power. In his fascinating book *An Experiment with Time,* Professor Dunne proposes the theory that all the time that is now, has been, or will be is like a river, and that you can navigate this river, forward, backward, and presumably sideways, in the vessel of your dreams.

Herder, the German philosopher, states that dreams are

but the ideals of all poetic arts, while Jean Paul Richter, another German author, thinks that dreams are involuntary experiences leading to the composition of poetry. Both these writers concur with other great ones of the past, such as Nietzsche, Kant, and Novalis.

F. W. Hildebrandt wrote in 1875, "Dreams help us to inspect those hidden depths of our existence which are mostly beyond our reach during our waking hours. Dreams bring us such refined insight into self-knowledge and such revelations of half-conscious dispositions and powers that on waking up, we may well admire the sharp-eyed demon that helped us find the hidden plot. A dream can warn us from within with the voice of a watchman stationed at the central observatory of our spiritual life. And our dreams can also warn us of the dangerous steps we have already taken!"

Most dreams are in the form of visual images. And through visual images we are able to explore the human mind. Jung, the brilliant Swiss psychiatrist, pointed this out concisely when he stated, "Visual images have the quality of the human soul!" The mental pictures you can carry over the threshold of your consciousness are unimportant mites when compared to the wealth of dream imagery.

Every human emotion and experience can be reflected in dreams. Consider for a moment the infinite possibilities. A dream may be happy or sad; joyful or tragic; frightening or reassuring; full of love or bristling with hostility; it may be religious or sacrilegious, inspiring, depressing, or amusing and so on ad infinitum.

Through the ages dreams—and their interpretations—have been recorded on cave walls and stone slabs, and one can imagine thereby that those dreamers compared notes with each other on the happenings which followed, and so through some shaggy scientific-minded cave dweller began the study of the omens, prophecies, and warnings contained in dreams which have since been woven into the very fabric of life, until they have become a part of art, literature, and religion as well as science.

The ancient Assyrians, Babylonians, Egyptians, and others did a great deal to disseminate the dream lore of their times, and centuries later when Artimedorus compiled his Oneiro-critica on this subject, it proved so popular that sixteen hundred years later its first English translation had been reprinted thirty-two times by the year 1800. But besides the Greek, there are ancient dream books in many languages, such as Hebrew, Latin, French, Italian, German, Arabic, Russian, and even Siamese. Needless to say, no book on this subject can ever be completely comprehensive, for to be so it would have to cover the whole of human experience and knowledge.

Friedrich Hebbell, who was a dedicated student of dream problems, stated that "In dreams fantasy gets even with the shameless imp, Reason." And Cicero, the Roman statesman and author (106–43 B.C.), wrote almost two thousand years ago, "nothing can be so silly, so impossible, or so unnatural that it cannot happen in a dream." And today, almost two thousand years and mountains of research later, it is still true that nothing is either impossible or ridiculous in a dream; because a dream can be likened to a very private script, written, produced, and directed by the dreamer. Sometimes the dreamer takes the leading role, but in all cases he or she is the *only* audience, and each time he or she falls asleep, there is an opening of a new show, because everybody dreams—every night! At this point you may be saying, "*I* don't; maybe other people, but not *me!*" Which may seem to be a reasonable reaction, since even those who know they dream may claim to remember times when supposedly they didn't.

But reasonable or not, the reaction must be completely discounted. According to extensive scientific research, at the University of Chicago, Walter Reed Institute of Research, Harvard University, Mount Sinai Hospital, as well as countless learned institutions all over the world, it has been conclusively proved that *everybody* dreams *every* night. You may be wondering *how* such a fact could have been proved. The answer is by monitoring the nightly sleep of thousands of volunteers. By measuring their heart action, respiration, eye and body movements, brain waves, and, when indicated by these physical responses, awakening them throughout the night to inquire, "Were you dreaming?" Invariably the response was "yes," even from those who previous to the experiment had insisted they never dreamed. Furthermore these scientific studies found that you have a minimum of three dreams a night, but you can have as many as nine. It has already been established that the congenitally deaf and/or blind dream, that children as young as eight months dream, that people of very low IQ dream no less than those of very high IQ.

You may be among the small minority who remember most of your dreams in vivid detail; or you may belong to the large majority who remember only vague parts of your dream, or you may be one of the sizable group who forgets everything. But no matter what you do or don't remember about your dreams, and regardless of who or what you are, it is certain that you *do* dream. Dreaming is a natural process like breathing, and there is no way, except for the right combination of drugs, or overindulgence in alcohol, that you can prevent it.

As a matter of fact recent experiments with "dream withdrawal" suggest that, if you deprive a man of his dreams, you take a chance that he will eventually act out his psychotic tendencies while he's awake, and this, in turn, gives rise to the hypothesis currently propounded in some scientific circles that as dreams allow one to go safely and quietly insane for a time each day, it is not, as heretofore believed, the sleep that is necessary for our well-being, but the dreams.

Be that as it may, the extraordinary power of the subconscious mind to dramatize problems or assimilate material only partially comprehended by the conscious mind is spectacularly documented in the field of science itself. One of the more recent examples is that of physiologist Otto Loewi who dreamed one night of an experiment which might prove his theory concerning the transmission of nerve impulses. He set up the experiment in his laboratory exactly as he had dreamed it, and it worked, subsequently leading to Loewi's receiving a Nobel Prize.

And of course there is the celebrated case of the late nineteenth-century German chemist Friedrich August Kekule von Stradonitz who dreamed he saw a snake eating its own tail, thus forming a large ring. The dream inspired him to run tests which led to the discovery that the atoms in the benzene molecule were, in fact, arranged in a large—six carbon atoms—ring rather than the straight line arrangement previously visualized. This is considered to be one of the most important flashes of creative work in the whole field of organic chemistry.

An interesting contemporary case of clairvoyant dream solution in a different type of scientific discipline is that of the brilliant astrologer Hugh MacCraig who was trying to work out a table that would give the position of the moon from the year 1800 to that of the year 2000 in three simple steps. Not only Mr. MacCraig, but The Astrology Association of England, as well as the mathematicians at NASA and other places, were also working on the problem with no success. One night, to quote Mr. MacCraig, he "prayed on it" as he was going to bed and he awoke at 3:00 A.M. to find he had dreamed the solution. This mathematical table, which was subsequently proved to be accurate, appears in his book *Ephemeris of the Moon,* published in 1952.

Many modern psychotherapists are now of the opinion that we can learn to interpret and use our dreams, which they believe to be mainly an extension of the situation we live in when awake. This theory is amazingly (and amusingly) similar to that of the ancient interpreters who considered not only the dream content significant but also the personality and social/economic position of the dreamer.

Dr. Stanley Krippner, of the Maimonides Medical Center Dream Laboratory, suggests that our dreams can often be used to expose problems that we may refuse to recognize consciously and by so doing can lead to positive corrective action.

There are a great variety of theories as to what shapes dream content, but all authorities agree that dreams represent mental activity that occurs when conscious control is removed. It seems very likely that current avenues of investigation of DNA and RNA will eventually show that certain types of dreams now classified as "clairvoyant," "precognitive," or "retrocognitive" are locked into one's genetic coding through the experiences or emotions of one's ancestors.

Dreams have been veiled in mystery since the dawn of time, and in this century, which has already seen men exploring space and walking on the moon, it seems reasonable to assume that the veil will be at least partially lifted. Whatever the current scientific advances may be, there are many who remain interested in the old traditions and superstitions of "oracles," "omens," and "portents" in dreams, and the purpose of this book is to offer to those, for pleasure as well as for information a reference synthesis of ancient and modern interpretations.

Interpretation

To interpret your dreams you must bear in mind that the first step is to learn to distinguish between a valid prophetic dream and one that has no subconscious or clairvoyant significance.

Dreams of a prophetic nature usually occur to you during the deepest part of your night's sleep; for most of you this will be between 2:00 A.M. and 7:00 A.M. By this time digestion has usually been completed, your body muscles are normally relaxed, and your mind is mainly free of the day's events. Dreams which occur under these conditions are generally worth your efforts at interpretation.

Persistent or recurring dreams can be traced, almost invariably, to some physical or psychological cause and as a rule have no prophetic significance. However, a dream that recurs only two or three times is a different matter and should be seriously considered.

Dreams which have no significance (although they may be more vividly recalled than meaningful ones) are:

Those that you have after you have overeaten or over-indulged in alcohol before going to bed.

Those that can be traced to external physical conditions, such as a man who dreamed he was being attacked by a tiger and awoke to find that his bridgework had somehow come out and his teeth were actually pressing into his thigh. Or you may dream that you are adrift on a floating iceberg and wake up to find the heat has gone off in your room and your blankets are on the floor.

There are also various noises: for instance, traffic, hammering, an airplane flying low, loud music, and so forth which may not actually awaken you but which can nevertheless influence your dream. You have, no doubt, at some time dreamed you heard bells ringing and you woke up to realize that your telephone or doorbell has been or is ringing.

If you have been deeply grieved or very frightened, it can influence your dreams, and dreams that occur during illness, fever, or following a shock must be discounted. Also dreams that you have after seeing a disturbing play, movie, or TV program.

And, obviously, dreams connected with people, things, or situations that have actively concerned you during the current day should be ignored.

A certain group of common dreams, which occur to almost everyone at some time, appear to be more easily recalled than others. This is because they produce decidedly unpleasant sensations, and dreams of this type should be considered as prophetic only when they cannot be attributed to external physical conditions as listed above. They fall into the following categories:

Falling.

Being helplessly pushed or drawn into danger by some irresistible force.

Being nude or nearly so and unable to cover oneself or find clothes.

Floating or flying through space.

Being unable to cry out for help in the face of visible danger.

Being unable to move away from approaching danger.

Unless the dreamer can be absolutely certain that no extraneous physical cause existed during these dreams, they should be ignored.

Prophetic dreams usually fall into one of the following categories:

PRECOGNITIVE—the interpretation of which usually foretells important events.

WARNING—the interpretation of which may suggest the nature of an impending danger.

FACTUAL—the interpretation of which simply confirms or emphasizes a situation that the dreamer knows about.

INSPIRATIONAL—the interpretation of which suggests a solution or course of action in regard to a personal or business problem.

The interpretation of dreams, like any other skill, becomes more interesting with practice. Perseverance is essential in learning a new language, and dream symbols are a language of the subconscious mind.

As a general guide it is best to assume that any action or event in which the dreamer does not take part but is merely an observer is a warning. However, where the dreamer is actually one of the participants in the drama, the message should be interpreted as one which personally affects the dreamer.

A useful list of some general rules for dream interpretation is as follows:

Clean or shiny objects or conditions are usually good omens, but dirty or dull ones forecast obstacles and/or difficulties.

Going up indicates success or improvement, going down signifies reverses.

Successful efforts in a dream are a good omen, but unsuccessful efforts forecast difficulties, except in the case of those specifically listed as dreams of "contrary" or "contrast" in meaning.

If a dream involves an illness to the dreamer, it is advisable to have a medical checkup.

Dreams involving members of the dreamer's family with whom the dreamer is on pleasant terms generally pertain to business advancement, but if the relations are unpleasant, the reverse is forecast.

In order to interpret your dreams with some degree of accuracy, you must remember that dreams are made up of many elements. There is usually one main factor or feature that will stand out in your memory and that is the one which you should consider first; but you should look up all the other elements as well and add them to the interpretation. You should not overlook even the most minor or minute detail as it may easily have an important significance.

For example:

Your dream involves attending a party; it is likely that you will have to look up foods flowers, strangers clothes and so forth before you can work out an interpretation.

If your dream concerns an unfamiliar room, you may have to look up furniture, wood, carpets, color, and so on, as all these details may have an influence on what the dream is trying to tell you.

When attempting to interpret a dream, there are a few basic rules to bear in mind:

Make sure the dream is potentially a prophetic one and not merely of the digestive or "cheese" variety.

That the feature of a dream which is most vividly and clearly recalled when you awaken is the most important element, and the significance of other aspects and factors of your dream must be related to its primary meaning.

The vividness and clarity of your dream is an indication of the importance of the event or warning forecast by the dream. A dream only half remembered or vague and hazy, if worth interpreting at all, is unlikely to have any important significance.

Timing. The imminence of the forecast interpreted from a dream may be calculated by the proximity of the dreamer to the main feature of the dream. For example, if the main factor was parsley, which signifies success through hard work, the success should materialize fairly soon if the dreamer were handling or eating the parsley, or if it were close at hand. If the parsley were just observed by the dreamer, or at a distance, the realization is likely to be delayed.

If the interpretations of the minor factors or details of a dream appear to contradict the significance of the main feature, it is an indication that the meaning or forecast of the main feature will be delayed or modified by the secondary interpretations.

The purpose of this section is to help you make the most of your dreams. According to Aristotle, "the skilful interpreter of dreams is he who has the faculty of observing resemblances." Try to cultivate that faculty and you will soon become adept at understanding what your dreams mean.

Abandon. The interpretation of this dream depends on its aspect. If, in your dream, you abandoned something of a distasteful nature, you will soon hear favorable financial news. However, if in your dream you abandoned someone close to you, it signifies trouble, but don't worry, you can overcome it by heeding the warning. If you dreamed you were a witness to an abandonment of any kind, it indicates you will hear some news which will be important to you. To dream you have been abandoned is a dream of contrary and means you will have a reconciliation or a quick recovery from trouble.

Abbey. If you saw this structure clearly and in daylight, it is generally a good omen. Peace of mind and freedom from anxiety will soon be yours. If seen in gloom or at night, it predicts sadness, but of a temporary nature.

Abdomen. A dream of contrary. If you dreamed you had pain in this region, you will have success due to good health and vigor. But if you dreamed of your abdomen being exposed in any way, it is a warning of unfaithfulness or treachery on the part of someone you trust. Be cautious with confidences.

Abduction. To dream you are being abducted indicates success against opposition whether business or social. If you dreamed someone else was being abducted, then you will soon get unexpected news.

Abhorrence. The interpretation of this dream depends on its aspect. If your feeling of distaste seriously disturbed you in your dream, it is a warning of danger or difficulties of an unforeseen nature; but, if you were merely annoyed by the feeling in your dream, you will overcome your problems.

Abject. To dream of being abject indicates coming financial reverses. If the abjectness altered during the dream, the reverses will be temporary. If, in your dream, you responded kindly to an abject approach, it means a financial benefit is on the way.

Abnormal. To dream of anything that is not normal— i.e., a horse with feathers, a woman who hops like a kangaroo, an airplane flying backward, etc., means you will shortly have a pleasing solution to your worries.

Abortion. For a man this dream portends failure in his current interest, whether it concerns love or money. For a woman it is a warning to look after her health.

Abroad. To dream of going abroad by ship means you will make an influential new friend in the near future. To dream of being abroad, in foreign places,

indicates an unsettled condition and a probable change of location.

Abscond. For a man this dream is a warning of treachery among his associates. For a woman it means that she must be careful not to give her affections unwisely.

Abstinence. A dream of contrary. To dream that you abstain (by choice) from drink or from any sort of temptation is a warning against over-confidence. But to dream that you abstain from necessity indicates that success and prosperity are on the way.

Abundance. If you dreamed of having an abundance of one thing, it is a warning to conserve your resources; but if you dreamed of having an abundance of a variety of things, it is a very fortunate omen.

Abyss. This is an obstacle dream. If you avoid the fall, you will overcome your difficulties; but if you fall into the abyss, it is a warning that you must be extremely careful in your business dealings.

Acacia. To see it in bloom or smell its fragrance is a lucky omen for your most secret hopes—or passions.

Academy. Any dream involving this type of institution promises new friends and experiences, but it also warns that these may lead to costly speculation. Be cautious.

Accelerator. Using it to increase the speed of a car (or any other vehicle) indicates that you will achieve your objectives through your own efforts. If, in your dream the accelerator jammed or you were unable to control it, it is a warning to beware of a habit which could turn into a vice if you're not careful.

Accent. If you heard yourself or others speak with an unfamiliar or foreign accent, you will hear news from a distance which could involve a hasty trip.

Accept. The interpretation of this dream depends on its aspect. If it involved a proposal of marriage and you accepted (or were accepted), it is a dream of contrary and you can expect a rocky road to romance. However, if you persevere, it may, in time, smooth out. If the dream involved the acceptance of money or anything else of value, it portends success in pending business matters. Acceptance of anything which is fake or counterfeit suggests you may be too trusting, so reexamine your current relationships. To accept an invitation is a forerunner to an inheritance or an unexpected gift.

Accident. The meaning of this dream varies greatly depending on the circumstances and surroundings, but as a rule it is a warning. If you dreamed of an accident, as such, you would be wise to avoid unnecessary travel for a few weeks. An accident at sea pertains to love affairs, on land, to business affairs. If possible, you should avoid the thing that was involved in the accident (for the twenty-four hours following the dream), i.e., if you dreamed of a car crash, walk for a day but be careful crossing streets! Steer clear of planes, trains, horses, knives, sharp instruments, fires, electricity, high places, or whatever pertained to the dream accident, for at least a day; and if you can't avoid them, take extra precautions. See also *Insurance*.

Accompany. To accompany a stranger in your dream means that your enemies will fall into their own traps. If you were accompanied by a stranger, you can expect some exciting and beneficial events before long. If you were accompanied by friends, expect a change of environment. If you had or gave musical accompaniment to singing, you will soon have cause to sing joyously.

Accordion. If you heard this instrument, the meaning relates to the sound; if it struck you as doleful, you may expect some sadness but not of a deep or lasting nature. If the sound was lively and bright, you will soon have some gay social times. If you were playing the accordion, your love and/or personal affairs will be totally satisfactory. See also *Music* and *Musical Instruments.*

Accost. If you were accosted by a man, a false friend may try to impugn your honor. However, you can expect money in the form of profits or a legacy if you were accosted by a woman, a beggar, or anyone known to you.

Accounts (Accountants). This is one of the rather rare straightforward dreams. If you were having difficul-

ties of any kind with your accounts, it is a warning not to lend money and to guard your credit. If, on the other hand, your accounts balanced easily, you may definitely expect a profitable proposition to come your way.

Accuse. To be aware of vague accusation is a warning to be on your guard against being used by unscrupulous people. If the accusation was clearly defined and you were able to defend yourself or prove your innocence, it portends trouble which you can overcome. If you were doing the accusing, it is a warning to reassess your personal relationships as you may be heading for trouble in that respect To be accused by a woman suggests some upsetting news is on the way, but if the accuser was a man, you will have a business success beyond your expectations.

Ace. The significance varies according to the suit. Hearts: success in love and/or wishes come true. Diamonds good luck concerning money. Clubs: success after quarrels concerning business. Spades: sadness and/or unrewarded labor. If you were not aware of the suit, you will be puzzled by a mystery you cannot solve.

Ache. This is usually a dream of contrary. A trivial ache is either due to a physical cause or is a warning to consult a doctor. A severe ache indicates an important event which will be beneficial to you. However, a headache is a warning against confiding your private affairs to anyone. See also parts of body—*Arm, Leg, etc., and Illness.*

Achievement. A dream of achievement is in direct line with its aspect—the bigger the achievement in the dream, the bigger will be the satisfaction coming your way.

Acid. Anything to do with acid is a dream of warning. Be cautious in regard to promises given or reliance on promises received. See also *Odor.*

Acne. See *Skin.*

Acorn. You will be immensely lucky if you dreamed of anything to do with acorns or the tree which bears them. They predict the successful outcome of any problems you may now have and prosperity and good fortune in all your plans for the future.

Acquaintance. If you made a new acquaintance in your dream or saw an old one, it is an indication that you will recover money (or something of value) you thought lost. A meeting with a slight acquaintance indicates a coming increase in social activity. To quarrel with an acquaintance suggests you should consult a doctor over some minor health problem.

Acquit. You're likely to have a rough time from hostile competition if you dreamed of being acquitted in court, but relax—you will overcome it suddenly.

Acrobat. The meaning of this dream varies according to its detail. If you watched an acrobatic performance, it would be wise to postpone any long-distance travel for at least a week. If you performed the gymnastics yourself, you will overcome your present difficulties sooner than you expect. If you dreamed of a friend or relation doing the acrobatics, it is a warning to look out for deception by the person involved. To observe an acrobatic accident or failure is a dream of contrary; you will have a lucky escape from danger.

Acrostic. A warning against making hasty decisions. Avoid unusual business risks, unless you dreamed of completing the acrostic, in which case your contemplated speculation will be lucky.

Acting. You must assert yourself in a more positive way to gain your ambitions. If your dream involved meeting actors or actresses, be careful not to repeat gossip or you could lose a friend.

Adam and Eve. To see either Adam or Eve in your dream is a good omen for some cherished plan. If you spoke to them or they to you, you will encounter a delay in the realization of your wishes, but the delay will be very temporary, so cultivate patience. If you saw Adam and Eve together in your dream you'll be tremendously lucky.

Adapt. If your dream involved adapting yourself to some difficult or unusual conditions, you can relax as far as your financial future is concerned.

Adder. This poisonous snake warns you against false friends and/or loss of prestige through deceit. If you killed an adder, you will triumph over an enemy. See *Snake(s)*.

Addition. You will have personal difficulties if you dreamed of adding up figures, but if your totals were correct, you will overcome the situation.

Address. To write a personal address is a warning against gambling of any kind, but if you wrote or saw in writing a business address, you will be fortunate in a speculation. To hear about, or discuss an address is a warning to be more discreet in confiding your personal affairs.

Adenoids. A dream of contrary if you had them removed; you will be much admired by some new friends.

Adieux. To dream of saying farewell to anyone is a warning to guard your health.

Adjustment. To adjust to anything mechanical in your dream is a happy omen of increasing success in business.

Adjutant. See *Armed (or Army)* and *Officer*.

Administrate. In connection with your own affairs, this activity indicates a coming inheritance. If it involved the affairs of others, you can expect an improvement in your business relations.

Admiral. This high-ranking fellow in your dream signifies success in your social life as well as in your career.

Admire. In certain respects a dream of contrary. If you were on the receiving end of the admiration, you may be in danger of losing useful friends through your own vanity; however, if the dream involved admiration for others, it indicates prosperity through good friends.

Adopt. A dream of contrary. If you were adopted yourself, expect an appeal for help from some unanticipated quarter (probably a relative). However if you did the adopting, your year ahead will be auspicious for speculation.

Adore. Adoration of any suitable person or object (i.e., husband, wife, children, religious things, etc.) is a forerunner to deep peace and contentment, but if the dream involved this emotion in respect of any unsuitable subject or object,

which left you with a feeling of guilt or unease, you may be in for a minor disappointment.

Adorn. Personal adornment of any kind in a dream is a warning of social difficulties ahead. If you refused the adornment, you will overcome the trouble. If the dream involved household adornment, you can expect a pleasant change of circumstances and/or location. See also *Clothes, Jewelry, Gift, Furniture,* etc.

Adrift. This is indicative of a problem you have been unable to solve, or unwilling to face up to, and is a straightforward obstacle dream. If you reached land safely, you will overcome your dilemma, but if you fell out of the boat or were upset by rough weather, it is a warning of serious difficulty due to indecision. If you were rescued in your dream, or managed to swim to safety, success will follow hardship.

Adultery. If you committed it, be on guard against giving your confidence to new friends; if you resisted it, you will have some disappointing setbacks, but they will be temporary.

Advance. This dream really means what it says. It is a fortunate omen to dream of advancement whether it involves you or someone else; it signifies satisfaction and success in any important undertaking, and a quick settlement if you have legal matters pending.

Advantage. Whether you took the advantage or someone took advantage of you, it is a good omen and presages family prosperity and general contentment.

Adventure. The type of adventure governs the interpretation of this dream, and while its meaning is quite straightforward, you must bear in mind that in this exceptional case the prediction pertains only to your FEELING about the adventure, rather than the details of it (i.e., pleased, amused, distressed, excited, ashamed, etc.), and you can expect an experience of a similar character shortly. So if your dream adventure left you feeling guilty—put up your guard! If the dream concerned an adventurer, or adventuress, you are probably in for a surprising change of environment.

Adversary. A dream of contrary. If your dream in-volved an opponent or a business, social, or professional rival, you may have some momentary difficulties, but you can rise above them with a little serious effort.

Adversity. This pertains to your finances and as with adversary is a good omen if you undergo the adversity; however, an exception to this generality is if the adversity was in a love affair, in which case you must guard against idle gossip.

Advertise. If you were advertising in your dream, avoid some speculative plan, but on the other hand if you read advertisements concerning others, your plans will materialize. It is especially auspicious if the advertisements had illustrations.

Advice. Beware of humiliating quarrels with friends if you gave advice in your dream, but if you received advice you will make some new and useful friends.

Affection. The interpretation here depends on the degree of affection in the dream. Any signs of reasonable good taste indicate a happy family life and/or personal relationships. However, any such demonstration of an embarrassing or abnormal nature suggests you may be influenced by ulterior motives in some current plans.

Affiliation. A dream of warning. Look out for a powerful enemy among your associates. Forewarned is forearmed.

Affliction. A true dream of contrary; the greater the affliction in your dream the more certain will be your success in life.

Affluence. A straightforward omen of improvement. The greater the affluence in your dream, the quicker will be the easement of your financial problems.

Affront. A dream of contrary. If you felt offended in your dream, you will soon have the satisfaction of sincere admiration from someone whose opinion you value. However, if you annoyed someone else, it is a warning to refrain from repeating rumors.

Afloat. The meaning of this dream depends on its aspect. If the water was calm and clear, a happy event is in view; if the water was rough or murky, you will be called on to cope with some difficulties not of your own making. See also *Water, Ocean, River, Ship, Drown,* etc.

Afraid. A dream of contrary, you will recognize your difficulties and find the courage to overcome them. See also *Fear.*

Africa. The interpretation of this dream depends on its details (such as animals, vegetation, etc.), but if you dreamed of this continent merely as a place, or on a map, you can expect a happy improvement in status in the near future.

Afternoon. Dream events that happen in the afternoons are generally favorable omens pertaining to personal affairs, but the interpretation depends on the details. See also *Fog, Rain, Sun,* etc.

Agate. If the agate you dreamed of was polished or in jewelry form, it is a warning not to allow yourself to be drawn into disagreements between your friends. See also *Jewelry* and *Stone(s).*

Age. To worry about your age in a dream, or to dream you are or have aged beyond your actual years, indicates you should see a doctor; but to see aged people in a dream is an omen of great good luck. If they are poor or ragged, you may have some difficulties ahead, but you can easily overcome these by positive bold action.

Agent. If you dreamed of negotiating with or through an agent, you will soon have a pleasant change of surroundings.

Agnostic. Religious disbelief in a dream is a reminder to be more circumspect in your associations with the opposite sex.

Agony. A dream of contrary. Whether it involved yourself or others, the greater the agony in the dream, the greater will be your coming joy. See also *Pain*.

Agreement. Look out for some careless oversight which may be detrimental to your immediate plans if your dream concerned an agreement, but if you actually signed the document in your dream, then guard against a financial setback.

Agriculture. Success, prosperity, and abundance due to diligence are forecast by a dream of this nature. See also *Farm, Wheat Harvest*, etc.

Ague. This illness pertains to business and is a dream of contrary. You will be gratified by some new business developments.

Air. The interpretation of this dream varies greatly according to its aspect. If the air was clear and enjoyable, it indicates success; however, cloudy, foggy, or misty air suggests you should postpone any important decisions for a few days and reconsider any proposed changes. See also *Clouds, Sky*, etc.

Air Brake. The sound of escaping air in your dream is a warning to reexamine your plans for some flaw which could upset your calculations.

Airedale. See *Dog*.

Airplane. If you piloted the airplane successfully, you may consider it an omen for unusual achievement in your business or in some extracurricular enterprise. Airplanes dropping bombs forecast disturbing news; flying in formation they portend financial gain (if the weather was good), but if the weather was bad, you may be in for a rough business ride. If you fell (or bailed) out of an airplane, you may expect some temporary reverses. If you were traveling by plane, you will probably hear news from a distance or concerning someone who lives far away. See also *Clouds*, etc.

Airship. See *Balloon*.

Aisle. If your dream involved the aisle of a theater, church, or building. it is a warning to be extremely cautious regarding an important decision you will soon have to make.

Alabaster. See *Stone(s)*.

Alarm. Hearing an alarm (fire, burglar, or clock) in your dream predicts an exciting and profitable time ahead. See also *Fright*.

Albatross. An omen of good luck and/or good news through strangers. See also *Birds*.

Alcohol. If you take it in moderation as a drink, it indicates success, but if taken to excess, beware of getting into a spot where you might have to make an embarrassing apology. As a chemical, it is a favorable omen, especially for those in the arts or sciences. See also *Drink*.

Alder. You will achieve happiness only by sticking to your high ideals, if you saw this tree in your dream. See also *Trees* and *Foliage*.

Aldermen. In general, this dream relates to any speculations you may be considering and warns you to go very slowly. It may also be considered a warning to be more circumspect in your business and/or social behavior.

Ale. You would be wise to stick to the simpler pleasures if you dreamed of drinking this beverage. See also *Drinks, Bar*, etc.

Alehouse. See *Bar* and *Hotel*.

Alibi. If you gave the alibi, steer clear of quarrelsome acquaintances; but if the dream involved someone else's alibi, there is an unexpected good time in the offing.

Alien. You will make valuable new friends if you dreamed of being an alien —but if your dream involved dealing or meeting with aliens, important changes are coming your way.

Alimony. A warning against careless pleasures if you paid it, but if you received it, you may expect to fulfill a wish that is dear to you. See also *Money*.

Alive. Excessive liveliness in a dream is a warning to guard your resources.

Allegory. A dream which seems to have allegorical significance predicts a series of disappointing discoveries.

Allergy. This is a good omen however you dreamed it. If the allergy was yours, you can expect some pleasant social news; if the allergy was someone else's, your immediate plans will flourish.

Alley. You will have an easy road ahead if you dreamed of an alley; unless it was a dead end, in which case success will come but only after some hard work.

Alley Cat. If you heard the noise of alley cats in your dream, it is a warning to avoid an indiscreet acquaintance in your immediate circle. See also *Cat*.

Alliance. See *Agreement*, *Contract*, etc.

Alligator. This dream is trying to alert you to an enemy. Be very cautious in any venture. See also *Animals*.

Allowance. If you received the allowance from a proper source (i.e., parent, guardian, business, etc.), it indicates a happy time ahead; however, if you gave the allowance or it came from a questionable source, beware of family quarrels.

Alloy. A dream involving the combining of metals indicates, for the unattached, a happy marriage; for the married, an increase in family responsibilities. See also *Metal*.

Allspice. To smell, taste, or use this spicy flavor in a dream is a happy romantic omen. See also *Herbs*.

Allure. To be conscious, in a dream, of the allure of someone of the opposite sex, indicates a probable rise in social status.

Almanac. For a woman to dream of an almanac is a warning not to sacrifice her personal obligations for the sake of social climbing; but for a man this dream signifies a profitable business deal.

Almond. You'll have a temporary sorrow if you only

saw the nuts; if you ate and enjoyed them, you'll be lucky, but if they tasted bitter, you should delay any contemplated changes for as long as possible. An almond tree in bloom promises joyous celebrations at home.

Alms. This is, in some respects, a dream of contrary, for if you dreamed you were begging or receiving alms, you will have an improvement in your financial status; you will also be lucky if, in your dream, you gave alms generously; but if you refused a beggar or gave reluctantly, the forecast is of some unexpected hardships to be overcome.

Almshouse. A dream of contrary; security will crown your efforts.

Aloes. See *Herbs,* also *Trees.*

Alpaca. You'll be lucky if you dreamed of this lovely material, and if you saw the charming animal from which the wool comes you can expect to receive an unusual gift rather soon.

Alphabet. Any dream involving letters of the alphabet indicates pleasant news on the way; if, however, your dream con-

cerned foreign letters, you may expect some clue to the solution of a mystery which has troubled you.

Alpine. Mountain scenery, at a distance, signifies unanticipated gains. See also *Climb.*

Altar. You will have a sudden release from pressing worries and/or good news from an unexpected source if an altar figured in your dream.

Alteration. Dreams of alterations to your home indicate you will soon be able to make pleasant changes; if the alterations involved clothing, you'll have to be strong to avoid some upcoming temptation.

Altercation. See *Argue, Quarrel,* etc.

Altitude. A warning to avoid an involvement with inferiors which could cause you serious embarrassment, especially if the height affected your breathing.

Alum. Luck and prosperity will be yours if you dreamed of having this tongue-puckering substance in your possession, or if you tasted it and it was sweet instead of bitter; but if you were aware of its disagreeable flavor, look sharp for a cuckoo in your business nest.

Aluminum. There are some happy days ahead if the metal was bright and shiny; if it was dull, you may experience an unexpected frustration. See also *Metal*.

Amateur. A dream of contrary; anything artistic done only for love (or fun) suggests an unexpected financial gain.

Amazement. An unusually exciting experience is in the offing if your dream involved this reaction.

Ambassador. An improvement in your social and/or financial status, through an influential friend, is likely to follow a dream concerning a foreign diplomat of high rank.

Amber. To give or receive this in a dream is an augury of an unexpected windfall of money, or recovery of a loss.

Ambition. A dream of contrary. If you gained it in your dream, be prepared for a setback, but if you were frustrated in your dream, you will attain your objective in time. Persevere!

Ambrosia. A dream of this godly food is a reminder that pride goes before a fall. Reconsider your personal actions carefully. See also *Food* and *Eating*.

Ambulance. No broad interpretation can be given, as this dream varies greatly according to its details, but it is generally a dream of warning against indiscretion in relations with the opposite sex. However, a full ambulance signifies the fulfillment of your hopes in a shorter time than you think possible.

Ambush. See *Hide*, etc.

America. Details, as always, must be carefully considered for an accurate interpretation, but in a general way to dream of going to, or being in, or observing America on a map is an omen of great happiness through family unity. Unless, of course, you are an American or live in America, in which case the national aspects of the dream have no significance and only the other details should be considered.

Amethyst. Peace of mind and contentment will soon be yours through some unanticipated good news if you dreamed of this lovely jewel. See also *Stone(s), Colors.*

Amiability. A dream of contrary if the display of amiability was toward you; be on your guard against gossip from a false friend. However, if your dream involved a demonstration of your own amiability, you will derive much satisfaction from some charitable efforts.

Ammonia. Avoid unnecessary risks of any nature for a few weeks after dreaming of this pungent substance. If, in your dream, you actually smelled its fumes, a medical checkup is suggested.

Ammunition. See *Bullet, Dynamite,* etc.

Amorous. To feel amorous in a dream suggests a friendship which will ripen into an exciting romance, but if you dreamed of an amorous person of the opposite sex, you should guard against a relationship which might involve you in a serious embarrassment, if not an actual scandal.

Amputation. A sort of dream of contrary. If the loss in

your dream was to someone else, be prepared for some unexpected difficulties ahead; but if you dreamed of the loss of one of your own members, you can look forward to an unanticipated important gain. See also *Hand, Leg, Arm,* etc.

Amulet. This talisman in a dream represents a decision hanging over the dreamer. Its interpretation varies greatly according to the details of the dream. See also *Stone(s), Jewelry, Carving, Colors,* etc.

Amusement. This is one of the straightforward dreams. The more you are entertained, the greater will be your coming satisfaction in life; but if, like Queen Victoria, you were not amused when you should have been, you can expect some minor annoyances.

Anaconda. See *Snake(s).*

Anagrams. Playing or watching this word game in a dream suggests a happy solution to current problems. See also *Games.*

Anarchist. Use extreme caution in any business or financial deal following a dream concerning anarchy or anarchists.

Ancestors. You will have some unexpected honor if you dreamed of ancestors, whether your own or not.

Anchor. Economize on things you don't really need for a few months. See also *Ship*.

Anchovy. You'll be lucky in love, cards, or anything else you may undertake, after dreaming of these tiny fish, whether they were canned or alive. See also *Fish*.

Ancient. See *Antiques*.

Andirons. If noticed in a brightly glowing fireplace, the portent is one of personal gratification, if in an unlit fireplace, a disappointing love affair is forecast.

Anecdote. If you told or heard an anecdote in your dream, you are likely to have an unusual social success soon.

Anemia. A dream of contrary. Your health will be good. See *Blood*.

Anesthesia. See *Ether, Unconscious, Sleep*, etc.

Angel. A favorable dream forecasting success, protection, happiness, and rewarding friendships.

Anger. A dream of contrary. If your anger was directed at someone you know, you will benefit materially through a friend; if the object or cause of your anger was unknown to you, you will soon be celebrating some joyous good news. See also *Rage, Animosity*.

Angleworm. See *Worms*.

Angling. You should resist the temptation to compromise your ethics. See also *Fish, Water*, etc.

Animals. To see wild animals in your dream is generally a good omen pertaining to business, but the interpretation depends on their attude; if they were calm, your affairs will prosper, but if they attacked you (or each other), you can expect some reverses. See also *Lion, Dog, Cat, Bull, Cow, Horse*, etc.

Animosity. Rethink a situation involving your morals if you were on the receiving end of the dreamed animosity. See also *Quarrel, Anger*, etc.

Ankle. As a general rule a dream involving your own ankles is an indication of success after a struggle. To dream of the ankles of someone of the opposite sex suggests an unwise love affair; but to dream of the ankles of your own sex signifies a solution to a puzzling predicament.

Announcement. An acceptable change in your life is imminent if you dream of hearing, receiving, or making a social or business announcement.

Annoy. A dream of contrary. Your plans will proceed smoothly.

Annulment. You will have cause for a happy family celebration if the dream involved your own marriage, but if it concerned the marriage of someone else, you will have some petty annoyance to overcome.

Anteater. Be extra cautious in your business dealings and take no financial risks for the time being. See also *Animals*.

Antelope. A sudden improvement in financial status is likely to follow a dream of seeing these animals in a natural surrounding, or having clothing or articles made of the leather; however, to see them in captivity or to hunt or shoot them indicates an untrustworthy business associate.

Antenna. An indication of good news concerning a bonus or extra profits coming your way. If, in your dream, you were putting up an antenna or aerial, you will recover something you thought irretrievable.

Anthem. All music, if it is melodic, is considered to be a favorable sign to the dreamer; an anthem heard relates to news from a distance, but if the dreamer was singing the anthem, it would be well to cultivate a higher resistance to the inclination to waste time. See also *Church*.

Antics. See *Magic*, etc.

Antidote. To dream of taking an antidote indicates a severe embarrassment or scandal through indiscretion. Be more circumspect in your personal relationships. See also *Poison*.

Antiques. A happy home life will be yours if you dreamed of looking at antiques. If you bought them, your financial independence will be slower in coming than you expect, but you will be helped along the way by an inheritance; if you sold them, don't lend or borrow money.

Antlers. An excellent omen of future happiness.

Ants. If, in your dream, you observed the interesting organized activity of these industrious creatures, a change of business or position would be beneficial; but if they were in food or on clothing, as pests, you will have a spell of frustration and hard work before achieving independence.

Anvil. Anything to do with an anvil in a dream is considered a forerunner to some really spectacular luck providing the noise was muted; if the noise was very pronounced, there will be an unexpected change of locale.

Anxiety. A dream of contrary. Your worries will soon be relieved.

Apartment. A straightforward dream. If the apartment was small and/or uncomfortable, you will have to persevere and try to avoid family quarrels; but if it was large and/or luxurious, you can expect a steady increase in prosperity.

Ape. Be on guard against a mischief-maker in your close social or business circle and pay more attention to your work, if you dreamed of an ape. See also *Animals*.

Apology. Whether the apology was given or received, this dream in any form pertains to friends. You may lose one and gain another, or perhaps be surprised by the return of a former one.

Apparel. To be concerned about your clothing is a dream of contrary. The more fashionable and elegant your attire, the more troublesome will be the problems crossing your path; therefore to be shabby, ragged or naked is a very lucky omen. However, an accurate interpretation of a dream concerning clothes often depends on color (if you were aware of it).

Apparition. The portent is of good news unless the apparition frightened you or made you feel ill, in which case a medical checkup is suggested. See also *Ghost*.

Appendicitis. Be more careful with your confidences! See also *Ache, Abdomen, Illness*.

Appetite. If you were aware of hunger, or your appetite was small, a medical checkup is suggested. A large appetite, in a dream, refers to money and is a warning to handle it with respect or your finances could become chaotic.

Applause. A dream of contrary. There is some ill-feeling and/or jealousy around you but you can overcome it if you try a bit of tact.

Apples. As with most natural products this popular fruit is generally a good omen, but the interpretation depends greatly on details. If the apples were ripe and sweet (or cooked and sweet), they are a promise of well-earned rewards. If they were green or bitter, you are in danger of loss through your own foolishness. See also *Fruit, Eating, Trees*, etc.

Appointment. Any dream involvement with appointments, whether making, breaking, changing, discussing, or what have you,

is a warning to alter, or better still, give up, some secret plan you have been harboring; it won't work out as you expected. See also *Calendar*, etc.

Appreciation. A sort of dream of contrary. If you showed the appreciation you'll be lucky, but if you received it you are likely to be in for some unexpected criticism.

Apprehension. Don't be persuaded to change your ways. The things you worry about most will never happen. See also *Anxiety*, etc.

Apprentice. A big success in business and/or love is imminent for you if you dreamed of learning a trade. If your dream involved teaching an apprentice, you can expect a windfall (or an inheritance) of money or valuable property fairly soon. See also *Learn, Teacher*, etc.

Approach. Curb a tendency to get involved in a family controversy. Following a dream of approaching someone, or of someone approaching you, is an especially auspicious time to mind your own business!

Approval. It's a happy omen to approve of something or someone in a dream, unless the approval was one you would not normally give, in which case you are being warned to open your eyes to a deceitful friend.

Apricot. Luck in everything but love is forecast by a dream of eating this fruit. If the apricots were dried or preserved, look for a meddlesome hypocrite among your associates.

April (Fool). If, in your dream, you were the April fool, you will have control over a new situation; be moderate in using this unexpected power. If the dream concerned someone else being fooled, your success will be delayed. If you dreamed of it being April when it isn't, you'll find yourself traveling, probably abroad, fairly soon.

Apron. As a general guide an apron in a dream represents a material gain and/ or a change for the better. If it was torn, you may expect a small but pleasing benefit. See also *Apparel* and *Clothes*.

Aquamarine. You'll have a happy love life if you dreamed of this lovely jewel, unless you lost it, in which case you should be careful where you give your affection.

Aquaplane. See *Sports*.

Aquarium. See *Fish*.

Aqueduct. You will experience some minor woes if the aqueduct in your dream was dry, but if there was water running through it, contentment and good health is your forecast.

Arab. See *Foreign, Dress, Costume,* etc.

Arbitrate. If your own claims or affairs were the subject of the arbitration, you will gain something you want. If you were the arbitrator, you'll need all the tact you can muster to get out of a tight spot.

Arbor. A fortunate omen for those involved in the arts, for others a warning against repeating hearsay.

Arcade. Intriguing temptations will be put in your way if you were walking in the arcade, but if you were merely aware of it or just looking into it, you must avoid repeating any confidences or your own may be betrayed.

Arch. Your efforts are in the right direction if the arch was whole and/or attractive, but if it appeared to be broken, or damaged in any way, a new line of endeavor is suggested.

Archer. If you are single, you'll soon find the right partner; if married, resist a temptation toward extra-curricular activity; it could be more costly than you anticipate. See also *Arrow, Sports,* and *Bow.*

Architect. Success with some difficult plan is forecast by a dream which involved an architect at work. See *Building.*

Archives. Anything to do with archives in a dream is a forerunner of unexpected legal entanglements.

Arc Light. See *Light,* etc.

Arctic. You'll achieve your highest ambition if you dreamed of this frozen area. See also *Ice, Snow, Cold.*

Arena. You would be wise to reject any new business venture or position offered at this time. It will have some hidden snags. See *Sports, Fight,* etc.

Argue. This is a lucky dream of contrary unless you lost your temper, in which case it is a warning against making impulsive decisions in important matters. Think carefully before you act.

Arise. With the sun, happiness, contentment, and fun. In the dark, after a few minor setbacks, you'll sing like a lark!

Aristocrat. Your material wealth will take a turn for the better if your dream involved this hybrid type, and if you were snubbed or made to feel inferior, it could be in the form of a windfall or inheritance.

Arithmetic. Dreams which involve doing problems predict petty annoyances you can solve with a little extra tactful effort. See also *Accounts.*

Ark. Good forces are at work for you and beneficial events will follow.

Arm. If the general aspect of the dream was pleasing, it is a promise of pleasant times ahead with good friends, but if the dream involved injury, accident, or discomfort to the arms, a medical checkup is suggested.

Armchair. Whatever favor you are seeking will be yours if you dreamed of sitting in or seeing a comfortable armchair. If you saw someone else in it or it was occupied by a dog or cat, you'll soon have an unwelcome guest or two. An empty armchair signifies a mystery which will take considerable time and perseverance to solve. See also *Furniture*, etc.

Armed (or Army). This kind of dream indicates obstacles to be overcome; if the army was marching, you will have to travel to achieve your goal. See also *Battle, Fight*, etc.

Armistice. A dream of opposite; you could lose a friend through careless gossip.

Armory. Seen from the outside this building suggests a rival to be reckoned with, but from the inside it forecasts a successful venture, especially auspicious if there is great activity going on.

Arms. See *Guns, Arm*, or *Body*.

Army. See *Armed*.

Aroma. See *Odor*.

Arrest. You'll have a sharp disappointment followed closely by an unexpected joy.

Arrive. To arrive yourself is a sure sign of efforts rewarded; to dream of others arriving is a warning against reckless speculation. See also *Travel*.

Arrogance. You will have great social satisfaction if you met with or observed arrogance in your dream.

Arrow. You've got an undercover antagonist among your friends if you dreamed of being hit by an arrow. A broken arrow is a warning to guard your business interests with more diligence; if you broke the arrow, it signifies a personal attachment which would be best severed.

Arsenal. See *Armory*.

Arson. An offer of a change for the better will soon come your way. See also *Fire* and *Flame*.

Art. You can expect a step up in your business or profession if you saw or discussed art in your dream.

See also *Pictures, Oil Painting, Museum, Statue(s),* etc.

Artery. A dream of contrary. If your arteries were weak or cut, you will be enjoying honor among your friends. See also *Blood, Vein(s), Body,* etc.

Arthritis. A dream of contrary. Your ailments are very minor indeed.

Artichoke. Be more circumspect in your affairs with the opposite sex or you could be seriously embarrassed.

Artillery. Stop trying to impress people who don't matter; no one can be liked by everyone. See also *Armory, Armed,* etc.

Artisan. See *Metal, Stone(s), Carving,* etc.

Artist. You are wasting your time on some unworthy pleasures if you saw an artist painting or drawing in your dream; if you were doing the artwork, you will have to revise your plans in order to achieve the recognition you want. See also *Oil Painting, Pictures, Sculpture, Museum,* etc.

Asbestos. See *Fire.*

Ascend. Any progress upward is a forecast of eventual success. The ease or difficulty involved in your rise is related to obstacles to be overcome, before you realize your ambitions.

Ashes. If the ashes got on you, you can expect some annoying but temporary reverses. If you were emptying the ashes, you may experience a financial embarrassment through your own carelessness. Sifting of ashes is an indication of prosperity. Ashes, as from a cremation, signify a probable unexpected inheritance.

Asia. There will be some surprising romantic developments for you or in your family following a dream of this location.

Asp. See *Snake(s).*

Asparagus. Resist an inclination to be influenced by others; you will be best served by using your own judgment. See also *Vegetable(s), Eating, Grow,* etc.

Aspen. See *Trees.*

Asphalt. See *Pavement.*

Asphyxiation. A dream of physical origin, possibly

due to asthma; see your doctor.

Aspic. A happy increase in social activity is indicated by a dream of jellied food. See also *Food* and *Eating*.

Aspirin. Be especially careful not to repeat confidences if you dreamed of taking or giving this drug. See also *Medicine*.

Ass. See *Donkey*.

Assassin. See *Crime* and *Killing*.

Assault. You will be given some information which will be of great value to you if you were assaulted in your dream; if others were assaulted, you may have to defend an attack on your character.

Assembly. See *Crowd*.

Assessment. See *Taxes*.

Assign. You will make a fast change of plans if you dreamed of the assigning of property or other interests.

Assist. To dream of receiving assistance signifies that you will need help and should not hesitate to ask for it; if you gave assistance in your dream, you will, in fact, succeed without it.

Aster. To dream of these hardy blooms signifies happiness and abundance; if you were gathering them, you will soon learn the solution to a mystifying puzzle. See also *Flowers*.

Asthma. There is no significance if you actually suffer from this ailment; for others, it is a warning against loss through carelessness or risky speculation.

Astonish. You're in line for a happy step-up if you were astonished; if you did the astonishing, you can expect some pleasing news, probably about money matters.

Astrology. You can expect important changes if your dream involved this ancient science. See also *Horoscope*.

Astronomer. Patient effort will be required if you are to achieve your highest ambition, so don't give up.

Asylum. For an accurate interpretation the details of the dream should be carefully considered, but as a general guide if you remained outside the building, you can expect to be asked for help which you should give unstintingly even though it may involve an effort on your part; if you were inside the building, or confined in the institution, you urgently need to find a trusted friend or professional advisor with whom you can discuss your secret worries.

Athletics. If you normally engage in the dreamed-of activity, it is probably a carry-over into sleep; otherwise it suggests strain or tension for which a short holiday or a medical checkup might be beneficial. See also *Sports*.

Atlas. See *Globe* or *Map*.

Atmosphere. Clear sunny atmosphere is a most fortunate omen of prosperity, domestic happiness, and faithful friends, but cloudy or overcast skies are a warning of stormy personal relations ahead.

Atoms. To see them in a dream suggests the breakup of a long-standing association, but don't despair— it will be for the best; if the atoms were simply spoken of or discussed without being seen, you'd better be prepared to economize for a while.

Atone. A dream of contrary. You'll soon have cause to rejoice.

Atrocity. See *Horror*, etc.

Attack. See *Assault, Fight, Quarrel*, etc.

Attainment. See *Achievement, Success*, etc.

Attendant. The interpretation varies according to the details, but in general, an attendant signifies an advancement or promotion in business, but if the attendant was dismissed, you may have an unfortunate love affair to cope with.

Attic. For the young, this dream is a warning against flirtation and/or promiscuity; but for the middle-aged it holds out a promise of comfort in old age.

Attorney. See *Law* (and *Lawyers*).

Auction. There's a possibility that a trusted acquaintance is trying to take an unfair advantage; be on guard.

Audience. A surprising distinction will come your way if you faced an audience; if you were in it, you will have cause to rejoice over the good fortune of a valued friend.

Auditor. See *Accounts.*

Auditorium. See *Audience, Hall, Music, Building,* etc.

Auger. See *Awl.*

August. In summer this dream is an omen of success in your current undertakings, but in winter it forecasts an unexpected trip.

Aunt. Curb a tendency toward impatience if your dream involved a paternal aunt, but if the aunt was on your mother's side, you will benefit through a family connection. See also *Relatives, Ancestors,* etc.

Australia. Get your affairs in order for an important change if you dreamed of this interesting continent.

Author. Your interests will widen considerably if you dreamed of being, meeting, or conversing with an author; however, if you observed an author at work, it is a warning of financial strain ahead. Don't lend money.

Autograph. Collecting them signifies a quick profit; signing them is a forecast of eventual success in your chosen endeavors.

Automatic. To see things working automatically in your dream is a suggestion to be more positive and determined in your personal and/or business relations.

Automation. You will soon be surprised by the solution to a mysterious turn of events.

Automobile. The meaning of a dream involving a motorcar depends very much on its aspect. If the car was merely a means of transport, it has, in itself, no particular significance, and other details of the dream should be carefully considered. However, if the car was speeding, you can expect some sudden news from a distance; an accident forecasts recovery of something lost; if the engine lost power or stalled or if you ran out of gas, you could be embarrassed by misplacing your confidence and/or affections.

Autopsy. See *Corpse.*

Autumn. In season this dream has no significance, but to dream of autumn at any other time of the year portends friendly forces around you where you least expect them.

Avalanche. To observe an avalanche in your dream predicts some rather formidable obstacles in your path; a change of plan would be advisable. If you were buried in an avalanche, you will have a spectacular stroke of good luck; if you dreamed of others being buried, the forecast is of a change of surroundings.

Aversion. Unfriendliness experienced in a dream is a warning to beware of deception in your close associates.

Aviary. See *Birds, Cage,* etc.

Aviator. You will soon be flying high socially if you dreamed of being or seeing or associating with an airplane pilot.

Avocado. Your love life will improve if you dreamed of this luscious pear. See also *Fruit, Eating,* etc.

Awaken. This rare dream is a most fortunate omen whether it was your own awakening or that of some other person.

Award. You'll be lucky if you dreamed of receiving or giving an award of any kind. Prosperity is just around the corner.

Awe. A warning against vanity and overconfidence are contained in a dream of inspiring awe in others; if you were awestruck in your dream, you must give closer attention to your responsibilities in order to avoid failure.

Awl. A warning against being led astray by bad companions.

Awning. A raised awning signifies new and strange experiences to come; a lowered awning suggests a change of occupation.

Ax. If the ax was bright and keen, it signifies gratifying rewards for work well done; if it was dull, it indicates a loss of prestige which could be averted by closer attention to your own business. See also *Hatchet.*

Axle. You will have opposition from an unsuspected quarter if you dreamed of a broken or damaged axle; but if it was being repaired, or a new one was being fitted, you will overcome your difficulties.

Azalea. Unexpected good news, probably about money, is forecast in a dream of these lovely blooms. See also *Flowers, Plant(s),* and *Colors.*

Baboon. You'll be lucky if you dreamed of this unusual animal. If you are single, you'll soon make a happy marriage; otherwise, you can expect some quick improvement in status; and if your prime concern is business, you can look forward to luck in your current undertakings.

Baby. If the baby was pretty, you will be fortunate through the help of friends. However, if the baby was ugly or in any way displeasing to you, look out for treachery in someone you are inclined to trust. Helpless or sick babies are generally a warning of difficulties ahead, so be cautious in your business and/or love affairs. A walking baby indicates sudden independence, and if you dreamed of many babies, great satisfaction and happiness are coming your way. See also *Cry*.

Bacchus. To dream of this Greek god signifies good financial news for a man; but for a woman, it is a warning to be careful in money matters.

Bachelor. The meaning of this dream depends on its aspect and your relation to it. In general, if the bachelor was young, your affairs will prosper; if the bachelor was old, you must be more circumspect in what you say or you could lose a valued friend. If you are a married man and you dreamed of being a bachelor, you will have a sudden change of circumstances. For a single man, it is a dream of contrary and means he will soon be running in double harness. For a single woman, it promises a new and happy relationship, while for a married woman, it signals the need for · more discretion with male acquaintances.

Back. In its broad interpretation this is a warning in regard to giving advice or lending money, but its meaning varies greatly according to its details. If you dreamed of a bare back, be prepared for some reverses or loss of status. If you dreamed of anyone turning his or her back on you, it indicates jealousy and envy among your associates which may cause you some worry, but it won't be serious. If they turned around and faced you again, you can be sure that the trouble will be temporary. To dream of your own back is an unusual and happy omen indicating that whatever your problems may be they will soon evaporate.

Back Door. Using the back door instead of the front door in your dream is an indication that some important changes are on the way for you. If it was friends who used your back door, be extremely careful in considering any new ventures. If you dreamed that burglars or strangers were trying to

break in your back door, it is the contrariest dream of all; look for a windfall of money!

Backgammon. If you dreamed of playing this game, you will soon be faced with a test of your character. If you won, you can expect an inheritance in the near future, or a valuable gift. If you lost, look out for a tricky business associate. If you were kibbitzing a game of backgammon in your dream, it indicates a coming triumph over opposition.

Bacon. Eating bacon in your dream means continuing prosperity in your life. Rancid bacon is a suggestion to see a doctor. Cooking bacon in your dream augurs a surprise, or gift, which will please you very much.

Badge. Whatever kind of security concerns you most, whether job, social, or financial, will be yours if you dreamed of yourself or anyone else wearing a badge.

Badger. A favorable omen indicating prosperity through your own efforts.

Badminton. See *Games* and *Sports*.

Bag. The significance of this dream varies greatly according to its details. If the bag was of paper and/or was empty, it warns of financial embarrassment which could be avoided by a little extra prudence. A cloth bag forecasts business success, and a leather bag indicates unexpected but pleasant travel. Full or heavy bags are an especially auspicious omen for your dearest wishes.

Baggage. Luggage seen in a dream forecasts a long trip or voyage, probably abroad. If you lost it, or were unable to locate it, an unexpected inheritance is indicated for you or someone close to you. Baggage being roughly handled or dropped is a warning against incurring debts. Having your luggage carried for you suggests happy changes ahead. See also *Travel*.

Bagpipe. See *Music* and *Musical Instruments*.

Bail. You are considering an unwise partnership if you dreamed of needing or supplying bail. Try to find a diplomatic way to sidestep the situation. See also *Arrest* and *Jail*.

Bailiff. If there was trouble with the bailiff, it is a dream of contrary and you will soon have some exciting good news regarding money. If the dream involved merely seeing, or being aware of, or being peacefully in the custody of this court officer, an improved position is indicated.

Bait. A temptation to drift along with an unwise alliance should be strongly resisted if you dreamed of baiting someone or of being baited. See also *Worms* and *Fish*.

Baize. A dream involving this type of material is a warning that your idleness might make someone else richer.

Bake. If you dreamed of baking anything yourself, you may confidently look forward to a rise in status. If the dream concerned a bakery or professional bakers, your year ahead will be prosperous. See also *Bread, Cake, Eating,* etc.

Balcony. This may be considered broadly as an obstacle dream, but you can overcome the difficulties by keeping calm. If the balcony collapsed or seemed dangerous, you will be likely to hear sad news of, or from, distant friends.

Bald. You need to be on guard against being cheated by someone you trust if you dreamed of baldness in others. A dream of your own baldness is a health warning; get a medical checkup. See also *Hair*.

Bale. Seeing baled material in your dream is an indication that the solution to your most pressing problem is near.

Ball. A good omen if the occasion seemed happy, and the music pleasant. However, if it was a masquerade, you are being warned against false friends. Playing ball games such as billiards, tennis, baseball, croquet, etc., signifies happy news.

Ballast. A dream of contrary. If the ballast was being taken on, it is a warning to guard your resources; however, if the ballast was being thrown overboard, you may expect some cherished hope to be realized.

Ballet. A good dream if you were dancing yourself; if you were watching a performance, it is a warning to look after your health.

Balloon. Toy balloons signify trivial disappointments; however, passenger balloons follow the classical interpretation, and ascending is favorable while descending portends setbacks.

Ballot. You will realize a wish you thought hopeless if you dreamed of casting your ballot in an election. Observing ballot boxes or others casting ballots signifies that a change of surroundings and companions would benefit you.

Ballroom. See *Ball, Room,* and *Dance*.

Balsam. Your health will improve if you saw or smelled pine in your dream. See also *Trees*.

Balustrade. You may expect a rash of petty annoyances over money matters if your dream involved sliding down. Going up, in any manner, signifies hard effort before reaching your goal. If the balustrade was broken or incomplete, there will be serious obstacles to some current plan.

Bamboo. See *Plant(s)*.

Banana. If you saw this fruit growing on a tree, you will be lucky in some small matters. If you ate it, you can expect a period of hard work with small reward. Spoiled bananas indicate disappointment in friends. See also *Fruit*.

Bandage. A dream of contrary. Good new influences are moving in around you. See also *Injury, Accident,* etc.

Bandanna. Petty worries and hard work if you wore it yourself. Observed on others it forecasts some happy family news.

Bandit. If you were the victim in the dream, your digestion was at fault; if you observed others being robbed, you are probably contemplating a line of action which you suspect will embarrass you and you'd be right, so don't do it! See also *Crime*.

Bandy. Bandy legs, your own or anyone else's, in a dream are a forecast of good luck on the way.

Banishment. Great prosperity is promised in a dream of being forced to leave your country, home, and loved ones.

Banister. See *Balustrade*.

Banjo. Your worries will soon fade away if you enjoyed the sound. See also *Music* and *Musical Instruments*.

Bank. A rather straightforward dream. An empty bank signifies losses. Tellers paying out money is a warning against carelessness in business matters, unless you were yourself receiving or depositing funds, in which case you can expect some form of money luck. See also *Money*.

Bankrupt. A dream of contrary if it involved your own bankruptcy; you will prosper. But a dream of bankruptcy involving others is a warning not to use shady methods in business and to avoid those who do. See also *Money* and *Law*.

Banner. Generally a good omen pertaining to personal affairs, but other details must be considered such as conditions; i.e., was it flying, torn, etc. See also *Flags, Colors*.

Banquet. There will be love, happiness, and abundant means within your family circle if you dreamed of an elegant banquet. However, if the occasion was in any way unpleasant or there were empty places at the table, you are being

warned against a tendency to be quarrelsome. See also *Food* and *Eating*.

Baptism. You will have a disappointment due to unforeseen circumstances, but you will subsequently find new doors opening to you.

Bar. You will be tempted to stoop to some questionable actions if you dreamed of tending a bar. If you were drinking or merely observing the activity in a bar, it is a suggestion to interest yourself in community affairs.

Barb. You may be heading for serious embarrassment through an unwise choice of companions if you dreamed of catching your clothes on, or being pricked by, a barb.

Barbarian. To be involved, in a dream, with savages is an auspicious omen provided you were not afraid, or if you were, didn't show it; however, if you were chased, or captured by them, you can expect some business snags.

Barbecue. You are likely to be imposed upon by friends or relatives if you dreamed of a whole animal being roasted.

Barber. For a man, this dream denotes success but only after delays and hard work; for a woman, it indicates less affluence than hoped for. See also *Hair*.

Barefoot. To be completely naked in your dream is a very lucky omen, but if only your feet were bare, you have some difficulties to overcome before you reach your goal.

Bargain. An auspicious dream for women; for men a warning to resist outside influences and rely on their own judgment.

Barge. You will outwit your competitors if the barge was loaded; if empty, it is a warning against making hasty decisions. If you only observed the barge in your dream, it forecasts a long trip quite soon.

Bark. Tree bark is a "Danger-Go-Slow" warning in regard to the opposite sex. See also *Trees*.

Barking. The interpretation of this dream depends on the nature of the sound; if it was angry or menacing, then the message is to beware of losses through so-called friends; if the sound was happy and welcoming, you can expect a beneficial happening soon. See also *Dog* and *Animals*.

Barley. This dream relates to your health and its significance follows the condition of the grain. If it was poor, stunted, or the field neglected, you should see a doctor.

Barmaid. This dream relates to sexual activity and is a warning to be more selective in choosing your companions.

Barn. The significance of this dream depends on its details. A barn in good condition and full, or partly so, is an omen of prosperity; conversely, an empty or derelict barn is a warning against risky investment.

Barnacles. You can anticipate a comfortable old age if you dreamed of this marine mollusk.

Barometer. Good business weather is predicted by a dream of this instrument, unless it was broken or damaged, in which case you should keep a tight grip on your spending for the time being.

Barracks. You will be protected from serious difficulties if you dreamed of this kind of abode.

Barrel. Upright, full, and in good condition a barrel promises financial security; but empty and/or rolling it suggests you should take measures to protect your position.

Barrier. Anything closed, such as a window, door, gate, fence, wall, etc., constitutes an obstacle dream, and its significance will follow on how you dealt with it.

Baseball. See *Games* and *Sports*.

Basement. You need to be firm about refusing plans which don't really appeal to you. See also *Cellar*.

Bashful. See *Shy*.

Basin. A dream of contrary. If the basin was full, you can expect some family troubles or disappointment in love. However, if the basin was empty, your success is assured.

Basket. A straightforward dream. If the basket was full and useful, you will have new opportunities; if it was empty or damaged, you are in danger of loss through your own carelessness.

Basketball. See *Sports, Games,* and *Ball.*

Bastard. A peculiar example of contrary meaning. If you dreamed of being one, you can expect some unusual honor to come your way; of someone else being one, you can look forward to an improvement in your social standing.

Bat. The augury is dependent on how you reacted to the bat. If you were frightened by it, you should avoid indiscreet discussion of your affairs; but if you were not afraid of it, you will be offered a new proposition which will be profitable.

Bath. If the bath was empty, it is a warning against decisions made, or actions carried out, in anger. If the bath was cold or too hot, you will have to revise some favorite plan, but if the temperature was pleasantly warm, your current expectations will be realized. See also *Water.*

Bathing. In the open sea predicts a fortune beyond your wildest dreams; in a lake, passing difficulties; in a river, a happy surprise

ahead; bathing with others, a friend will approach you for help. See also *Water.*

Battle. You are apt to be involved in serious quarrels if you dreamed of a battle. If you were on (or observed) the winning side, it is a happy omen for your current love interests.

Bauble. See *Jewelry, Beads,* etc.

Bay. The meaning of this dream depends on its aspect. Travel is predicted if you saw the bay from a height or scenic viewpoint. If the water was rough, you can expect a period during which your cash will go out faster than it comes in; but if the water was calm or only gently ruffled, there is unusual social success in store for you.

Bazaar. You will soon have cause to rejoice if you dreamed of being at, seeing, or assisting in, one of these busy places.

Beach. The interpretation of this dream varies greatly according to its details. You will be likely to need financial help if the dream involved working on a beach. Lying on a beach is a dream of contrary; you will soon be almost too busy with a new venture. See also *Sand*.

Beacon. See *Lighthouse*.

Beads. You will have a good share of social success if you dreamed of looking at beads. If they were being strung or counted, it signifies the receipt of unexpected money. Lost or dropped beads represent some small disappointment. See also *Jewelry* and *Rosary*.

Beak. See *Birds*.

Beam. A heavy beam of wood indicates a burden you will have to bear. A light beam of wood suggests an unanticipated reward for a past favor. A steel beam portends money from a forgotten source. See also *Light*.

Beans. A dream involving beans is a warning of difficulties ahead, unless you were cooking them, in which case they indicate an increase in income.

Beard. This is a good omen for men (and for women if the beard was on a man), and the fuller or more luxuriant the beard the better will be your coming luck. But a dream of a beard on a woman is a warning against gambling of any nature. See also *Hair*.

Bears. A caged bear signifies future success; a dancing bear indicates luck in speculation; fighting off or killing a bear suggests victory over hostile opposition. See also *Animals*.

Beasts. Seen in a dream most unusual animals represent difficulties and problems which will cause considerable worry unless you managed to drive the beasts away, in which case you will overcome the troubles with small effort. See also *Animals*.

Beaten. This is a dream of contrary in a peculiar way, for if you dreamed of beating, or being beaten by, friends or loved ones, it is a fortunate omen for personal or family affairs; however, if strangers were involved, it is a warning not to procrastinate in dealing with current domestic problems. If the dream concerned the beating of animals or carpets, it indicates difficulties arising from lack of organization which are within your power to overcome if you concentrate.

Beauty. A dream of beauty is an excellent omen forecasting success in both love and business affairs.

Beaver. This industrious animal is a symbol of substantial comfort achieved through your own efforts, unless you killed or injured it which suggests you are ignoring some good advice through obstinacy. Calm down and listen to your conscience. See also *Animals.*

Beckon. Your immediate future will be full of pleasure and satisfaction if a friend or relation beckoned in your dream, but if a stranger did the beckoning, you can prepare yourself for minor reverses.

Bed. A strange bed forecasts an upturn in business affairs; your own bed promises security; making a bed suggests that you should expect some unexpected visitors.

Bedbugs. Unpleasant news may be expected if you dreamed of seeing these nasty creatures. If you killed them or managed to get rid of them, you will eventually improve your situation.

Bedclothes. In some respects this is a dream of contrary which pertains primarily to your finances. If you are well off and you dreamed of having lots of bedclothes, it is a warning against serious reverses through lack of proper supervision of your investments. But if your income is on the modest to poor side, you can expect a comfortable improvement shortly. To dream of putting a bolster on a bed signifies an embarrassing marital situation coming up; to put fresh slips on pillows predicts an approaching opportunity which should be grasped. However, if your dream specifically concerned the condition of the bedclothes, then its significance must be interpreted according to whether the bed was clean and neatly made, pleasant or unpleasant in appearance, white or colored linen, etc., and such details should be looked up under their separate headings.

Bedfellow. A strange bedfellow of the opposite sex is a forecast of a change of residence; if you were in bed with someone of your own sex or with a friend, your happiness could be threatened by your own foolish actions.

Think it over! Seek advice.

Bedroom. A strange bedroom, pleasantly furnished, indicates a change for the better; your own bedroom signifies harmony in current affairs.

Beef. You would do well to keep your private affairs to yourself if you dreamed of raw or bloody beef. If you refused a serving of beef, it augurs a coming need for help and/or dependence on the generosity of a friend; however, if you ate the beef and enjoyed it, you can expect a business turn for the better. See also *Food, Eating,* etc.

Beehive. Dignity, honor, and wealth are signified by a dream of a beehive, unless it was empty, in which case financial difficulties are forecast.

Beer. It is a good omen if you dreamed of pouring or drinking the beer, especially if there was foam on it. But if the beer was flat or stale or others drank it, you are being warned not to be persuaded to enter into some unworthy intrigue which could backfire and damage your reputation.

Bees. These busy creatures are a forerunner of great good fortune in business matters, even if they stung you. However, if they were dead, listless, or you killed them, you could suffer a loss by putting too much trust in "friends." If you heard the bees buzzing, expect good news.

Beeswax. Beeswax in a dream represents love affairs, so the interpretation must be made from the other elements involved; i.e., how the material was used. See also *Ironing, Sewing,* etc., and under individual listings of kinds of wood.

Beetles. A dream involving these unpleasant creatures is a warning of hostility and jealousy among your associates. If you killed the insects or managed to get rid of them, your difficulties will be very temporary.

Beets. To see them growing or harvested indicates prosperity after hard work; to eat them forecasts happiness in matters of love. See also *Vegetable(s)* and *Colors.*

Beggar. A dream of contrary. You will receive unexpected help if you dreamed of begging or of giving to a beggar. If your dream involved refusal, you will be disappointed by someone on whom you counted.

Begonias. See *Flowers* and *Colors*.

Behead. Another dream of contrary. Your success is assured if you dreamed of being beheaded; if the beheading involved others, success is still predicted but only after discouraging delays.

Behind. See *Buttocks, Body,* etc.

Belch. A dream of warning to be more circumspect in your behavior.

Belfry. This dream meaning is in line with its aspect. If the belfry was high and in good condition, good news is predicted; but if it was demolished or in bad repair, be prepared for a change involving reduced circumstances. See also *Church* and *Bell*.

Bell. You will receive disappointing news if you heard a single bell ringing in your dream, but if you heard many bells, the news will be joyous. Church bells signify a warning against problems arising from people pulling against

you. See also *Church*.

Belladonna. A modest commercial success is indicated if you dreamed of belladonna. See also *Plant(s)*.

Belle. A dream of contrary. Whether you played this role in a dream, or were involved with one who played it, it is a forerunner of trouble in family affairs.

Bellows. Be prepared to struggle through a period of difficulties of your own making if you dreamed of using bellows. If you merely observed them in your dream, it indicates a tendency to waste effort on meaningless things. Change your tactics.

Belly. See *Abdomen*.

Belly Button. See *Navel*.

Belt. A dream of contrary. To wear a belt or put one on signifies a wish for a change of surroundings, but to observe a belt or take one off indicates a need for more security. In either case, energetic positive action is suggested. See also *Leather* and *Colors*.

Bench. To be seated on a bench signifies important business news; a moss-covered bench foretells a minor loss; a stone bench predicts a significant profit; and a wooden bench augurs a small but pleasing gain.

Benediction. See *Blessing, Church,* etc.

Benefits. You will need to guard against problems arising from uninhibited actions if you were the recipient; but if you were the benefactor, you'll be lucky in your current interests.

Bequests. A dream of contrary. If you bequeathed in your dream, you will receive something of value; but if you were the recipient of a dreamed bequest, be prepared for a small loss.

Bereavement. Another dream of opposite portent. News of a birth, engagement, or wedding is likely to follow. See also *Funeral, Death, Grief,* etc.

Beret. See *Hat, Head,* etc.

Berries. To see them growing or harvested is a sign of increasing social status; to pick them signifies financial improvement through your own efforts; to eat them predicts achievement of comfort but not wealth.

See also *Blackberries, Strawberries, Raspberries, Fruit, Eating, Colors,* etc.

Best Man. For a man to dream of fulfilling this important function signifies coming happiness in love and/or family affairs. For a woman it foretells future security. See also *Wedding.*

Bet. The wind of change is blowing in your direction if you dreamed of betting yourself; if you observed others doing the betting, look sharp for mischievous competitors in business and/or love affairs. See also *Gambling, Money,* etc.

Betrothed. See *Engagement.*

Beverages. See *Drink* and *Alcohol.*

Bewilder. See *Confusion.*

Bewitched. Any dream involving this reaction is a warning to stop wasting your time with meaningless people and activities.

Bias. To be aware of prejudice in your dream suggests you could use some competent advice concerning your personal relationships. See also *Cloth* and *Sewing.*

Bible. You will reap an unexpected reward for an act of pure kindness if you dreamed of the Holy Book. See also *Read*.

Bicycle. A bicycle represents assistance in your endeavors, so to interpret the meaning of your dream, you must consider whether you were riding it, pushing it, etc., also whether you were going uphill, on the flat, or downhill, the appearance and/or condition of the bike as well as details of location, weather, etc.

Bid. See *Auction*.

Big. You'll have great success with the opposite sex if you dreamed of being a bigger person than you actually are. If the dream involved others being very big, it signifies prosperity ahead.

Bigamy. For a man, this dream connotes loss of virility and suggests a medical checkup. For a woman, it indicates a need for more discretion in choice of companions.

Bilious. You are being warned against high living and low company if you dreamed of being bilious. See also *Illness*.

Billiards. Legal action and/or family quarrels over property are apt to follow a dream about this game, unless you are a regular player, in which case the dream has no significance.

Bills. A dream of contrary. If you were worried about or received bills in your dream, you can expect a happy run of good luck in financial matters; but if you paid, collected, or sent bills out, you'd better get in contact with generous friends or relations because you'll be needing assistance.

Bind. Embarrassing personal entanglements are indicated by a dream of binding things up, or being bound up yourself. Reexamine your current relationships with an eye to being more selective in future.

Binoculars. If the binoculars were properly used in your dream, they are a fortunate omen; but if they were used for peeping or spying, you may soon have to defend your reputation, so avoid all actions which could be misinterpreted by your detractors.

Birch. See *Trees*.

Birds. Birds are generally considered a most fortunate dream omen, especially so if they are brightly colored, singing, and/or flying. Dead or injured birds are an indication of coming worries unless they are birds of prey, in which case the worries will be short-lived. Birds' eggs in a nest signify money, broken birds' eggs forecast disappointment, birds hatching in a nest indicate delayed profits. An empty nest is a warning not to be drawn into family arguments. To be aware in your dream of the beak of a bird is a forecast of a change of residence, whether for better or worse depends on the other details of the dream.

Birth. You are sure to have good news soon after a dream of the birth of, or giving birth to, a child. If the birth involved animals, it signifies defeat for anyone working against your interests. Multiple births indicate an increase in material wealth. Of course if the dreamer happens to be pregnant, there is no significance.

Birthday. Dream of your own, or another's birthday, and good luck will surely come your way. A dream

of birthday presents has the same significance.

Biscuits. See *Bread, Eating,* and *Bake.*

Bishop. This high church official, in a dream, has, through the ages, been considered a harbinger of unpleasant news, so brace yourself! See also *Church* and *Clergy.*

Bison. See *Buffalo.*

Bit. To dream of applying a bit to wood or metal suggests that you can solve your own problems by taking positive action.

Bite. You may uncover a secret that you'd rather not know if you dreamed of being bitten by an animal or insect. There is a suggestion in this dream that you refrain from prying into the affairs of others.

Bitter. To experience this sensation in taste or feeling indicates that you would be well advised to think before you speak or you could incur the enmity of someone who might frustrate your ambitions.

Black. Bubble, bubble, toil and trouble will be yours if you dreamed of anything black, unless you saw it at a funeral, in which case it predicts success, especially in love affairs. See also *Colors*.

Blackberries. Whether you saw them, picked them, or ate them, blackberries predict reverses. Pull in your belt and be prepared to struggle for a while.

Blackbird. You can expect a dreary drag for the next few months if you dreamed of seeing a blackbird. However, if it was flying or singing, the significance alters to one of a successful venture. See also *Birds*.

Blackboard. News is on the way if a blackboard figured in your dream. If you observed white writing on the board, the news will probably affect your immediate plans.

Blacking. See *Shoes*.

Blackmail. You are being warned against indiscreet behavior with the opposite sex if someone tried to blackmail you in a dream. If you were the blackmailer, you would be wise to avoid any type of gambling for the time being. See also *Crime*.

Black Maria. A dream of

contrary if you were in the police wagon; you can expect an improvement in status. But if you observed others being taken away, it predicts a temporary setback. See also *Arrest*.

Black Sheep. If you were called a "black sheep" in your dream, it's a warning to guard your tongue. To see a black sheep forecasts some unexpected profit. See also *Sheep* and *Animals*.

Blacksmith. Your current projects will turn out better than you anticipated if you saw a blacksmith in your dream. See also *Anvil*.

Bladder. A warning against physical overexertion. Get a medical checkup. See also *Body*.

Blade. If the blade was dirty or rusty, see your doctor. If clean and shiny, it indicates helpful new friends. See also *Cut* and *Knife*.

Blame. A dream of contrary. If you were being blamed, you will have some unusual business luck; but if the blame attached to others, look out for hypocrisy among your close associates.

Blanket. A sort of dream of

contrary, the significance of which depends on your circumstances. If you are well off and dreamed of buying or receiving new blankets, you should guard your investments; if you are not well off, you may expect an improvement in your financial position. Soiled or ragged blankets warn against trickery by someone you trust. See also *Colors*.

Blasphemy. A dream of contrary if you heard it; you will realize your ambitions. If you used it, you will suffer embarrassment through false friends. See also *Curse* and *Profanity*.

Blast. You can expect smoother sailing in all departments of your life if you dreamed of hearing or setting off a blast. See also *Explosion*.

Blaze. See *Flame* and *Fire*.

Bleach. See *Hair*.

Bleat. You can expect new and pleasant interests if you heard young animals bleating in your dream. See also *Lamb* and *Animals*.

Bleed. See *Blood*.

Blemish. You will have great

success with the opposite sex if the blemish was on the neck, chest, bust, or arms; but if on the body or legs, you will have to be very careful indeed to avoid being involved in a dangerous scandal! See also *Face*.

Blessing. If it occurred in a church, the forecast is for an easement of your burdens, whatever they may be; however, if you pronounced the benediction, you will have to struggle to overcome the obstacles that face you.

Blight. To see blighted plants is a warning against promiscuous behavior with the opposite sex.

Blind. A dream of warning; whether the dream involved others who were blind or your own blindness, it is a straightforward sign of deceit among those you trust most.

Blindfold. Reexamine your plans and motives; if your dream involved a blindfold, you've got a queasy conscience.

Bloat. Good luck will follow a dream of seeing others who were bloated, but if you were bloated yourself, it signifies some annoying news.

Block. Start economizing. If your dream concerned a block of any hard or solid material, you can expect to need financial help soon. See also *Stone(s), Metal,* etc.

Blond. See *Hair*.

Blood. Be prepared for a period of hard work against hostile forces if you saw blood in your dream. If you were bleeding, try to avoid any sort of controversy with friends or relatives; however, if the blood was that involved in a transfusion, you can expect your difficulties to be very transitory.

Blossoms. Happiness, prosperity, and contentment are promised in a dream of trees, shrubs, or flowers in bloom. See also *Colors, Plant(s),* etc.

Blot. You will solve a mystery which has been puzzling you for some time if you dreamed of a blot on clean paper. If you made a blot on a document, you may expect a sudden improvement in your affairs. See also *Ink* and *Writing*.

Blotch. See *Blemish* and *Skin*.

Blotter. You can expect to hear some astonishing news regarding a friend if you saw a clean blotter in your dream; if the blotter was much used and/or worn, it signifies quarrels with family or close friends on the horizon. Curb your tongue! See also *Colors, Ink,* and *Writing*.

Blow. See *Wind, Storm(s),* etc.

Blows. A dream of contrary. If you received the blows in your dream, you can expect an improvement in your status; if you defended yourself, it signifies a return of something you thought was lost. If you struck the blows in your dream, it signifies a coming embarrassment. See also *Fight*.

Blue. See *Colors*.

Blunder. A dream of contrary, and the more clumsy and awkward the dream action was, the greater will be your success.

Blush. To dream of blushing predicts that you will discover a false friend; to observe blushes in others is a warning against repeating gossip.

Boa Constrictor. See *Snake(s)*.

Boar. If you chased it or ran from it, be prepared for a disappointment. If you killed it, you can expect a promotion. See also *Animals*.

Boards. See under individual listings of kinds of wood.

Boat. The interpretation of this dream depends on its other aspects, such as the condition of the water, clear or murky, rough or smooth, river, lake, or ocean; at anchor or moving speedily or slowly. You may take it that the boat is a dream symbol for your life and the details must be applied in relation to it. See also *Ship*.

Body. It's a happy omen of success to see a body in your dream and this is so whether the body was beautiful or deformed. A female body pertains to social success while a male body signifies business achievement.

Bog. A dream of contrary. You will overcome your obstacles by refusing to become discouraged. Persevere.

Bogey. See *Apparition* and *Ghost*.

Boil. You are being warned against allowing your emotions to influence your judgment if you dreamed of boiling water. See also under *Food*.

Boils. See *Blemish* and *Skin*.

Bolts. An obstacle dream, and also a dream of contrary. If you were bolted in, you may expect a change of location; if you were bolted out, it signifies some difficulties of your own making, unless you broke the bolt, in which case you will eventually overcome the obstacles now facing you.

Bombs (or Bombers). These represent a threat to your way of life which you can avert by judicious action.

Bone. Meat bones signify business reverses; human bones indicate a coming inheritance; fish bones suggest a medical checkup.

Bonus. New social contacts will prove unexpectedly useful in business if you dreamed of receiving a bonus. See also *Money*.

Book. You can anticipate slow but steady progress and a calm pleasant life ahead if books were the main feature of your dream.

Bookcase. See *Furniture*.

Bookkeeper. See *Accounts*.

Boomerang. A warning to guard against dishonest associates if you dreamed the boomerang came back to you; if it didn't, you can expect a change of residence.

Boots. New and/or comfortable well-polished boots forecast promotion and financial security; but if they were shabby and/or ill-fitting, you would be well advised to give more serious attention to your personal affairs.

Booty. See *Treasure*.

Borrow. Prepare to retrench if you dreamed you had to borrow anything; however, if someone borrowed from you, you'll have help over any financial hump you may encounter.

Bosom. See *Breast*.

Botany. See *Plant(s), Flowers,* etc.

Bottle. The interpretation of this dream varies with its details. If the bottle was full, it forecasts quick prosperity; if empty, sudden reverses. If you spilled the contents, you can expect petty worries and domestic quarrels.

Boulder. See *Rock(s)*.

Bound. An obstacle dream. Don't give in to mental jitters and follow the advice of more experienced heads and you can avoid the pitfalls.

Bouquet. A fresh bright bouquet signifies a happy social occasion. If it was wilted, a medical checkup is indicated. See also *Flowers* and *Colors*.

Bow (and Arrow). Your good luck will vary according to how well you hit the target, so a bull's eye will make good fortune phenomenal! If you missed, then you may expect some difficulties due to your own foolishness. If you were hit by an arrow, look out for a false friend in your close circle.

Bowel Movement. In a way, this is a dream of contrary, as the more embarrassing the situation was in the dream, the better is its omen. If it occurred in bed, it signifies coming abundance; in public, the forecast is of great financial success. To observe feces on the street or step in them is an omen of sudden money luck.

Bowl. The meaning of this dream is in line with its aspect, but influenced by its details. You can expect some disappointment if the bowl was empty, but filled, it signifies good prospects for all your dearest wishes. See also *Colors* and nature of contents.

Bowling. A generally fortunate dream whether indoors or out, especially if you were playing.

Box. You can expect an upset in your plans if your dream featured an empty box, but if there was something in the box, you can overcome your obstacles. See also under nature of the contents.

Boxing. Be careful about repeating confidences after a dream involving a boxing match or you could lose an important opportunity which is coming your way.

Boy. Any dream featuring boys, even if they were fighting, is a generally good omen for your future.

Bracelet. Whether your main concern is money or love, this is a fortunate dream, unless you lost or broke the bracelet, in which case prepare for a disappointment in love or a financial setback. See also under *Metal, Silver, Gold, Jewelry,* etc.

Brain. Pleasant and/or profitable news from an unexpected quarter is forecast in a dream featuring animal brains; however, if the dream involved human brains, it is telling you that you need to show more consideration for those you love.

Brake. You will be offered a new opportunity which will increase your responsibilities if you dreamed of braking a vehicle; if the brake failed or made a noise, you would be wise to consider VERY carefully before accepting any new offer, as there is apt to be a well-hidden snag. See also *Automobile, Train, Airplane,* etc.

Brambles. You can expect some reverses if the thorns scratched you; if not, you will soon be much happier than you are now.

Branches. A generally good omen. See also *Trees* and *Hedge,* etc.

Brandy. You could lose valuable friends by being too materialistic if your dream featured brandy, unless you bought (or paid for) it, in which case your personal affairs will take a turn for the better.

Brass. Be extremely cautious about dealing with new acquaintances after a dream featuring brass, and depend on your own judgment more. See also *Metal*.

Brassiere. Obviously, the interpretation varies according to the sex of the dreamer. For a man, any dream featuring this bit of lingerie is a warning to be on guard against adverse influences in his immediate circle of associates. For a female it promises a welcome increase in social activities. See also *Bust* and *Breast*.

Bravery. A dream of contrary. You are apt to put yourself at a disadvantage by not facing up to some present problems if your dream featured acts of bravery or heroism. See also *Coward*.

Brawl. See *Fight*.

Bray. This donkey sound, heard in a dream, is considered to be the fore-runner of unpleasant (but not disastrous) news. However, you must be sure the donkey was BRAYING; if it was making any other sound, it mitigates the prediction to one of good news. See also *Donkey*.

Bread. If the bread in your dream was dark, stale, and/or hard, you can expect a sudden outcrop of annoying family worries; however, if it was fresh, white, and tasty, your future is secure, which is also the case if you dreamed of baking the bread yourself. See also *Bake* and *Eating*.

Break. Be prepared for a period of unrewarding struggle if your dream featured breaking, broken, or damaged articles of any description. The more valuable or important the broken item, the longer will be the trying period. There are two exceptions to this rule: broken eyeglasses signify success where you expected failure, and breaking (or broken) bones (human) forecast an unexpected legacy. See also under *Glass*, *Furniture*, etc.

Breakdown. See *Health* and *Nervous*.

Breakfast. All the details of the meal, such as the food involved, etc., must be considered for an accurate interpretation, but as a general guide, if you were eating alone, you must guard against restlessness and hasty speech, but if you were breakfasting with others, you can gain your objectives by being patient and diligent.

Breast. You will soon make a new, valuable, and lasting friend if your dream involved resting your head on someone's breast. See *Bust*.

Breastbone. See *Wishbone, Bone*, etc.

Breath. If the breath was pleasant or the breathing steady and/or deep, it signifies success and satisfaction in your efforts; however, if the breath was in any way unpleasant or the breathing difficult, a visit to your doctor is advisable.

Breeding. Dispose of existing obligations before considering new ones if you dreamed of breeding animals.

Breeze. See *Wind*.

Brewing. Eventual content-

ment, but only after a rather long period of worry, is suggested by any dream featuring brewing.

Bribe. An unfortunate omen whether you offer the bribe or accept it. Avoid any form of gambling or speculation for the time being, and stay far away from anyone you suspect might try to exploit you.

Bricks. Bricks in a dream forecast upset conditions due to sudden change, unless you were laying them or observing them being laid, in which case your circumstances will slowly but steadily improve.

Bride. You'll be lucky if you saw or were a bride in your dream, but the details must be considered for an accurate interpretation. The condition of the bridal dress, for instance; whether the general atmosphere was happy, etc. All these factors should be looked up. If you kissed or were kissed by a bride, you will have a small but pleasing inheritance. See also *Wedding*.

Bridegroom. You will have an unexpected delay in some cherished plan if your dream featured a bridegroom, but don't give up; new tactics can succeed. See also *Wedding*.

Bridesmaid. The significance is the same as for Bridegroom, except that it refers to romance. See also *Wedding*.

Bridge. The meaning of this dream depends on its aspect and your relation to it. As a general guide if it was daylight and the structure was in good repair and you crossed it without difficulty, it signifies a satisfactory change and prosperity. If the structure was damaged in any way, you are warned against making any changes for the time being. See also *Water, River*, etc. If your dream involved the game of bridge, you are apt to be disappointed in a business matter. See also *Cards, Games*, etc.

Bridgework. See *Teeth*.

Bridle. You will be obliged to take on some unwanted task if you dreamed of putting a bridle on a horse; however, you will eventually be glad of the experience gained. If it was difficult, or the bridle was broken or very worn, it is a warning not to be persuaded into a clandestine affair. See also *Horse*.

Briefcase. The meaning depends on details of color, condition, etc., but as a general guide: a well-worn case predicts business success; a new briefcase is a warning against making changes or decisions without adequate investigation; a full briefcase is telling you to pay more attention to your personal affairs, and an empty one predicts success with your current plans. To lose your briefcase is a dream of contrary and forecasts an unexpected profit, but to find one suggests that you must watch your step very carefully indeed to avoid a business disappointment.

Bristles. Firm bristles are a forecast of good luck in your future plans, but soft bristles signify a social disappointment.

Broadcast. Success is predicted in a dream of listening to a broadcast; if you were doing the broadcasting, the dream was telling you to persevere with your current plans.

Broker. Don't speculate for at least a month if your dream featured a broker (or brokers) of any kind.

Bronchitis. An obstacle dream. If the affliction was

temporary in your dream, you will overcome your difficulties by your own efforts; however, if you were not aware of a recovery in your dream, you will need help, so ask for it.

Brooch. See *Jewelry*.

Brood. Any kind of brood (except chickens) observed in a dream indicates a financial improvement. See also *Chickens*.

Brook. See *Water*.

Broom. Your general luck will soon improve if the broom was new; however, if it was dirty or worn, you'd better look out for an insincere friend, unless you threw the old broom away or got rid of it in some manner, in which case you can expect to benefit through a good friend. If you hit someone (or something) with a broom, it signifies a surprising change for the better.

Broth. All your affairs will prosper if you dreamed of drinking or cooking broth. See also *Eating* and *Cooking*.

Brothel. Oddly enough this is, in a way, a dream of contrary. For either a man or woman a dream of visiting such an establishment signifies an improvement in domestic affairs.

Brother. The meaning varies according to context and sex of the dreamer. For a woman it signifies great domestic security, but for a man it indicates family quarrels ahead. An objective dream of unity between brothers is an indication of financial stability.

Brother-in-Law. The same as for Brother.

Brown. See *Colors*.

Bruise. There is a distinct warning against too much high living in a dream of bruises on yourself or someone else. If the bruises were on the legs, your reputation could be at stake. Slow down! See also *Body*.

Brussels Sprouts. See *Vegetable(s)* and *Eating*.

Brutality. See *Horror*, etc.

Bubbles. Your immediate worries will vanish as if by magic if you observed bubbles in your dream; however, if you were making the bubbles, you are being warned against extravagance. Be more realistic in your attitude toward money.

Buckle. A fastened buckle signifies loyal and affectionate family ties; an unclasped buckle indicates a necessity for positive action to avoid domestic or romantic upsets; a dream of fastening or trying to fasten a buckle suggests you should give more diligent attention to your business affairs.

Buffalo. Large profits are forecast in a dream involving this rare animal, unless you killed or injured it, in which case be extra careful concerning any new venture offered.

Bugle. If you heard it, you can expect good news from a distance; if you played it, you can count on generous rewards for your efforts.

Bugs. There is a warning in this dream against unfortunate influences around you, unless you succeeded in driving the bugs off or getting rid of them in some way, in which case it is a dream of contrary and signifies imminent money luck. See also *Insects*.

Building. The meaning of this dream is in line with its aspect. The building(s) represent your life achievement; therefore if the structures were imposing, well kept, beautiful, and/or impressive, you can expect eventual luxury; if they were modest but pleasant in appearance, you can expect comfort but not wealth; and if they were old and/or dilapidated, you'd better start saving for the rainy days ahead.

Bull. You have some tough competition facing you in business and/or love if your dream featured this animal, unless it was very light or white, in which case you'll have a stroke of great luck when you least expect it. If you dreamed of a bullfight, you are being warned to take decisive action to clear up an unpleasant personal situation.

Bulldog. This fellow is a warning against any sort of legal pettifogging. Don't even park overtime at a meter, not to mention fiddling your taxes—you'll regret it!

Bullet. Don't expose yourself to any possible whisper of scandal if your dream featured the sound or sight of a bullet; if you were hit by a bullet in your dream, you'd better have a medical checkup.

Bullfrog. You can expect to make new and interesting friends if you saw the bullfrog; if you heard it, you can count on contentment in the near future; but if you caught it, you'd better look in your nest for a cuckoo!

Bull's-eye. Important news is on the way if you hit a bull's-eye in your dream, but if someone else was doing the shooting, be careful where you put your trust.

Bum. See *Tramp.*

Bump. A dream of warning. Be extremely circumspect in all your actions if you dreamed of bumping or being bumped.

Bundle. Don't expose yourself to any kind of criticism if you dreamed of wrapping or carrying a bundle. If someone else had the bundle, it indicates a surprise, probably in the form of an unexpected invitation.

Bunion. See *Feet.*

Bunk. See *Bed* and *Sleep.*

Burden. This dream is an omen of success, providing you were not yourself carrying the burden; if you were, you can expect an increase in your responsibilities.

Burglar. A dream of contrary. Burglars in your dream predict an increase in worldly goods, and if you caught them, it will probably be by way of an inheritance.

Burial. Another dream of contrary. You will no doubt have news of a marriage, be invited to a wedding, or hear of a birth. However, if your dream was one of being buried alive, it is telling you to avoid doing anything which you know or suspect to be even marginally unethical. See also *Funeral, Cemetery,* and *Death.*

Burlap. Your current projects will give great satisfaction if your dream featured this material.

Burning. A dream of contrary signifying a coming increase in prosperity, unless it was a very large building that was burning, in which case you are being warned to guard your finances.

Burns. You'll be lucky if you dreamed of burns, especially of the hands or feet. After this kind of dream is a good time for a little speculation, but stay well within your means.

Burro. See *Donkey*.

Bus. Traveling by bus indicates progress toward your heart's desire; waiting for a bus signifies setbacks which will be very temporary. A bus accident predicts a period of frustration due to financial embarrassment.

Bush. The message here is in the action. If you were only aware of the bushes, you will have an offer which involves a change of location; if you (or anyone else) hid in or under the bush(es), it is a warning not to do anything at this time that the world can't know about; if you cut the bush or saw it burning, be prepared for the revelation of an embarrassing secret.

Business. Be prepared for a sticky time ahead if your dream concerned business; you will probably have to fight against some hostile, or even dishonest, competition. However, if the dream involved business documents, you can expect the situation to resolve in your favor.

Bust. Any dream featuring a bust whether beautiful or not is a good omen, and the larger the bust the more fortunate the omen. Even a wounded bust predicts money luck. If the dream involved a suckling baby, you can expect to be very happy indeed in the near future. See also *Breast, Art, Sculpture,* and *Statue(s)*.

Butcher. Be very cautious about signing any documents if your dream featured a butcher or a meat market. If the dream involved killing animals or slicing meat, a medical checkup is suggested.

Butler. See *Servant(s)*.

Butter. A fortunate dream no matter what form it took. Even rancid butter signifies a secure future.

Butterfly. Social success, romantic success, and/or domestic happiness is forecast by a dream of these gaily colored creatures.

Buttermilk. If you drank it, you will be worried by some past indiscretion, but the difficulty will soon pass.

If you threw it out, or gave it away, you must avoid hasty decisions (or actions) regarding matters of importance.

Buttocks. The meaning of this dream varies according to its details, but it is a generally good omen. Whether the buttocks were your own or someone else's, you can anticipate happy times ahead. If they were animal buttocks, the indication is of financial luck. If the dream involved being kicked in the buttocks, you can be sure of a steady rise in status; but if you did the kicking, you will have to cope with some foolish jealousy in your immediate circle.

Buttons. If the buttons were bright and/or broken, you must take steps to break away from a worrying

emotional situation. If the dream involved losing a button, it indicates a need to curb extravagance to avoid financial embarrassment.

Buying. A dream of contrary. Indiscriminate buying in your dream indicates a need to conserve your resources; however, if you were buying carefully, you can expect a stroke of money luck.

Buzzard. This ugly bird in a dream is a strong warning against repeating idle gossip which could boomerang on you, especially if you observed it eating. See also *Birds*.

Buzzer. You can look forward to a happily stepped-up social life if you heard the sound of a buzzer in your dream.

Cab. Riding alone in a cab (or taxi) means you will gain (or retain) a comfortable life through your own efforts. If it was at night and you were with a companion of the opposite sex, you are in danger of being involved in a scandal through your own indiscretion. Don't gossip!

Cabin. If you dreamed you were in a ship's cabin, there is rough domestic weather ahead, or alternatively you could be drawn into the legal troubles of a friend or associate. Try to steer clear of controversy for the time being. However, if the cabin was in the woods or at the beach, you can look forward to happiness in domestic affairs.

Cage. The interpretation of this dream depends on the circumstances of the dreamer. To see a cage full of birds means a release from anxiety which could come through a sizable inheritance. An empty cage denotes an elopement or a loss of opportunity through carelessness. Two birds in a cage signify success in love affairs. Re animals in cage, see *Animals.*

Cake. A fortunate dream signifying satisfaction in both social and business affairs. Very sweet cake indicates a legacy and/or for those employed a promotion. Thickly iced cake predicts gay times ahead. To eat cake in a dream is more fortunate than to bake or buy it, although anything to do with cakes is lucky.

Calendar. Most dreams involving calendars signify gradual reduction of worries.

Calf. A suckling calf is a sure sign that all your hopes will be realized. A butchered calf indicates a disillusionment; a frisky calf is a happy omen for marriages or affairs of the heart. For a man to dream he is admiring the calf of a woman's leg is a warning to guard his credit.

Call. To hear your own name called by someone you cannot see or identify predicts important news soon to come. If the voice was that of a friend or relative, the news is likely to concern an illness in the family. If the call you heard was for someone else, or you were calling for someone, the news is likely to involve a divorce or a break of some nature.

Calm. A dream of contrary. You can expect some hectic activity if the calm you dreamed of was the variety following a storm; however, if your dream involved calming people or animals, it signifies stormy weather ahead in your family or love affairs.

Camel. You will have to work hard and diligently to overcome your obstacles if your dream involved one (or more) of these hardy animals, unless it (or they) carried a burden, in which case there is some unexpected wealth, possibly in the form of an inheritance, coming your way. If you were riding on a camel or saw them in a herd, your future is very bright indeed. See also *Animals*.

Camera. A dream of warning. Whether you or someone else used or had the camera it signifies insincere friends around you. Be especially cautious about giving any confidences of a personal nature.

Camp. A generally good omen. If it was a holiday type of camp, it signifies a beneficial change of occupation and/or location; and if it was a military camp, the augury is for great success in business ventures.

Camphor. A warning against casual and/or promiscuous sex affairs. There are unfriendly influences around you at the moment, and scandal or illness could result. Slow down! See also *Odor*.

Can. The significance depends on the details and the action. If the dream involved many cans and they were full, you can expect some good news to reach you quite soon. If you opened a full can, you will discover some very useful secret knowledge; if you drank from a can, you will have unanticipated joy; however, if the can featured in your dream was empty, discarded, or you threw it away or cut yourself on it, you may have serious financial difficulties ahead. Reexamine your plans for an alternate road.

Canal. As a general guide this dream pertains to future security, and if the canal was full, the portent is good, if it was empty or nearly so, or there were weeds to be seen, there is a suggestion to cut your extravagance. If the dream featured canal locks, you'd better look for a cuckoo in your nest of friends. See also *Water*.

Canary. A certain promise of happiness ahead, so don't allow any current worries to depress you. See also *Birds, Cage,* and *Colors*.

Cancer. A dream of contrary, but also a warning. The prognostication here is of a long life providing you avoid overindulgence in

the fleshpots. See also *Illness*.

Candle. Lighted candles in a dream promise improvement in all your affairs; however, unlighted ones portend an impending disappointment in domestic or love affairs. If your dream featured candlesticks being carried, you can expect a most welcome increase in social activity. Short and/or guttering candles signify the opening of new opportunities for you. See also *Flame*.

Candy. Whether you made it, ate it, received it, or gave it away, it's a sign that you'll soon be happy even if at this moment you don't believe it. There is, however, an exception to this generality; if the candy was sticky, the dream is telling you to mind your own business; even charitable impulses can sometimes backfire. See also *Eating*.

Cane. If your dream featured cane growing, it predicts increasing profits; if the cane was cut, avoid any kind of speculation for at least a month. If your dream involved carrying, or observing someone else carry, a cane, it signifies success in business and/or love but only after irritating delays. To be beaten or to beat someone with a cane is a warning to postpone any contemplated changes for the time being. A broken cane or a sword cane is a dream of contrary and indicates a victory when and where you least expect it. See also *Walk*.

Cannibal. Whether the dream featured cannibals or cannibalism, it is a warning to avoid being tempted into anything risky or underhanded no matter how promising it appears.

Cannon. Unusual achievement is predicted if you saw or heard cannon in your dream. If the dream featured cannonballs, you can expect some delightful experiences with the opposite sex. See also *Guns*.

Canoe. If your dream featured paddling your own canoe, you must look up the details (*River*, *Lake*, *Water*, etc.) for a correct interpretation; but if the canoe was empty, it signifies a need to make new friends.

Canopy. You can look forward to a secure life if you dreamed of being under any kind of canopy; this type of cover in a dream represents protection. See also *Cover*.

Cantaloupe. Whether they were growing in the field, on the vine, or harvested, these delightful melons signify love, peace, and prosperity; however, if you dreamed of eating cantaloupe, it signifies a minor physical upset.

Canyon. You'll need all the tact you can muster to avoid quarrels and/or disagreements over money matters if your dream featured a canyon, especially if it was wooded. You would be well advised to postpone any business discussions for a few days.

Cap. Whatever your sex, it is a good omen to dream of wearing a cap; your worries will evaporate and your troubles will prove temporary, unless the cap was noticeably shabby, torn, and/or dirty, in which case you may expect some minor reverses in any business which concerns you. However, if the cap involved was a military one, it predicts a great triumph in spite of serious opposition. See also *Head* and *Hat*.

Capsule. Success with the

opposite sex is forecast in a dream concerning anything in capsule form.

Captain. For a man, this dream augurs a rise in status whether the captain is military, naval, or air; for a woman, it warns against jealous friends. See also *Ship, Airplane,* etc.

Captive. A dream featuring captivity suggests tension and overstrain, probably due to overspending; cut down on extravagance of any kind unless the captives were animal, in which case you should soon be finding life most enjoyable.

Car. You can forget about great luxury, but modest comfort will surely be yours if your dream featured a railroad or cable car. See also *Automobile, Carriage,* and *Cart.*

Carbon. Carbon copies or carbon paper are a warning against deceitful associates and/or mischief-making friends. If the carbon was of the motor variety, it is a caution against too much high life.

Carcass. A high degree of prosperity is forecast by a dream of carcasses in good condition and in a proper place (such as a meat market or butcher shop); but if they were abandoned or appeared deteriorated, you'll have a long row to hoe before you get what you want.

Cardinal. An ecclesiastical cardinal seen in all his colorful glory follows the ancient rule that high-ranking churchmen are harbingers of unpleasant news; but on the other hand, a bird of this variety promises family harmony and/or business expansion, plus happy social events ahead. See also *Church* and *Birds.*

Cards. Using a deck of cards yourself or observing other people using a deck signifies financial reverses through carelessness and/or trickery; however, certain cards and suits have specific meaning and if observed in the dream should be collated with the action. The face cards signify as follows:

King.
    CLUBS: You will be helped by a friend.
    DIAMONDS: Danger from an older man who has a position of power.
    HEARTS: True love.
    SPADES: Opposition in your ambitions.

Queen.

CLUBS: You need to un-snarl your love life.

DIAMONDS: Good news concerning property.

HEARTS: Happy romantic news.

SPADES: A niggling worry through a misplaced confidence.

Jack.

CLUBS: Deceit and trick-ery could cause you a loss.

DIAMONDS: A pleasing gift or small inheritance.

HEARTS: Happiness through a new romance.

SPADES: You've got a rival and/or opposition in whatever concerns you most.

See also *Ace* and *Numbers*.

Cargo. An enjoyable minor trip is forecast in a dream of cargo being loaded; however, if it was dropped or thrown overboard you could be inconvenienced by someone else's financial problems. Be careful with your money.

Carnations. The significance varies according to the color and the action. If you were just aware of the flowers you will have an unusual social success. If your dream involved gathering the blooms you may expect a pleasant sur-prise, probably in the form of a valuable gift. White carnations predict a grati-fying increase in status; bright red ones forecast an exciting love affair; pink ones indicate a happy do-mestic situation, and dark red or odd colored ones are an omen of prosperity through the help of good friends. See also *Flowers.*

Carnival. See *Mask* and *Ball.*

Carol. A happy contented year ahead is forecast in a dream of hearing carols sung or played. See also *Singing.*

Carousel. See *Merry-go-Round.*

Carpenter. This busy fellow is one of the happiest sym-bols you can dream up. Whether you were one, observed one, or hired one, you will have love, re-spect, leisure, *and* the means to enjoy it!

Carpet. An omen of general good luck, unless it was shabby and/or soiled, in which case you are being warned to get out (or stay out) of debt. See also *Furniture.*

Carriage. You could be deeply embarrassed by questions concerning your social companions if your dream featured one of these old-fashioned, horse-drawn vehicles. Guard against subjecting yourself to unkind gossip.

Carrots. These tasty roots in a dream prophesy an unexpected legacy or money windfall. See also *Vegetable(s)* and *Eating*.

Carry. Profit through the actions of others is forecast if your dream involved being carried by someone. See also *Burden*.

Cart. Prepare for a long period of hard work and not much joy if you dreamed of riding in, or driving, a cart. If you only observed the vehicle, you must still expect the slog but it will be a short one. See also *Hay*.

Cartoon. Whether they were animated cartoons or comic-strip variety, if they amused you in your dream, they predict a period of disappointment in romantic matters but good luck in business.

Carving. The meaning of this dream depends on the circumstances. If you were carving for others, you can expect someone else to get the lion's share of profits

from your current efforts; but if you were being served, you can be sure of reaping your just rewards. See also *Cut, Meat, Eating,* etc.

Cascade. Happiness, interesting variety of life, and modest success are presaged in a dream of water cascading over rocks.

Cash. See *Money*.

Cashier. Financial worries are apt to follow a dream in which you met with, or acted in the capacity of, a cashier. Guard your credit.

Casket. Sadness (but not grief) may be expected following a dream of a casket containing a body, but a dream of contrary indicating good luck if the body was your own. An empty casket signifies a lost friend, but not necessarily through death. See also *Funeral, Death,* etc.

Castanets. The sound of these instruments in a dream suggests a physical disturbance. See your doctor.

Castle. If your dream involved visiting or living in a castle which was in habitable condition, it forecasts a comfortable future with interesting travel;

however, if the castle in your dream was in ruins, you are being warned to curb your romantic passions and/or your temper, whichever applies.

Castor Oil. See *Laxative*.

Castrate. A dream of contrary. Whether the castration was your own, someone else's, or involved animals, its augury is that of eventual triumph over all obstacles and/or opposition to your aims. See also *Operation*.

Cat. A generally unfortunate omen indicating treachery and deceit among those you trust. If you killed the cat, you will defeat the purpose of your detractors; if you chased it away, you may expect a sudden stroke of luck. See also *Animals*.

Cataract. See *Cascade*.

Catastrophe. A radical change in your life-style is predicted if you dreamed of witnessing or participating in a catastrophe. If you escaped injury and/or gave assistance in any way, the change will be a happy one; otherwise you would be well advised to avoid any form of risk in the year ahead.

Caterpillar. Another rather unfortunate omen regarding trouble from unforeseen jealousy and treachery. Be extremely careful of your actions following this dream or you could be put in a humiliating position with no defense.

Cathedral. Seen from the outside this building presages attainment of your highest aspiration; the inside predicts failure to reach your ultimate goal, but some satisfying rewards during your struggle to get there.

Cattle. The significance of this dream depends on the action. If the cattle were peacefully grazing, it is a good omen of "easy come" prosperity. If you had to drive the cattle in your dream, you will also be successful but only through hard and diligent effort. Black or large-horned cattle suggest that your business affairs receive closer attention in order to avoid a loss.

Cauliflower. Whether you are married or single, you are likely to be experiencing a more agreeable way of life soon if your dream featured cauliflower. See also *Cooking, Eating,* and *Vegetable(s)*.

Cavalry. See *Horse*.

Cave. An obstacle dream. If you found your way out, you can expect eventually to overcome your difficulties; but if you failed to get out, you must prepare for an escalation of your worries for a rather long period. Dreams involving cave dwellers are an omen of marital happiness.

Cavern. Another form of obstacle dream. If you observed the cavern entrance from outside, you can expect that your circumstances will gradually improve; however, if you were in it (or fell into it) and couldn't get out, you may be up against some hostile influences which could frustrate your ambitions. The seriousness of your opposition would be indicated by the depth of the cavern. If it seemed very deep, you should reconsider your goal.

Cedar. Any dream featuring the smell or use of this aromatic wood is an omen of happy contentment with your lot, whatever it may be. See also *Trees*.

Ceiling. A cracked or damaged ceiling is a warning against possible trickery from inside your close circle of associates; but if the ceiling appeared well preserved and/or nicely decorated, its omen is the same as that of a canopy.

Celery. Happiness through love and abundant good health are promised in a dream which involves crisp celery. See also *Vegetables, Eating,* and *Cooking*.

Cell. You are being warned against carelessness with your commitments if you dreamed of being confined in a cell. Failure to keep your promises could lead to loss of valued friends. See also *Jail*.

Cellar. A dry and/or well-stocked cellar is an indication of expanding profitable business interests. If the cellar was dank, musty, and/or empty, it predicts financial worries or reverses which you may be able to mitigate by some thoughtful forward planning.

Cello. If your dream involved putting new strings on the cello, you can expect to hear sudden good news; if a string broke while the cello was being played, it predicts an unexpected break in a personal relationship. See also *Music* and *Musical Instruments*.

Cellophane. A dream featuring cellophane relates to new opportunities you are, or will be, considering. If the cellophane was colorless, the indication is that the proposition(s) involved have no hidden snags. If the cellophane was colored, the interpretation will be accordingly influenced. See *Colors*.

Cement. A happy augury whether the cement was used on bricks, stones, paper, plastic, china, or what have you. It signifies a rise in status and/or income. See also *Glue*.

Cemetery. A dream of contrary. If the cemetery was well kept, it signifies coming happiness and prosperity; however, if the general appearance of the place was dreary, you must expect a bit of trouble first. See also *Funeral, Death,* etc.

Cent. See *Penny* and *Money*.

Ceremony. Whether the ceremony was civil, religious, or fraternal, the dream was telling you that your friends are reliable.

Certificate. This dream was reminding you that big oaks CAN be the product of little acorns, so try to cooperate more with your associates in small matters and you may gain more from the important ones.

Chaff. You are being warned against repeating idle gossip which could jeopardize your reputation if your dream featured chaff in any form, unless the action pertained to separation of the seed, in which case you will succeed with your current plans but only after painstaking effort.

Chagrin. See *Embarrassment*.

Chains. A dream of contrary. Whether your dream featured your own, someone else's, or unattached chains, you will soon be free of all your worries. For gold or ornamental chains see *Jewelry*.

Chair. An empty chair signifies unexpected news; sitting in a comfortable chair predicts comfort; a rocking chair indicates unanticipated gains through efforts other than your own (possibly an inheritance). See also *Furniture*.

Chalk. You must be prepared for a serious setback in your current plans if your dream featured chalk in any form. If you heard squeaky chalk in your dream, your disappointment will be due to your own indiscretion. Guard your tongue! See also *Blackboard*.

Challenge. You must be extra careful to avoid offending influential people if you dreamed of being challenged; think everything over twice and then don't say it. If, in your dream, you did the challenging, you can expect someone of the opposite sex to give you a hard time.

Chameleon. This little creature in a dream is a warning to be wary of strangers for the time being.

Champagne. To dream of a champagne party is a warning against overextending yourself financially, unless it was a wedding party, in which case it predicts success in affairs of the heart. See also *Wine* and *Drink*.

Champion. A sort of dream of contrary whether the dreamed-of championship was your own or someone else's. It predicts modest success in small matters.

Chandelier. Brilliant success both socially and in business is predicted in a dream which featured a beautiful lighted chandelier. If the chandelier was unlit, you may achieve the rise in status but more slowly. If your dream involved yourself (or anyone else) hanging (or hanging onto) a chandelier, you are being warned against extramarital affairs and/or sexual promiscuity. See also *Furniture*.

Change. If the main feature of your dream was the general impression of "atmosphere" of change, it is a straightforward omen and you should be prepared to adjust to a change which may not be entirely to your liking. However, if the change involved an alteration in the direction of a walk, drive, or vehicle, the dream is a warning against procrastination in making decisions. Be more positive. See also *Coins, Sex,* and *Clothes,* etc.

Chant. You will have some reason for pride and joy if you heard chanting in your dream.

Chapel. Unlike other religious buildings, a chapel in your dream is a fortunate omen whether you found yourself inside or outside.

Charades. Delayed success but with some compensations along the way is predicted in a dream featuring a game of charades.

Charity. A dream of contrary. The more charitable you were in your dream, the greater will be your financial embarrassment in the next twelve months; however, if you received the charity in your dream, you can look forward to a rapid increase in income or other money luck.

Charm. You may expect an improvement in all departments of your life if you dreamed of mixing with charming people. For charms see *Jewelry*.

Charter. Whether you chartered a vehicle or were a charter passenger in one, some sudden good luck should be yours.

Chase. No luxury, but a comfortable old age through your own efforts is forecast in a dream where you participated in, or observed, a chase.

Chastise. A dream of contrary. You will have cause to be proud if you dreamed of being chastised; if you did the chastising, you should be prepared for some minor re-

verses. If the dream involved children being chastised, it might be wise to get a medical checkup.

Chatter. The yakety-yak of chatter in your dream was your subconscious suggesting that you be much more circumspect or much less kinky in your relations with the opposite sex.

Cheat. A dream of contrary. If you dreamed of being cheated, you can expect a stroke of luck; however, if you were the cheater, you can expect to be cheated.

Check. Another dream of contrary. The more and the larger were the checks you signed in your dream, the greater will be your money luck in the near future. However, the reverse is true if you received payment by check in your dream; you are being warned to be extra cautious in current transactions.

Checkers. Win, lose, or draw, a dream featuring a game of checkers promises a happy future whether you played or just kibitzed.

Cheeks. You should find your love life and/or close personal relationships improving following a dream of your own cheeks. See also *Skin* and *Face*.

Cheering. Another contrary dream. If you were doing the cheering, you are likely to have cause to regret some impulsive action; if you heard others cheering, it is a warning to curb your extravagance.

Cheese. The significance of a cheese dream varies greatly according to its details. As a general rule eating cheese signifies success in love. Smelly cheeses such as Limburger, Brie, etc. predict financial and or social embarrassment, but mild or processed cheese signifies a need for a change. If you were making cheese in your dream, your current ventures will be successful beyond your expectations. Dry and/or grated cheese signifies a stroke of money luck.

Cherries. Cherries growing on a tree predict business troubles brewing, so go slow in any new ventures, but a cherry tree without fruit is an omen of happiness and good health. Ripe cherries in a bowl (or off the tree) signify success in love, but green or spoiled cherries are an augury of tears and disappointment, so don't put much trust in any recent romance.

Chess. This ancient game in a dream is an omen of annoying obstacles in your path. You can expect a strenuous business period ahead, but don't despair; you can win if you persevere and vary your tactics by using a little imagination.

Chest. A large chest is a warning against getting into debt; a small chest forecasts success in love; an empty chest is a forerunner to a minor disappointment; a full chest is an augury of family solidarity but only after disagreements and quarrels. See also *Bust, Breast,* etc.

Chestnuts. The meaning varies greatly with the action. If you were splitting or opening the chestnuts, you will solve a mystery or a problem which has been plaguing you. If you cooked the nuts, you are in danger of being exploited by someone you trust; eating chestnuts in a dream predicts happy relations (sexual and/or social as may apply) with the opposite sex. Lucky you.

Chew. You will have a disappointment due to your own foolishness if you dreamed you were chewing; if you observed others chewing, you can expect some pleasant social invitations; and if the chewers were children, you can expect some pleasant developments in all that concerns you. See also *Gum* and *Eating*.

Chickens. This dream is telling you not to count them before they're hatched!

Chilblains. A dream of contrary. Something which has been causing you considerable anguish will suddenly be cleared up. See also *Skin* and *Itch*.

Children. If your dream featured children (of walking age upward), its augury is one of happiness in domestic affairs and/or business interests, whichever concerns you most. See also *Baby*.

Chill. See *Cold*.

Chimes. If the sound was pleasant and tuneful, they herald better times ahead; but if they were discordant, be prepared for a period of hard work without much joy.

Chimney. You must consider the aspects of the chimney to interpret its meaning. If it was a very tall one, its augury is of unusual achievement; an average-height chimney indicates favorable times ahead but nothing spectacular; if there was smoke coming from the chimney, it predicts good news on the way. A chimney in bad repair or cracked suggests that some expected troubles will materialize; but if the chimney actually collapsed or fell·down, you will soon have cause for celebration. Sparks rising from a chimney are a warning to avoid antagonizing an influential colleague.

Chin. Generally a good omen pertaining to business luck, but other details must be looked up for an accurate interpretation. Double chins on yourself or others predict fortunate events to come. Chinning (athletically on bars) suggests you are needlessly concerned about a situation which you can easily handle. Hitting or being hit on the chin predicts startling news. See also *Skin*.

China. Abundance and happy domestic affairs are forecast in a dream featuring china, unless it was cracked and/or broken, in which case you can expect a change that may not be entirely to your liking but will eventually prove beneficial.

Chinese. Chinese people or objects observed in a dream signify a satisfactory solution to all your problems. However, if the objects were damaged or the people seemed unfriendly, you may expect to make (or receive surprise guests from) a long journey.

Chips. Gambling chips signify successful speculation; wood chips indicate petty annoyances; and potato chips predict a change for the better in your personal and/or love affairs. See also *Cards, Gambling, Eating,* etc.

Chisel. If the main feature of your dream was the use of the chisel, it is telling you that you CAN get what you want but it won't come easy; however, the other material details must be considered. See also *Stone(s), Bricks, Sculpture,* etc.

Chloroform. If you (or others) took the chloroform willingly, you can expect an improvement in a worrying situation; however, if there was a struggle involved in giving or taking the chloroform, the dream is of physical origin and a medical checkup is advisable.

Chocolate. Oddly, a dream featuring chocolate drinks, candy, or anything of this flavor does not, as one might expect, indicate luxury, but it does predict good health and modest contentment.

Choir. You can prepare for a period of minor frustrations if the choir was inside a church; but in any other location, the singing of a choir heralds the arrival of pleasant news. See also *Music.*

Choke. The best general interpretation of a dream which involves choking is the old saying that "The things you worry about most never happen."

Chop. A dream of chopping down trees or chopping anything into pieces is a dream of contrary which signifies the healing of disturbances or rifts in your close circle or family. See also *Ax, Hatchet, Cut,* or *Meat.*

Chorus. See *Music, Singing,* and *Choir.*

Christ. Although your ultimate contentment may be preceded by some trials, you will achieve peace of mind by making a good adjustment to your life conditions if you dreamed of Jesus.

Christen. Strangely enough this usually joyful occasion is not an auspicious omen in a dream. It signifies hard work for little reward.

Christmas. To dream of Christmas out of season presages happy family and social times ahead.

Chrysanthemum. To smell them predicts hopes fulfilled; to pick them forecasts increased social activity; and to give or receive them indicates an unexpected increase in status through influential friends. See also *Colors* and *Flowers.*

Church. As with a cathedral it is a lucky omen if your dream featured the outside of the building; however, if the interior was involved, it signifies some impending troubles, but don't get depressed—they are likely to turn out to be small blessings in disguise. A dream of a churchyard is a promise of better things to come.

Churn. If you dreamed of a churn in use, you can be sure of always having the necessary things in life. If the churn upset, it indicates a disappointment in someone you have trusted. See also *Butter, Cheese,* etc.

Cider. Misplaced confidence is the message in a cider dream, so be prudent and don't confide for the time being. See also *Drink.*

Cigar (or Cigarette). Whether you were offering them, smoking yourself, or observing someone else with them, this form of tobacco in a dream is a lucky omen pertaining to prosperity.

Cinder. If, in your dream, you merely observed the cinders, you can expect a temporary setback in your present plans; but if your dream involved shoveling them, or handling them in any way, the forecast is for improved times ahead. To have a cinder in your eye, indicates that you will be surprised by a request for help. Give it if you can.

Cinnamon. This pleasant

spice in a dream, properly used, indicates an exciting increase in social opportunities; however, inappropriately used, it forecasts disappointment in the character of a friend.

Cipher. A straightforward omen of failure regarding some cherished ambition if the cipher involved was a zero. Reexamine your situation for a possible change of objective. See also *Code*.

Circle. As opposed to a naught, a circle in your dream is a forecast of success beyond your highest hopes, unless the circle was badly drawn, in which case you will still achieve your aims but only after some delay.

Circumcision. Advancement through new influential friends is forecast in a dream of circumcision whether your own or that of an infant.

Circus. If your dream involved being with children at a circus or taking them to one, it is a sign of exceptional luck in financial matters; otherwise, it is a warning to be more careful of the impression you make on others.

Cistern. A full cistern de-

notes full success; a partly full cistern indicates modest achievement; an empty cistern suggests lack of reward through lack of effort. If your dream involved falling into a cistern, it is a warning to avoid stepping on influential toes.

Clairvoyance. You are likely soon to be contemplating a change of occupation if your dream featured the possession and/or use of psychic powers. Consider carefully, but don't make the change unless there is some means of ensuring it will be for the better.

Clams. See *Oyster*.

Claret. See *Wine* and *Drink*.

Clarinet. The instrument itself has no significance in a dream. See under *Musical Instruments* and *Music*.

Clay. You can expect to make satisfactory progress toward your goals if you dreamed of modeling or working with clay. See also under *Bricks*, *Sculpture*, and *Earth*.

Cleaning. A clear, straightforward warning note from your conscience is contained in a dream of cleaning, and the harder or busier was the dreamed cleaning activity, the more urgent is the warning against allowing yourself to be drawn into anything even slightly unethical, no matter how pleasurable and/or profitable it may appear. See also *Wash, Teeth,* etc.

Clergy. You are likely to have disappointing (but not serious) news following a dream featuring churchmen of this level.

Cliffs. An obstacle dream of warning. Avoid any speculation or risks for the next few months unless you were successfully scaling the cliff, in which case the augury is reversed and indicates satisfactory rewards for your efforts.

Climb. Whether up mountains, hills, stairs, or what have you, an increase in status and/or prosperity is forecast in a climbing dream; even if the effort seemed to tax your stretch beyond endurance, you will still succeed, but only after surmounting strong opposition.

Cloak. A cloak (as opposed to a cape) featured in your dream signifies protection against any hostile influences around you.

Clock. If your dream involved noticing a clock, hearing it tick or buying it, etc., it is a straightforward warning to stop wasting time. If you heard a clock strike, it is a suggestion that you can improve your lot by taking positive action. To wind a clock signifies a happy love affair in the offing.

Clogs. You are likely to enjoy a passionate but short-lived love affair if your dream featured wearing, buying, or observing others in clogs.

Closet. An empty clothes closet is a warning against getting into debt; a full closet signifies unusually large business profits; a well-stocked linen closet is a sign of a happy family future, but an empty linen closet is a forerunner of family quarrels or rifts.

Cloth. The significance depends on the kind of cloth, the color, and other details, but as a general guide: Linen signifies increased income; Woolen promises security; Velvet or Brocade forecasts success in love affairs; Silk predicts a happy social life; and Cotton indicates a need to guard against loss of reputation through indiscreet behavior. To cut cloth on the bias predicts a message of distress from a distance. See also *Colors, Cut, Sewing,* etc.

Clothes. The portent of a dream concerning clothes varies greatly with the details. It is a dream of contrary with respect to quantity, as the more clothes you had in your dream the more urgent is the warning to prepare for difficulties ahead. However, if you were only partly dressed, or stark naked, money luck is on the way. On the other hand, the act of putting on clothes in a dream signifies success ahead, whereas undressing is a forecast of reverses. Shabby or soiled clothes are a warning against business dealings with, or through, friends. Tight, uncomfortable, or back-to-front clothes suggest a need to protect your reputation by cooling down your sexual activities. See also *Colors, Costume,* etc.

Clouds. The meaning of this dream depends on the details and the action. Storm clouds in a dark sky predict sorrow through a broken friendship. Floating white clouds in a clear sky forecast better times in store; banks of white clouds indicate happy experiences with the opposite sex; and oddly enough if your dream involved the sun being obscured by passing clouds, it is a certain promise of sunnier financial times ahead.

Clover. You'll soon BE in clover if your dream featured this pleasant plant, and if it was in bloom, you can expect your good fortune to extend to love as well as business affairs.

Cloves. Whatever your worries may be they will vanish like a magician's coin if you dreamed of eating or using this sharp spice.

Clown. You will be annoyed and aggravated by the discovery that some of your thoughtless actions are being misinterpreted if a clown featured in your dream. You might benefit from a change of companions.

Club. A dream involving club activities is a forerunner of unpleasant news. To be hit with a club is a dream of contrary; you will be much admired. To hit someone else with a club predicts an improvement in status.

Clumsy. A dream of contrary. The more clumsy or awkward you were in your dream the greater will be your ability to handle any life situation which may confront you. If your dream involved observing the clumsiness of others, it predicts new and interesting contacts.

Coach. See *Carriage*.

Coal. A dream in which the blackness of the coal, coal mine, or coal pit was a feature is a warning to retrench and prepare for a period of financial embarrassment. However if the coal was burning brightly or you were stoking a coal fire, you can expect a promotion or satisfactory reward for past efforts. If you delivered the coal or gave it away, the augury is of sudden social advancement. To shovel coal presages many obstacles to overcome before you succeed. See also *Digging*.

Coat. A dream of contrary as regards condition. A new coat signifies business reverses, whereas an old, shabby, or torn coat means prosperity and/or money luck. To hang up a coat indicates favor in the corridors of power. If you helped someone on with a coat, you can expect to be asked for a loan, but if someone helped you on with your coat, you will have to borrow. Losing a coat predicts discovery of a false friend; but to lend or give one away indicates a widening of your social circle.

Cobbler. See *Shoes*.

Cobra. *See Snake(s)*.

Cobweb. You'll be lucky if you dreamed of cobwebs in an acceptable place such as a wine cellar, attic, etc.; but if they were where they shouldn't be, for example on clothes, furniture, or books, they predict difficulties through secretly hostile competition; however, if you brushed them away, you will easily overcome the difficulties. See also *Spider(s)* and *Web*.

Cocaine. You can expect a business improvement if you dreamed of cocaine used in a medical way; however, if your dream featured the addictive aspect of this drug, it predicts some cause for sorrow. See also *Drugs*.

Cock. A lucky omen, especially if you heard a cock crowing; it predicts joyous news. But if the cocks were fighting, look out for family disagreements. See also *Fowl*.

Cockatoo. Don't allow yourself to be influenced by gossiping friends if you dreamed of this exotic fellow. See also *Birds*.

Cocktail. See *Drink*.

Cocoa. You can rely on the integrity of your friends if you dreamed of drinking or serving cocoa.

Coconut. Whether you ate it, saw it, smelled it, or opened it, coconut in a dream forecasts an unexpected gift, probably money.

Code. Whether received or sent, coded messages in a dream are a warning against deceit. Reexamine your judgment about those you trust.

Coffee. The meaning here depends greatly on the details and the action. If you drank the coffee and it was good, it augurs surprising good news; if it was bitter, you will have cause to break off a friendship. If you ground the coffee, it is a favorable omen signifying unusual domestic happiness; but if you spilled coffee in your dream, you must expect a series of small disappointments.

Coffin. See *Casket*.

Coins. If the coins were counterfeit, the dream foretells a minor illness; otherwise it is a fortunate omen of unexpected gain. However, this is, in a way, a peculiar dream of contrary in that the smaller or less valuable the coins are in the dream the greater will be your gain.

Cold. A dream of contrary. The lower the temperature was in your dream the more comfortable and secure will be your estate in life. However, if your dream involved yourself or anyone else having a cold, or getting a chill, you are being warned to guard your credit.

Collar. This dream pertains to love affairs. If the collar was clean, your mate or current heart interest, as the case may be, is reliable; but if the collar was soiled or torn, you could either be deceiving yourself or being deceived.

Collect. A dream of collecting things such as stamps, antiques, etc. is a sign of making new and interesting friends; if a money collection was involved and you contributed, you can expect some minor, but pleasing good luck. If you were soliciting the funds, it signifies an unexpected short trip.

College. This dream predicts upcoming petty annoyances unless a professor was involved, in which case it forecasts a slight advancement in status.

Collision. This dream is telling you that you'd better take positive action in regard to making a decision. If you don't trust your own judgment, seek friendly (or professional) advice but stop dithering.

Colors. You can expect increasing security and success in all your affairs if you dreamed of a mixture of bright colors. Individually, or if one color stood out in your dream, the significance is as follows: Blue indicates liberation from worry and/or help from outside sources; Black is an unfavorable omen unless it featured in a funeral or other appropriate situation, in which case it forecasts difficulties to be overcome; Brown means money luck; bright Red is a warning to curb your temper; deep Red forecasts unexpected good news; Green pertains to travel or news from a distance; Gray indicates a period of "marking time"; Lavender or Mauve foretells minor disappointment or transitory unhappiness; Orange suggests that an expected change in your situation will be delayed; Pink predicts unusually great success; Purple is a forerunner to happy social affairs; Yellow forecasts setbacks and struggles before improvement can be achieved; White is a certain promise of success in all that concerns you.

Dreams involving people of a color other than your own are generally lucky omens pertaining to money and/or business, unless the people were some exotic shade like green or blue, in which case the dream probably had a digestive origin and no significance.

Column. You will achieve recognition through the help of influential people if your dream featured any kind of column.

Comb. Combing your own hair in a dream suggests that you will have to take action to solve some bothersome problems. Combing someone else's hair is a sign of misplaced trust. Be careful where you place your confidence. Losing your comb in a dream predicts a coming disenchantment in love; borrowing a comb or lending one forecasts financial difficulties for which you will require help, but don't worry, you'll get it. If your dream involved observing a comb or seeing someone else using one, it signifies that you need to be firm in shaking off an association which no longer interests you.

Combat. An obstacle dream with a straightforward meaning. If you won the fight, your current undertakings will be successful; but if you lost or the outcome was indecisive, you can expect some difficulty and worry. However, if the dream feature was a battle of wits rather than a physical fight, you can expect a happy outcome to an annoying personal situation.

Comedy. A sudden development of events which will advance your interests can be expected following a dream involving comic humor and/or fun, but the other details of the dream should be considered for its full portent. See also *Laughter, Theater, Colors, Costume,* etc.

Comet. You must expect difficulties due to sudden opposition and/or rivalry if you dreamed of this unusual type of heavenly body, unless your main concern at the moment is a love affair, in which case it signals sudden success.

Command. The augury here depends on the action and reaction; if you gave the commands and they were obeyed, you can expect some quick improvement in your life; but if your demands were ignored or refused, you will have to make an effort to avoid clashes with influential friends and/or associates. If the commanding was done by someone else, the dream has the same significance, except that it applies to someone with whom you are closely involved rather than to yourself.

Commandment. A dream featuring any (or all) of the ten commandments is a warning that your behavior is in some way causing you mental anxiety. Be your own best friend and change your ways.

Commencement. See *Graduation.*

Committee. A committee in

your dream signifies an upheaval in your affairs. Try to be philosophical in the face of possible sudden changes.

Communion. This religious ritual featured in a dream predicts sad, but not grievous, news, unless the service was out of doors, in which case the omen is reversed and the news will be joyous.

Communist. Activities of a communist nature in a dream portend misunderstandings followed by a long period of peace and comfort.

Companion. You can expect a general improvement in all that concerns you if the main aspect of your dream was one of pleasant companionship, unless the dream involved a departed or former companion, in which case it forecasts some unexpected anxieties.

Compass. You are in for a period of general upset in both domestic and business affairs if your dream featured a compass, unless the needle pointed north, in which case you should continue along your present lines and success will follow.

Compassion. See *Pity*.

Compete. A dream of contrary. The more successful was the dreamed competition the rockier will be your road ahead and vice versa.

Complain. You should avoid controversial subjects or behavior which could be misinterpreted following a dream featuring complaints, unless you were doing the complaining, in which case you may expect an important addition to your circle of friends.

Compose. Provided the writing and/or reading of music is NOT one of your skills, you will receive a valuable present, possibly in the form of useful information, if you dreamed of writing or reading a musical composition. If composing is one of your skills (but not your profession), this dream predicts an opportunity to make a change. See also *Music*.

Concert. Unanticipated good news will follow a dream of attending a concert, unless the general atmosphere was in some way unpleasant, in which case the forecast is of minor illness. See also *Music, Hall, Gather*, etc.

Condemn. A dream of contrary. If, in your dream, you did the condemning or observed others being condemned, your own actions will be subject to criticism; but if, in your dream, you were condemned, you can rely on those you trust.

Condole. To offer condolences in a dream is a straightforward omen of sadness, but to receive condolences is a dream of contrary and signifies happier times to come.

Conductor. If your dream featured the conductor of a public carrier, it predicts foreign travel; but if it involved an orchestra (or musical) conductor, you can expect some unusual money luck.

Cone. Every interpreter of dreams from Ptolemy to Freud agrees that anything in a cone shape or form represents exceptional sexual or sensual pleasure; so if you've had it, you'll have it again, and if you haven't, you will!

Conference. A business or professional conference predicts profitable news; a political conference indicates increasing responsibilities; a spiritual or religious conference augurs a rise in social status.

Confess. If the dream involved hearing a confession, you are being warned to be on guard against being tricked into betraying a confidence; if the dream concerned making a confession, it predicts a welcome change of circumstances.

Confetti. Fantastic social success is forecast in a dream featuring this paper symbol of celebration.

Confide. To receive confidences signifies better times ahead; to give confidences predicts unexpected gain, possibly through new friends.

Confusion. If the main feature of your dream was an overall or general atmosphere of confusion, you are being warned to continue along your present lines, as any changes you are contemplating could prove awkward at this time; but if your dreamed confusion was purely personal, it predicts recovery of a long-lost hope.

Congratulate. A dream of contrary. To receive congratulations predicts a coming need for commiseration, but of a minor order; to give congratulations to others is a forecast of coming personal success.

Congress. A calm and happy life is foretold in a dream of being a delegate to, or observing, a session of Congress.

Conjurer. See *Magic*.

Console. See *Condole*.

Conspiracy. Another dream of contrary. To be the victim of a conspiracy in your dream predicts great social success; but to be a party to a conspiracy against others suggests that you are in danger of tempting trouble through your own foolish actions. Think things over again.

Constipation. Your conscience is telling you to curb your selfishness and be more considerate of others if your dream concerned your own or someone else's constipation. See also *Bowel Movement* and *Feces*.

Contamination. Immediate reverses but long-term success are forecast in a

dream concerning any type of contamination.

Contentment. A dream of warning against egocentricity. Overconfidence could trip you up; consider the other person's point of view occasionally or damaging clashes could develop with your friends and/or associates.

Contraband. Any type of illegal dealings in your dream are a warning to reconsider some dangerous path you are contemplating. This is a time to think it over well and then forget it.

Contract. A promotion is in the offing for you if you dreamed of signing a contract; if you refused to sign it, the step-up will be much greater than you might be expecting.

Convent. Happiness and contentment with whatever your lot may be are forecast in a dream featuring this type of cloister or its inmates.

Convict. To dream of convicts or that you are yourself a convict is a dream of contrary; you will soon be free of all worries unless the dream involved an escape, in which case you must be prepared for some ups and downs due to rivalry from an unexpected source. To be convicted is a sign of coming prosperity.

Convulsion. A dream of seeing anyone having a convulsion is a warning that you can no longer afford to carry others, so be firm in cutting leaners or clingers adrift. If you dreamed of having a convulsion yourself, you are in danger of being legally cheated by someone you trust. Make sure your affairs are in order.

Cookies. Trivial disputes are indicated in a dream of eating, giving, or receiving cookies. See also *Bake*.

Cooking. One of the most fortunate dreams going; whether someone else was doing the cooking or you were doing it yourself, it is a promise of every material comfort in the near future. A dream of cooking broth or soup predicts an eventual rise to a position of great power.

Copper. Success will come, but perhaps not as quickly as you hope if your dream involved this metal alloy. Possibly you should adjust your sights a bit. See also *Metal*.

Copulate. See *Intercourse*.

Copy. You are in for a period of changes for the better, and any issues hanging in the balance, especially with a legal aspect, can be swung in your favor by careful handling if your dream involved copies or copying.

Coral. In a dream this represents friends, and its meaning varies according to its color as follows: Red suggests a warning to curb your temper or you might lose a valuable friend; Pink indicates happy social times ahead; White predicts a widening circle of admiring new friends.

Cord. Tying a cord in your dream predicts satisfaction through your own achievement; untying, forecasts domestic or love trouble; breaking a cord indicates that you should take the initiative in cutting loose from an unsatisfactory relationship. See also *String* and *Rope*.

Cork. To pull a cork signifies good news; to push in a cork predicts the sudden solution to a personal problem; to hear the pop of a cork indicates a light-hearted love affair; to see a cork or objects made of cork means money luck. If the main feature of your dream was the use of a corkscrew rather than the cork itself, the dream is warning you to avoid casual affairs at the present time; and if the dream in-involved being cut or scratched by a corkscrew, you would be wise to curb your extravagance and avoid getting caught in social rounds which are beyond your means.

Corn. You could hardly have a better dream than one of corn. Whether it featured cornfields, corncobs, popcorn, or corns on feet, it is a happy omen of success in all that deeply concerns you.

Corner. An obstacle dream if the corner was anywhere indoors or enclosed; it is warning you not to force any issue for the time being or the tide could turn against you. If the corner was outside or in the open, it predicts new opportunities which will change your life-style. If the main feature of your dream involved turning a corner, you can expect a very pleasant surprise.

Cornet. See *Musical Instru-*

ments, Metal, Brass, Horn, Music, etc.

Coronation. A succession of modest successes is forecast in a dream featuring the pageantry of a coronation ceremony.

Corpse. A dream of contrary in that it predicts a full and happy life if the corpse was that of a stranger. If the dead person was known to you, it signifies an estrangement or unhappy love affair. If your dream involved a number of corpses but without any particularly distressing aspect, it is a forecast of success where you least expect it. If your dream featured a medical examination of a corpse, such as an autopsy, it portends an unusual new and interesting experience to come. See also *Casket, Funeral, Death,* etc.

Cosmetics. For a woman, a dream of using or buying cosmetics is a very fortunate omen, and also for a man, providing the cosmetics were appropriate for a male; but if a man dreams of using or buying women's cosmetics, it is a warning of possible business or professional reverses due to loss of reputation, and he would be well advised to reconsider his current activities and/or choice of companions.

Costume. You can expect an astonishing turn of events and/or some really astounding news if your dream involved wearing or observing fancy dress. The omen is especially fortunate if the costumes were worn by children or very young people.

Cot. You are in for a period of beneficial changes if you dreamed of sleeping on a cot, unless the cot broke under you, in which case you are being alerted to a possible sudden letdown by someone on whom you rely.

Cottage. Comfort and serenity, as opposed to acclaim and luxury, are promised in a dream featuring a cottage or bungalow, unless the structure was derelict or deserted, in which case it signals a significant time for sorting out your personal concerns.

Cotton. Picking cotton or seeing it growing in a field is a symbol of great prosperity in later life; medical or medicated cotton predicts unexpected visitors

or news, probably from abroad. See also *Cloth.*

Couch. You are in danger of lulling yourself into a false sense of security if your dream featured a couch either occupied or empty. This dream is telling you to listen to the advice of trusted friends.

Cough. A warning of impending danger of loss through fire, flood, theft, or carelessness. Take all possible precautions and make sure your insurance is in order.

Counterfeit. A warning dream. Anything counterfeit in a dream indicates that you may be deceived regarding support you expect from others, so try to arrange to stand on your own feet, unless your dream involved the destruction or rejection of the counterfeit object, in which case it signifies triumph over danger from an unknown enemy.

Counting. Counting money in a dream forecasts an increased income, but counting anything else indicates that you may be carrying too heavy a load of obligations. Try to shift some of them elsewhere, or, if possible, detach yourself.

Court. A dream featuring a court of law predicts imminent financial reverses; however the long-term outlook is optimistic if you avoid wasting time and energy on vain regrets. Look forward!

Cousin. Freedom from worry will soon be yours if you dreamed of a cousin or cousins. See also *Relatives*.

Cover. A dream featuring covers, or covered objects, furniture or whatever is telling you that your decisions and/or arrangements can work out well, but they may require more outlay than you anticipate, so you should be prepared to stretch yourself. See also *Blanket*.

Cow. An omen of good luck and prosperity if the animal was contented, grazing, chewing its cud, good looking, and/or being milked; however, if it was skinny, ugly, or it chased or attacked you, it represents threats to your most cherished plans, and the forecast of the outcome depends on the degree of the animal's disagreeable appearance and/or the outcome of the action. If you escaped, you will overcome all obstacles; but if you were trapped or injured, you must be prepared for a period of hard work without much joy. See also *Calf*.

Coward. A dream of contrary. You will stand up to any test of your character if your dream featured an act or feeling of cowardice.

Crab. Look sharp for tricky rivals in business and/or love if you dreamed of this crusty fellow, unless you cooked or ate him, in which case it might be an auspicious time for a bit of cautious gambling—but don't plunge!

Crabapple. See under *Trees*.

Crackers. Baking crackers or seeing them baked is a fortunate dream signifying happy social times in the offing. Eating crackers is a forerunner of domestic or lover's quarrels. If your dream featured a messy or crummy aspect of the crackers, such as sitting, stepping or lying on them, or having to clean them off of anything, it predicts some embarrassing petty annoyances through disloyal friends or associates. Reassess your personal relationships.

Cradle. An unhappy omen

signifying difficulties arising from poor health if the cradle was empty. Otherwise, see *Baby*.

Cramps. An unexpected reward for past favors is forecast in a dream of having cramps.

Cranberries. See *Fruit, Berries,* and *Colors*.

Crane. If your dream featured this bird on the wing, it is a good omen, but if it was on the ground, it signifies troubles of your own making. The meaning of a mechanical crane in a dream depends on the action. If you were operating it, you can expect a promotion in your job or an increase in status through widened responsibilities, whichever applies; if you observed the crane lifting, it signifies a relief from worries or solution to troublesome problems. A broken crane is a warning that you are in danger of biting off more than you can chew. Better reconsider.

Crash. Whatever its origin or cause, a crash in your dream heralds an important achievement, and the louder or bigger the crash the more noteworthy

will be the accomplishment.

Craving. Be prepared to consider a flattering offer if your dream concerned an intense feeling of longing.

Crawl. A dream of crawling forecasts difficulties in affairs of the heart.

Crazy. See *Insanity*.

Cream. See *Milk*.

Credit. If the main feature of your dream was the use of your credit, you may have to cope with the result of someone in your family, or close circle, being less than honest with you. If your dream involved the use of credit other than your own, you can look forward to a period of easy money.

Creek. The significance here varies according to the details and action. If the creek was dry, it portends a disappointment probably to do with business; if it had a normal amount of water running, it augurs some pleasing new experiences; if you were swimming in it, you can expect some exceptional luck to come your way; but if you only observed others in it, you are being warned to pay more attention to your own interests or others may benefit from your efforts.

Cremation. If your dream concerned your own cremation, you are being warned against allowing yourself to be influenced by others. In important matters rely on your own judgment. If the cremation of others was involved in your dream, it predicts a valuable acquisition, probably by inheritance. See also *Fire* and *Funeral*.

Crew. See *Sailor(s)*.

Crib. An empty crib is an augury of temporary domestic upsets; however, to see or put a baby in a crib indicates happiness through good health and modest prosperity. See also *Baby*.

Cricket. To hear or see crickets indoors in your dream forecasts family joy and a long life. If the crickets were in the open, they are warning you to guard against loss through indiscretion. Keep your private affairs and your plans to yourself. See also *Games* and *Sports*.

Cries. A dream of contrary. Joyous happy cries herald sad tidings, whereas cries of sadness or distress predict glad tidings.

Crime. In certain respects a dream of contrary. To witness or hear of a crime in your dream predicts a pleasant change of circumstances; to commit a crime is an omen of success in all that concerns you deeply. If the crime involved was an assassination, you can expect some sensational news; if you were caught in the act, it is a warning to guard your tongue and curb your temper. See also *Blackmail, Kidnap, Killing,* etc.

Cripple. You can expect an appeal for help from a relative or associate if your dream featured a handicapped person or persons. You would be well advised to give the assistance, as it will eventually turn out to be bread on the water. If the dream involved being crippled yourself, you can rely on getting whatever help you may be needing. See also *Crutches*.

Crochet. See *Knit*.

Crocodile. The meaning here depends on the action. If you merely observed him, he's a warning against untrustworthy associates who are trying to influence you adversely. Stand firm. If he chased or threatened you, good luck is sure to follow, unless he caught or injured you, in which case you are in for a painful disappointment or business reverse; however, if you killed a crocodile or saw a dead one, you will have success beyond your wildest expectations.

Crocus. Crocuses in a dream signify happy new beginnings, so don't waste time and energy in regrets concerning past events. Interesting new doors are about to open on your horizon.

Cross. Joy and triumph, but only after a hard struggle and some grief, is predicted in a dream featuring a cross of any description.

Crossroad. This symbol means what it indicates, and you'll soon be faced with an important decision if you dreamed of standing at or observing crossroads. Listen to advice, but in the final crunch rely on your own judgment or on your intuition if necessary.

Crow. This black fellow is an unhappy omen. He's usually a forerunner of sadness though not necessarily grief.

Crowd. Increasing happiness and/or widening opportunity for betterment is assured in a dream featuring an orderly, good-natured crowd. See also *Mob*.

Crown. A paper crown signifies a temptation which could degrade you if you do not resist it; a flower or foliage crown is a good omen for all your concerns; a gold crown signifies unexpected honors; a silver crown indicates the clearing of a health problem; a plastic crown suggests benefits through influential friends.

Crucifix. Wherever or however featured in your dream, a crucifix symbolizes fortitude in your trials and good hope for your future.

Cruelty. Whether the victim was you or someone else, mental cruelty in a dream signifies frustration; perhaps you would be wise to be more flexible in your attitude and/or aims.

Crumbs. Anything but will be your lot if you dreamed of them; great loaves of glad tidings will soon come your way, and if your dream featured birds feeding on the crumbs, you can expect a valuable gift or even an inheritance to follow.

Crush. The action of crushing anything in your dream indicates that you are under tension and/or pressure in regard to making an important decision. Be as independent as possible if you are certain you're working along the right lines, but if you have serious doubts, then get professional advice rather than friendly opinions.

Crust. Of similar portent to that of crumbs, except that this symbol relates exclusively to material matters.

Crutches. An obstacle dream. If during your dream the crutches were discarded, you will overcome the difficulties; if not, you are in for a long struggle and perhaps it might be wise to consider a shift either of your goal or your method of approach to it.

Cry. To hear a baby crying signifies surprising good news; any other crying indicates news of a friend or associate in distress. Be sure to give sympathetic response.

Crystal. When seen with the light shining through it, a prismatic crystal signifies a quick solution to any problems, puzzles, or mysteries that may have been troubling you. Crystal glassware, household articles, or items of adornment promise happy social events ahead. See also *Jewelry* and *Glass.*

Cuckoo. This odd fellow ought to be a symbol of fun because he's so amusing, but to see or hear him, in the flesh, is a forerunner of upsetting news, probably concerning a divorce or broken love affair. However, if he was a clock-type cuckoo, his song heralds a happy home improvement.

Cucumbers. If the cucumbers in your dream were being eaten, they signify news of a recovery from a serious illness or return of a lost friend. If they were being cooked, you are in danger of making a big business boo-boo. Reconsider any recent decision involving radical changes. See also *Vegetable(s).*

Cup. A full cup is a sure sign of increased prosperity, but an empty cup predicts reverses, so pull in your horns and prepare to retrench for a time. A decorated cup or one of gift quality indicates that you can avoid social embarrassment by heeding the advice of a loyal friend.

Cupboard. A straightforward symbol that means what it says. If your dream cupboard was bare, it predicts lean times in the offing; if it was full or reasonably well-stocked, you can expect your interests to flourish. If your dream involved putting supplies in a cupboard, it signifies recovery of losses through your own efforts.

Curb. A dr2am featuring a curb, of stone or any other material, is a warning against overextending your credit, business, personal, or social, whichever applies.

Curls. Exciting changes for the better, if they were being cut; otherwise, for a woman, they signify a new romantic interest, but for a man, they indicate possible damage to his reputation through unwise choice of companions, and he would do well to reassess his personal relationships.

Currants. An augury of splendid new opportunities if the fruit was ripe and red, but if it was dark and/or dried up, it signifies a period of struggle and frustration. See also *Berries*.

Curse. You are in danger of losing the respect of friends and/or colleagues if you uttered curses in your dream. Curb your temper and impulsive actions. However, if the curses were directed at you, a rise in social status through new and influential friends may be expected.

Curtain. An obstacle dream pertaining to hidden opposition. If during your dream the curtains were opened, you will discover and outwit the hostile hypocrite. If your dream featured the hanging or selection of new curtains, you may expect increased social activity.

Cushion. A dream of contrary. The more cushions there were in your dream the more you will have to economize during the coming year, unless the cushions were torn and shabby, in which case they signify small gains.

Custard. Be prepared for a season of boredom and frustration if you dreamed of this bland type of food.

See also *Food* and *Eating*.

Cut. To dream of yourself or anyone else being cut by a sharp edge or object is a warning that indiscreet gossip or behavior could be very costly. Cool it! See also *Knife, Blade, Razor, Ax, Cloth,* etc.

Cycling. See *Bicycle.*

Cyclone. A dream of a cyclone is a warning to avoid taking risks of any description whatsoever for at least six months. Lie doggo on as many pending issues as possible during that period.

Cymbals. A passionate new romance is likely to follow a dream of hearing or playing this percussion instrument. See also *Music* and *Musical Instruments.*

Cypress. This tree on its own signifies sad news concerning friends. See also *Trees.*

Daffodils. You can forget any worries concerning your personal or love affairs if you've dreamed of these lovely spring flowers. Seen growing out of doors in a garden, or in a field, they indicate an unusually long and happy future.

Dagger. If you saw a dagger in your dream, you can expect news from a distance. To carry a dagger is a warning to be more circumspect in your actions or you might become involved in an unpleasant situation; to see others with daggers or someone stabbed by a dagger signifies triumph over hostility.

Dahlias. This dream pertains to financial matters and is a harbinger of good news, especially so if these flowers are seen indoors or in a vase.

Dam. Water churning over a dam is a warning against impulsive action of any nature, but particularly in regard to changes of employment or investments. After this dream, it is advisable to reconsider your plans.

Dance. This dream is mainly favorable. If it featured ballet dancers or dancing it predicts new friends and gay social times ahead; if you saw young people dancing together, you'll have great success in your love affairs; children dancing, you'll have some unexpected joy; and if you were dancing yourself, all your enterprises will flourish.

Danger. A dream of contrary. You will overcome your difficulties if you faced the danger. If the danger was of a physical nature and you avoided it, it is a warning to look after your health.

Darkness. Be prepared for a setback; however, if you managed to grope your way to the light, you will achieve great success. If you were walking in the dark, you will recover something you had given up for lost.

Darn. If you were doing the darning in your dream, you can expect the healing of a breach which has distressed you; if the darning was observed on a garment or someone else was doing it, you are being warned against idle gossip lest you alienate someone whose respect you value. See also *Mend*.

Dates. To eat them predicts a marriage, not necessarily your own but one that concerns you. To see dates growing or harvested is a forecast of business success.

Dawn. A clear sunny dawn predicts some splendid new opportunity on your horizon; but a gray or rainy dawn suggests some trials to be overcome.

Deafness. To dream of losing your own hearing is the forerunner of great financial success; to dream of others being deaf signifies a happy solution to your present problems, unless you were trying to communicate with a deaf-mute, in which case you must expect a period of frustration before you get what you want.

Death. If you dreamed of being dead yourself, it indicates an approaching release from all your worries and/or a recovery from illness. If you spoke with someone who is dead, you will soon hear very good news. To dream of a death frequently signifies news of a birth. To be aware of a dead person you cannot identify portends an inheritance which may not be personal but could be indirectly beneficial.

Death's Head. This kind of a skull featured in your dream predicts that you will inadvertently uncover a secret that you'd rather not know. Be extremely careful how you use or react to it, as your handling of the situation could affect your future.

Debt. A dream of paying

debts indicates a lucky period ahead, but if you were repaid a debt, you'd better be prepared to take a loss, so if you're inclined to gamble, govern yourself accordingly.

Decay. Whatever the nature of the decayed material, this dream is telling you that you've got some stormy weather ahead.

Deck. To be on the deck of a ship is a lucky omen, providing the water is calm or pleasantly rolling; otherwise it predicts some unexpected trouble the size of which will be in ratio to the roughness of the sea. See also *Cards.*

Decorate. A dream of decorating anything, inside or out, is a prediction of celebrations to come. See also *Colors, Paint,* etc.

Deed. You are being warned against speculating either with money or with personal relationships if you dreamed of signing or of a signed deed; but if you refused to sign or the deed was unsigned, you can be your own best friend by keeping your plans to yourself.

Deer. If the deer was cap-tive or in an unnatural surrounding, it signifies emotional upsets and/or disappointment in some trusted friend; however, in its natural habitat it augurs the cementing of a new and pleasant friend-ship. To kill a deer or see a dead one is a warning to look out for a backbiter masquerading as a friend.

Defend. If your dream involved shielding or defending someone else, you can be sure your trust is well placed. If you defended yourself or some-one else defended you, you should avoid forcing any important issues for the time being, as someone you count on for support could suddenly fail you.

Deform. A dream of deformity, whether your own or that of others, signifies a need for some house-cleaning. You're harboring a viper in your nest and you'd better clean it out before you get stung!

Delay. For an accurate interpretation the details of the dream must be correlated to its action, but as a general guide: this dream portends a season of upsets and/or family disagreements, unless it was a delayed bus, train, or airplane which was featured, in which case it indicates some upcoming problems connected with money or financial affairs.

Delirium. You're bottling up something you need to get off your chest if you dreamed of being delirious; a sympathetic and trusty ear could avoid an embarrassing explosion, so try to find one. If your dream featured others in a delirious state, you will get help from an unknown source.

Deluge. Avoid controversy of any kind with friends, family, or associates after a dream of a heavy downpour. Arguments at this time could have unexpectedly unhappy, if not unfortunate, repercussions. Play everything very cool for the time being.

Demolish. See *Destruction*.

Dentist. See *Teeth*.

Depart. See *Travel*.

Derelict. Anything derelict in your dream is telling you to buck up. You can overcome your present frustration by using your common sense plus a bit of ingenuity. Have a bash; you have nothing to lose but your discouragement.

Desert. In bloom, and/or in clear sunny weather, a dream featuring a desert predicts contentment and good success in your efforts; but if the weather was bad or if there was a sandstorm, you can expect some immediate difficulties due to hidden opposition, but the outcome will be better than you expect.

Desertion. A dream of opposite. If you dreamed of deserting someone or something, you can expect to lose a friend through foolish gossip, but if, in your dream, you were deserted, you can count on true friends who will rally to your cause whenever needed.

Design. To see or make designs of any kind is a prediction of increasing responsibility without commensurate financial reward; you'll have to content yourself, for the time being, with the status aspect.

Desire. See *Craving*.

Desk. A closed desk forecasts a disappointment; it could be in business but is more likely to be of a romantic or social character. An open desk, whether you were seated at it, working at it, or just observed it, indicates satisfaction with all matters which closely concern you. To rummage in or clean out a desk predicts new and influential friends.

Desolation. A desolate house or district in a dream forecasts the acquisition of articles of great material value, most likely by gift or inheritance but could be by lucky accident.

Despair. You'll have no cause to if you dreamed about it; everything will come up roses before long.

Dessert. See *Eating, Fruit, Food*, etc.

Destroy. A sort of contrary dream in that it is an unfortunate omen if you break or destroy anything not your own property. To see or find it destroyed signifies an unexpected triumph or gain.

Destruction. To dream of the destruction of buildings, other structures, or their environment by aggression or natural causes is a warning to curb your temper; ill-considered or impulsive reactions could be very costly just now.

Detail. You can expect to have some really complicated puzzles to sort out if your dream featured small details of any kind.

Detective. This fellow in your dream signifies what he does. You can expect to learn the solution to a perplexing problem which has been plaguing you.

Detest. Petty family quarrels are likely to follow a dream in which you detested something or someone; however, if you had the feeling of being detested, it's a reverse omen of coming admiration.

Devil. The meaning of this symbol of evil depends greatly on the details. If you dreamed of him surrounded by his traditional instruments of punishment, you'd better get some professional advice concerning the guilty secret you're hiding. If your dream involved fighting him off, you will outwit those who are trying to harm you; if he spoke to you, it signifies a great temptation you will find difficult to resist; and if your dream meeting with him was congenial, you would be well advised to have a medical checkup.

Devotion. See *Love*.

Dew. This moist blessing of nature is a most fortunate dream omen; all your hopes will bloom into reality, especially if you walked in it.

Dial. Use of a telephone dial predicts the repayment of a loan you have written off or a small gain from a forgotten investment. A watch, clock, or instrument dial indicates a need to check on the safety of your savings and/or investments; this is especially urgent if the dial or dials were either cracked or broken.

Diamonds. Strangely enough, these glittering symbols of affluence are not particularly fortunate dream omens. If, in fact, you own them, or are in a position to have them, they signify losses though not of a serious order; on the other hand if your financial position doesn't allow for diamonds, their appearance in your dream indicates coming profits, although perhaps not as large as you might be expecting. See also *Jewelry*.

Diapers. For a man this dream predicts a change of job or position to one of greater responsibility; for a woman, it forecasts a temporary separation from her husband or fiancé, or a break with her current boy friend, whichever applies.

Dice. For a woman, a dream featuring dice is a warning that she is contemplating a romantic affair which she suspects might be foolish; it would be. For a man, this dream is telling him that the immediate financial success he is so ardently pursuing may be too costly in the long run and he would be wise to reassess his actions and perhaps take life a bit more calmly. Anyone who dreams of throwing a spectacular winning streak at dice can expect a windfall of money, useful perhaps, but not big enough to affect his or her lifestyle.

Dictaphone. If you only noticed the machine in your dream, you will hear news of a friend's promotion; however, if you dreamed of using the apparatus yourself, it signifies a good rise in your own status.

Dictate. To give dictation in a dream signifies an unexpected complication in your current plans; to take dictation indicates an important improvement in your business affairs. Of course, if your normal activities include giving or taking dictation, then the dream has no significance.

Dictionary. A dream featuring this book of words is a warning that you are in danger of losing a friend through inconsequential controversy. Try to be less contentious; it's not worth losing a friend to win an argument.

Diet. The meaning here is as dreary as its practice; a dream concerning this exercise in restraint predicts upcoming financial reverses, unless you are actually in one, in which case you are probably just hungry.

Difficulty. An obstacle dream of contrary. The bigger and more worrisome was your dreamed difficulty the smaller will be your real one.

Digging. The significance of this dream varies according to the circumstances of the dreamer. For a person in business or in a job, it signifies that hard, or harder, work will be necessary to attain what he

wants. For a professional person, it indicates that a further course of study or acquisition of higher qualifications would be beneficial to his or her aims. If you don't fit either of the foregoing categories, then the key to the meaning of the dream lies in the effort involved in the action; if the soil was soft and/or the digging easy, you are in for a happy period of easy living; if the digging was hard and slow going, you can expect to have to struggle for a while yet.

Dike. You are worried about carrying or taking on responsibility which you secretly fear will prove too much for you if your dream featured this type of water barrier; either talk it over with a trusted friend or get professional counsel.

Dime. See *Coins*.

Dimples. Noticing dimples on anyone in a dream signifies passing love affairs. Don't take any declarations of undying devotion seriously after this dream however much you may fancy your current attachment.

Dinner. Any meal, as such, is a dream of contrary,

and the more elaborate its general aspect the greater are the difficulties it predicts; therefore a frugal meal indicates success with minimum effort. However, any details which were noted in the dream should also be considered for an accurate interpretation. See *Food, Eating, Vegetable(s), Meat,* etc.

Diploma. Whether it was received, given, or only observed, for a man a dream of a diploma predicts wealth and distinction through his own efforts. For a woman, however, it is a dream of contrary and a warning of possible downfall through excessive vanity. She would do well to curb her extravagance before it curbs her.

Dipper. To dream of drinking from any kind of communal dipper is a warning to guard against the impulsive breach of family or personal confidences; no matter what the provocation, hold your tongue or you'll regret it.

Director. A dream of being appointed to or offered a place on a company board signifies good business news and/or good news concerning any issues with a legal aspect. To resign or lose a directorship in your dream suggests a possible loss of status through your own foolish actions. Whatever your secret indiscretions may be you'd best consider the consequences of exposure and cool it for the time being.

Directory. The use or appearance of a telephone or other type directory in your dream signifies a propitious time for having a flirtation and/or a flutter at gambling, but don't go off the deep end.

Dirge. An omen of contrary. To hear a funeral dirge in your dream predicts a celebration but concerns a friend or relation rather than yourself.

Dirt. To dream that your person or your clothes are dirty in the ordinary way of carelessness or neglect is an indication of illness and a medical checkup is suggested. To dream of stepping or falling into dirt or trash predicts a change of residence for the better. A dream of throwing dirt or having it thrown at you is a warning that someone in whom you have confided will attempt to use the information against you. Forewarned is forearmed; be prepared to defend yourself. See also *Earth, Dust, Manure,* etc.

Disappearance. To be aware, in your dream, of the magical disappearance of yourself, others, and/or material objects predicts that though you will soon be perplexed by a variety of problems you won't be overcome by them.

Disappointment. A real contrary one. The dreamer is assured of success in the precise matter of the dreamed disappointment.

Disaster. Another forecast of opposites. To dream of being in or witnessing a disaster is a forerunner of improved circumstances.

Discipline. Being disciplined in a dream augurs recognition for work well done, but if you dreamed of handing out the discipline, you better hold on to your money, because someone will try to con you out of some.

Discoloration. You may expect to suffer a setback in your social ambitions if you dreamed of having or observing a black eye and/or any other body discoloration. See also *Bruise.*

Discord. If the discord was

in the form of disputes, arguments, or a sensed unfriendly atmosphere, you will hear news of a divorce or a broken romance. See also *Music.*

Discover. It's a happy omen if you suddenly discovered someone or something in your dream; you should soon come into an inheritance. If you were the one discovered, it's a promise of seeing new faces in new places, so get ready to travel.

Discuss. To dream of hearing or being involved in a lot of palaver is a warning to avoid letting others influence you when it comes to important decisions. Rely on your own judgment.

Disdain. A dream of being treated with contempt is telling you that you could lose useful contacts by being oversensitive; if your dream involved contempt for others, you are being reminded that pride goes before a fall.

Disease. To dream of disease in general is a dream of contrary and signifies happy times ahead. If the dream involved the illness of someone known to you, it predicts good luck for that person. There is however an exception to the rule of contrary in this case, which is that if your dream specifically concerned a venereal disease, it is a warning that someone is trying to impugn your character. Beware of overconfidence.

Disfigure. A dream of contrary if it featured your own disfigurement; you will have unanticipated joy. However, if it involved the disfigurement of others, you are in danger of being deceived and/or actually cheated by someone you trust. Avoid any business dealings with friends for the time being.

Disgrace. This dream pertains strictly to love and/or domestic affairs and is a most favorable omen whether it involved your own disgrace or that of others.

Disguise. You are considering some devious plan or unethical course of action if your dream featured others in disguise; better reconsider carefully, as you could be seriously embarrassed, if not actually damaged, by treachery from your associates in the matter. If you were yourself disguised, you are being warned against a tendency to be oversecretive. Try talking over your worries with a trusted friend.

Disgust. Whether you showed or observed disgust in your dream, you can expect a series of petty annoyances and minor frustrations for a short period of time.

Dish. The portent here depends on the condition of the dish (or dishes). If it was full, it signifies good fortune; empty, the augury is of a static period of marking time unless the beauty of the empty dish was the main feature, in which case the dream predicts luck in love affairs. Broken, damaged, or dirty dishes are a forerunner of family quarrels or domestic problems.

Dishonesty. You will be tempted to take a step backward in order to take a later one forward if your dream involved dishonesty of any kind. Rely on your own intuition in the matter.

Disinfect. If your dream involved disinfecting or a disinfectant, it is telling you that, although you may be on the road to, or even on the brink of disaster, help will come out of the blue.

Disinherit. A dream of disinheritance predicts a sudden spectacular change for the better in whatever concerns you most.

Dislocation. Following a dream of a dislocated joint, any offer or plan which would require a change of business, job, or residence should be considered with extreme caution and only after careful investigation.

Dismiss. You are being warned to pay closer attention to your responsibilities if you dreamed of being dismissed from a job; if your dream concerned dismissing someone else, you should reconsider a break in a personal relationship which you are contemplating. Lay the person aside if you must, but you'll regret it if you throw him or her away.

Disobedience. To be aware of disobedience in your dream predicts an important problem involving a decision you will find difficult to make. Get advice from a more experienced head than your own before you commit yourself.

Disorder. To dream that your clothes are in disorder is a warning against scheming friends or associates; a dream of disorderly rooms or surroundings indicates a trip or news of something you thought lost.

Dispute. See *Argue.*

Disrespect. See *Disdain.*

Distance. A dream in which the people, things, or action seemed to be a long distance away predicts that you will have to wait to achieve your present desire until you have overcome an obstacle from your past.

Distort. Sudden strong rivalry in business or love, whichever is your prime concern, is forecast in a dream featuring facial or any other type of distortion.

Distress. You'll make a gain where you expected to take a loss if you dreamed of yourself or others being in distress.

Distrust. See *Doubt.*

Disturb. To dream of yourself or anyone else being disturbed is a symbol of personal trouble. Consult a doctor, minister, or other qualified counselor.

Ditch. An obstacle dream—money troubles if you were in the ditch, romantic troubles if you fell into it; but whatever the difficulties may be, they won't be serious ones, and, if in your dream you got out of the ditch or jumped over it, you can be sure of an ultimate benefit from the experience.

Divan. See *Couch.*

Dive. Diving symbolizes a serious temptation or ordeal with which you are or will soon be faced. The prediction of the outcome of your action depends on the condition of the water; if it was clear, you will be gratified with the result, but if the water was murky and/or choppy, you can expect to have unpleasant repercussions.

Dividend. A dream concerning dividends is a warning that someone may profit from your efforts if you don't guard against carelessly given confidence.

Divorce. The significance of this dream depends upon the marital status of the dreamer. If married, it is a dream of contrary and you can rely on your mate; if single, it is a warning that your affections are probably misplaced.

Dizziness. Have your blood pressure checked, and if it proves to be normal, expect to be upset by a sudden passionate attraction to a new acquaintance.

Dock. To dream of seeing the dock from on board a ship portends a surprising and beneficial turn of events. A dream of a busy dock or dockyard indicates an increase in material wealth; but if you were alone on a dock or observed a deserted dockyard, the prediction is one of sadness.

Doctor. He's a good man or woman to have in your dream because he or she forecasts an improvement in all departments of your life.

Document. Business or legal documents in a dream are usually a warning against speculations, unless the documents were in an indigenous place such as a notary or lawyer's office, in which case they portend a coming increase, possibly for inheritance.

Dog. As a general rule dogs

in a dream are a good omen and symbolize friends. Of course the interpretation varies according to the action and other details but is fairly straightforward. If the dog was friendly and affectionate, it signifies pleasure and happy times with friends; a fierce or snarling dog suggests disagreements or untrustworthy friends; and if it bit or attacked, you are being warned to look out for actual deceit or harmful trickery from someone you have trusted. To hear a dog bark happily signifies pleasing social recognition, but if it barked fiercely, you are being warned of possible legal troubles, so don't fiddle your taxes or park your car too close to a hydrant. To see dogs fighting indicates that you may be called on to arbitrate in an argument between friends, in which case you must be extra tactful to avoid ending up the odd man out. If the dog in your dream was an exceptionally large one, it signifies protection through a powerful friend. See also Colors.

Dole. See Charity.

Doll. It is generally agreed that dolls, being a symbol of childhood, predict social and/or domestic happiness. If you bought a doll in your dream, it indicates a small but pleasing profit or gain; however, for an accurate interpretation, other details of your dream should be examined. See also Children, Baby, Colors, Gift, etc.

Dollar. A silver dollar or dollars mean good luck in your current interests. For paper bills see under Money.

Dolphin. These amusing, intelligent mammals are a sign of advancement through your own mental vigor, but other details of your dream should also be considered, such as the condition of the water, the location and/or action of the dolphin, etc.

Dome. The dome of a building seen in your dream signifies unexpected honor or recognition for yourself or someone closely connected to you.

Domino. This fancy-dress costume featured in your dream indicates some small difficulties which you can easily overcome by simply ignoring them.

Dominoes. You should avoid

any risk or speculation for a few months following a dream of playing this game. If you only saw the dominoes in their box, you are being warned to delay the purchase of anything valuable at this time or alternatively be sure to get an expert opinion no matter who offers you the article.

Donation. See *Collect.*

Donkey. Love and/or sexual affairs are symbolized by this patient and often stubborn animal; therefore the interpretation of your dream depends on its action as related to your circumstances. As a general guide it is considered favorable for your affair(s) if you were riding or sitting on the donkey, unless it balked, threw you off, kicked you, or otherwise gave you a hard time, in which case that's exactly what you can expect. A donkey braying in your dream is telling you that you could be severely embarrassed by the exposure of a discreditable affair or illicit relationship. Better reassess your recent behavior and companions. However, if the donkey in your dream was a white one, the significance (whatever the action) is altered

to one of increased sexual vigor, great personal success, and loyal friends.

Door. Closed or locked doors usually signify vain regrets over past or missed opportunities; save your energy. An open door, especially if it reveals a pleasing vista, predicts a realization of your highest hopes. More than one door in a dream means that you will soon be able to choose from a number of good opportunities.

Doorbell. A symbol of pleasant excitement. If you pushed it, you will soon have an interesting new friend; if you heard it ringing, you can expect to have an opportunity to engage in a happy new activity.

Dope. See *Drugs.*

Dormer. See *Window.*

Double. See *Pair(s).*

Doubt. To experience the feeling of doubt in your dream signifies that you need not doubt those in whom you have placed your trust. If, in your dream, you sensed that you were being doubted, you will need patience to overcome an annoying obstacle in your way.

Dough. Kneading or seeing dough in your dream is an omen of good health and prosperity.

Doughnuts. Whether you ate them, bought them, fried them, or just observed them, these round goodies in your dream forecast travel, so if you weren't expecting to, you'd better get ready, and if you were expecting to, you'd be smart to be prepared for a longer trip than you anticipated.

Dove. White doves signify happy domestic affairs and/or a peaceful solution to any disagreements which may be troubling you. A flock of doves predicts sudden travel or the return of an old friend from a distance. The cooing of doves promises reciprocal love, but the voice of a turtledove heralds some approaching sadness.

Draft. Fluctuations in your fortunes from which you will learn useful lessons for the future are forecast in a dream of sitting or standing in a draft. See also *Soldiers*.

Dragon. You will get an enormous boost in your progress toward financial success from a powerful and influential personage if you dreamed of a dragon. And if you don't now know such a big wheel, you soon will.

Drain. A drain in a dream is a warning of low vitality; it would be wise to get a medical checkup and include a blood test.

Drake. See *Ducks*.

Draperies. Decorative draperies (as differentiated from curtains) predict coming luxury, and the more elaborate the draperies the greater will be the wealth, unless they were faded, torn, otherwise shabby, or obviously shoddy, in which case they signal possible losses through lack of attention to your own best interests. Stop taking the line of least resistance unless you're sure it also happens to be the right one.

Drawbridge. Your diary will soon be full of exciting engagements if your dream involved an opening drawbridge; if the bridge was closed, it signifies a satisfactory conclusion to one or more pending matters. If the bridge in your dream was being lowered, it was telling you that you may have to take a step backward in order to take two forward.

Drawers. A closed drawer means that you will have to outmaneuver an unsuspected rival for something you want. An open drawer signifies a new opportunity, and if the drawer is full it signals a propitious time for undertaking a new venture. An empty drawer indicates success but only after hard work. A locked drawer or trouble opening one suggests unforeseen obstacles in your path, but persevere, you can overcome them with patience.

Dreams. A dream within your dream portends a deferment of your highest hopes but nevertheless a definite improvement in your present circumstances.

Dress. To dream of having or seeing an attractive new dress augurs some imminent social satisfaction. An embroidered dress signifies casual sexual pleasures. See also *Clothes* and *Colors*.

Drift. The sensation of drifting experienced in your dream is reminding you that your problems won't disappear if you ignore them, so you'd better get down to some positive action to sort them out.

Drill. The use of any kind of mechanical drill is a sort of dream of contrary in that the harder the drill was working in your dream the more urgent is its warning to you to stop frittering away your time and energy in meaningless activities.

Drink. The significance depends on what the drink is and its condition. Water which is cloudy, dirty, warm, or hot predicts loss of money and/or status due to unfortunate circumstances; but a drink of clear cool or cold water is a very fortunate omen for anyone but particularly for students or those in academic life, as for such it augurs honor and achievement through knowledge. To drink milk is also a happy omen of coming success. Fizzy soft drinks such as Coca-Cola, etc. signify exciting happenings ahead, and any very sweet, syrupy drink predicts a passionate love affair. However, drinking from a bottle indicates an unsatisfactory romantic experience. See also *Wine, Brandy, Colors, Bar,* etc.

Drive. You'll have a stroke of money luck if someone else was driving you, but if you were driving yourself, it is a warning to avoid gambling and be cautious in money matters for the next few weeks.

Dromedary. See *Camel*.

Drool. To do or observe this infantile action in your dream predicts opportunities for extraordinary sensual pleasures. Try to remember that moderation in all things is the better part of valor!

Drops. A dream featuring anything being measured in drops predicts a small but gratifying increase in material wealth, possibly by inheritance, or alternatively it may signify a slow but steady advance in your position if you are employed.

Drought. A short period of tough luck followed by a sudden release from worry is forecast in a dream featuring parched and sere land or fields.

Drown. An unfortunate omen pertaining to business interests, unless you (or the drowning person) was revived or rescued, in which case you will get a chance

to recoup your losses through the intervention of a friend.

Druggist. See *Pharmacist*.

Drugs. The meaning of this dream varies greatly according to the details of its action. If you dreamed of being drugged to the extent that it interfered with, or altered, your normal movements and/or behavior, it is a warning that there is active jealousy around you from someone who would not only be ready and willing to make capital of any mistake you might make but might even try to mislead you into making one. Be extra careful of your actions following this dream. Drugs used in a dream as an antidote to pain predict an increase in income, but to take drugs as a lark signifies that someone is trying to lead you astray. If your dream featured addiction or an addict, it is telling you to stop drifting and take a more positive role in life. A dream of giving or selling drugs suggests that you have some dishonesty around you and you'd do well to reassess your current companions. Of course the foregoing applies only if you don't actually use drugs.

Drugstore. If your dream involved a drugstore, it indicates that you would benefit from a change of occupation.

Drums. To hear drums in your dream forecasts great success and to play them yourself signifies great joy. See also *Toys, Musical Instruments,* and *Music*.

Drumstick. A dream of drumsticks being used on anything but a drum, or of having drumsticks without a drum, is a warning that you could be severely embarrassed if you are not careful about being absolutely aboveboard in all your dealings and/or statements. To dream of eating the drumstick of a fowl is an omen of good luck.

Drunk. If your dream featured your own intoxication, you are being warned that too much high living in low places leads inevitably to the slippery slope. Slow down! A dream of others who were drunk indicates a loss by way of a loan which will not be repaid; but don't worry, it won't be important to you.

Dry. A dream of drying yourself signifies that you can successfully handle your own affairs. Listen to qualified advice but do what you think best. If your dream involved drying others or others drying themselves, you may have to ask for help from a friend; don't hesitate. Drying of dishes or cooking utensils in a dream predicts petty annoyances; drying clothes suggests a need to shake off some conditions that are holding you back, or some people whose attitudes are depressing you. Get on with it!

Ducks. You'll be lucky if you dreamed of ducks, unless they attacked you, in which case you can expect to have an insignificant loss, but not necessarily financial. If you saw them flying, they forecast monetary gain; swimming, they signify happy family unity; to see a duck and a drake together is a forerunner of happy romantic news.

Duel. You have some mischief-makers in your family or among your close companions; try to sort them out before their meddling causes a serious rift.

Duet. To hear, or sing in, a duet in your dream is a

fortunate omen signifying happiness in love and/or domestic affairs. See also *Music* and *Singing*.

Dumb. Whether it was yourself or others who were unable to speak, a dream of dumbness is a warning to keep your business to yourself and avoid any speculative ventures for the time being.

Dump. You can expect, in the near future, to be obliged to help someone out of a tight spot (not necessarily financial) if your dream featured a trash dump, refuse heap, or junkyard.

Dumplings. Making or eating these tasty morsels in your dream augurs a release from anxiety; if they were made of potato, you will suddenly get cooperation where you have previously encountered opposition. See also *Eating, Food, Cooking,* etc.

Dun. A dream of contrary. Being dunned for payment in your dream portends an unexpected large profit or increase in income, unless you actually are in a financial mess, in which case the dream is simply asserting a threat to your mental welfare

and you should try to work out a sensible plan with your creditors.

Dungeon. An obstacle dream. If you couldn't get out, you would probably benefit from a change of plans, but if you managed to escape, you can expect to achieve your aims in time but only by diligent effort.

Dunghill. See *Manure*.

Dunk. Performing this breach of good manners in a dream presages an increase in material wealth if you dunked bread or toast; if you dunked cake or doughnuts, it indicates delayed success.

Dusk. This type of half-light in a dream signifies some annoying but not serious difficulties ahead, most likely to do with romantic matters.

Dust. Not an auspicious omen. It signifies an approaching period of annoyances, petty quarrels, and minor embarrassments; however, if you managed to clean it off, the adverse aura will soon disperse. To dream of seeing a cloud of dust gathering or rolling indicates a new problem on your horizon which will only be overcome by prolonged effort.

Dwarf. All your problems will disappear as if by magic if you dreamed of being or seeing a dwarf, unless the dwarf was ugly or malformed, in which case you are being warned against a false friend, so be cautious about sharing secrets.

Dye. The act of changing colors in a dream symbolizes success through the use of constructive initiative and good judgment. If your dream featured dyed hair, it pertains to your business or professional career; if the dyed items were garments or cloth, your success will be in a social sphere. The only exception to the foregoing is if your dream involved anything being dyed black, in which case the dream predicts a passing sadness concerning your own decision to make a break in a personal relationship which has become incubustic.

Dying. The significance is substantially the same as that of death except that its prediction is less imminent. See also *Illness*.

Dynamite. To be aware of unexploded dynamite in your dream predicts that some danger or problem which has been worrying you will either not develop or will prove to be groundless. If you dreamed of seeing or hearing a dynamite explosion, you are being warned to abandon a new plan or venture you have been considering; it won't work.

Dynamo. A dream of a dynamo suggests that you have been burning the candle at both ends, either with work or play; slow down before you break down!

Dysentery. If you had this disagreeable bacterial attack in your dream, you can expect to receive a valuable gift, possibly in the form of profitable information. If your dream involved others being afflicted, it forecasts a celebration in the offing.

Eagle. If you see an eagle flying, your business prospects are very rosy indeed. And should this noble bird happen to be perched in a high place, you will have fame as well as fortune. If you see it on a mountaintop, you will achieve beyond your highest ambitions. However, should the eagle attack or frighten you, you will have to overcome some difficult obstacles before reaching your goal.

Earrings. For a woman, any dream featuring earrings pertains to personal relationships and as a general rule is a warning against repeating gossip which could lead to embarrassing rifts. However, other details should be considered for an accurate interpretation. For a man, a dream of wearing earrings himself signifies an interesting development concerning his work, but otherwise they pertain to romantic relations and other details of the dream should be collated. See *Jewelry, Gold, Silver, Colors, Gift,* etc.

Ears. A dream of other people's ears indicates you will hear some startling news. If your ears ached or you had trouble with them in your dream, it is a warning to look out for an untrustworthy person in your immediate circle. If the ears were very large, you will get help from an unexpected source; if they were very small, you will discover a false friend.

Earth. To dream you are lying on the earth signifies news of a sad nature; but if you are being buried in earth, you will be lucky in some kind of gamble.

If, in your dream, you see someone tilling the earth, or you observe earth which has been tilled, you will participate in very substantial profits.

Earthquake. This is a rare dream and its meaning varies greatly. For those who live in an earthquake area, it merely indicates some minor difficulties to be overcome. But for others it signifies a complete change of circumstances and/or environment from which they can eventually reap a rich reward, but only through diligence and perseverance.

Easel. If you dream of seeing an artist painting at an easel, or a picture on an easel, you will have a comfortable life sooner than you expect.

East. A dream in which this direction is the main feature indicates the formulation, or cancellation, of a plan involving an important change of location. See also *Compass*.

Eating. The interpretation of this dream differs greatly according to the circumstances and other factors involved, so you must look up the various foods, fruits, vegetables, meat, etc. However, as a general guide eating with guests is a happy omen, but to eat alone is a warning to guard against a loss of status or valued friends.

Eavesdropping. A dream in which others are eavesdropping is a warning that you are facing a dilemma from which it will be difficult to extricate yourself. But any dream in which you are the eavesdropper is a forerunner of unanticipated good luck.

Ebony. You should be very careful about what you put in writing, or about signing petitions or documents following a dream featuring this shiny black wood.

Echo. In this curious dream, if the echo was of your own voice, you can expect to have a strange experience, probably with the opposite sex. If the echo is near, you will hear good news concerning others; if far away, the news will be from a distance.

Eclipse. A very unusual dream probably arising from a subconscious worry concerning your health or that of someone close to you. In either case a medical checkup would be helpful.

Ecstasy. A sort of dream of contrary in that it indicates boredom with the present state of your sex life. A hiatus and/or a change, whichever is feasible in your case, would be advisable.

Eden. A rare dream warning that you will have to be on guard against strong rivals masquerading as friends or well-wishers.

Editor. To dream of seeing one indicates a need to pay closer attention to your general personal interests; to dream of being one predicts an unexpected delay in your current undertakings.

Education. A dream of contrary. If your dream featured getting or extending it, the prediction is that any success you achieve will be purely commercial; if, on the other hand, your dream concerned a lack of it, you will probably attain recognition in a cultural endeavor.

Eels. Live eels in a dream signify troubles which can be overcome by diligent effort. Dead ones are a warning to guard your fi-

nances; if you are considering a new business venture or investment, you'd better double-check to make certain there is no hidden snag which could put you under financial pressure. Alternatively, if your love or sex life is your primary concern at the present time, this is a dream of contrary and dead eels are an indication of overindulgence, whereas live ones suggest underindulgence, so be guided accordingly.

Effigy. A dream of seeing an effigy is telling you that you will have to face up to the deceit, among your acquaintances, which you now suspect.

Eggs. Eggs are a generally good omen for whatever concerns you most. They augur domestic contentment and/or prosperity and abundance. Eating eggs signifies good (or improving if you're not well) health. If your dream involved finding eggs in a bird's nest, it predicts an unexpected windfall of money. However, if the eggs in your dream were cracked, rotten, broken, stale, or otherwise unpleasant, they are a warning of disappointment through unwisely placed trust. Brightly colored Easter eggs signify a coming celebration of a happy event. See also *Colors*.

Eight. See *Numbers*.

Eighteen. See *Numbers*.

Elastic. A dream of elastic material or elasticity signifies that you will have to stretch yourself to the outside limit of your capabilities but that you will find the exercise both stimulating and rewarding. If the feature of the dream involved snapping elastic or the use of rubber bands, it forecasts a coming request for help which you should try to give.

Elbow. The significance here varies greatly depending on the action. A dream of using your elbows effectively in a crowd is a forecast of notable achievement, but to be elbowed yourself is a warning that you are in danger of being cheated or unjustly sued. A pain in the elbow is a signal of unexpected opposition; clean or pretty elbows predict pleasant social occasions, but dirty ones indicate unhappiness through troublesome friends or relatives. A broken elbow is a warning against mismanage-

ment in your business affairs. See also under *Bone*.

Elderberries. Whether you picked them, ate them, cooked them, or whatever, these wild berries in your dream predict that you will be faced with a mess not of your own making, but don't be unduly worried, you'll be able to cope.

Election. Quick success with your current short-term plans is the forecast if your dream featured taking part in an election.

Electricity. The interpretation of this mysterious force is greatly influenced by the details and action, so all aspects should be carefully integrated, but as a general guide:

Cross-circuiting or fused wires indicate possible business reverses or property loss due to carelessness.

Being shocked by a live wire or by static electricity signifies sudden surprising news.

Turning electricity on forecasts unexpected recognition for past efforts or favors.

Turning it off indicates depression or discouragement probably due to low vitality; try a vacation or a tonic.

A sudden general power failure in your dream suggests that you suspect you are wasting your energy; reassess your ambitions and consider a possible change of direction.

To be aware of a live wire (as opposed to being shocked by it) in your dream portends sudden opposition which you will have to circumnavigate by the use of careful diplomacy. Tread softly and don't try to force issues for a few weeks.

See also *Lightning*.

Elephant. These big animals if in a normal friendly mood are an omen of great good luck. Performing they signify helpful friends and/or associates. Working, they indicate assured success in all your undertakings. If you fed it, watered it, rode, or sat on it, you may expect a sudden rise of status or other improvement through a sheer lucky break or the discovery or return of something you thought irretrievable. Even the adverse aspect of this beast, which is if it frightened or attacked you, isn't really dreary, as it signifies annoying but temporary obstacles to your progress.

Elevator. This follows the general rule in the chapter on interpretation. Up is good, down is discouraging, but other factors should be considered. See also *Metal*, etc.

Eleven. See *Numbers*.

Elf. Help from unexpected, or even unknown, sources will be yours if you dreamed of these mystical, magical characters.

Elk. However featured, this noble animal in a dream is a sex symbol and signifies that you'll have no need to worry about your attraction and/or ability in regard to sex relations.

Elm. A carefree life during which all things come easily is forecast in a dream of a lofty elm, unless it was wormy or otherwise diseased, in which case its augury is still favorable but does not exclude occasional setbacks. See also *Trees*.

Elope. A dream of contrary. If you were eloping, the dream predicts a romantic disappointment or break; if your dream involved the elopement of others, someone will try to persuade you to make a sentimental journey which would be disappointing if not actually distressing. Don't be tempted.

Embalm. To dream of assisting or observing an undertaker at this job indicates that you are contemplating an action which you suspect will be misinterpreted; you're right, so forget it. It might cause you more embarrassment than you think possible.

Embankment. An obstacle dream if it was a high embankment; you may have to back up and park for a while before you can go forward again. If it was a low embankment, it predicts the resumption of a past relationship which will prove to be beneficial in an unexpected way.

Embark. See *Travel.*

Embarrassment. Another dream of contrary. The greater was your dreamed embarrassment the bigger and more satisfying will be your coming success. If your dream concerned the embarrassment of others, it is reminding you to be firm in rejecting outside influences and relying on your own judgment.

Embassy. If your dream concerned a social function at an embassy, it is a straightforward forecast of a coming opportunity to mix socially with influential people. If your dream concerned the official or business aspect of an embassy, it is telling you that achievement without effort is not possible for you; you'll have to go after what you want, it won't come and sit in your lap.

Ember. See *Fire, Burning,* etc.

Embezzle. A dream which involves embezzlement by yourself or others suggests that you have some knotty problems and/or secret fear of such a complex nature that you would be wise to seek professional help as soon as possible.

Embrace. A sort of dream of contrary. To dream of being embraced predicts that impulsive behavior, if not controlled, will subject you to unfair criticism. To dream of embracing others, or observing others embrace each other indicates basic family unity in spite of quarrels or differences of opinion.

Embroidery. To do it yourself is a forecast of personal happiness and contentment, but to observe it being worked by others or on garments, household items, or cloth is a warning that there is hidden opposition and deceit in your close circle.

Emerald. In the mysterious East this valuable jewel is interpreted as one of the greatest possible harbingers of good fortune; however in the West its meaning is somewhat qualified to one of assured success but only following trials and frustrations.

Emigrate. Pull in your belt and prepare to economize because you'll have some unexpected demands on your resources if your dream featured emigrants or emigration.

Employment. A dream of contrary. You'll have a choice of opportunities if you dreamed of being out of a job; if you dreamed of employing or offering jobs to others, it's a warning that overconfidence can be expensive, and a reminder that a bit of extra effort usually pays dividends.

Emptiness. To be aware of emptiness, or to find something empty when you ex-

pected it would be full, suggests that you are contemplating some venture or activity which would turn out to be an exercise in futility. Don't try anything unfamiliar for a time following this dream. An exception to the foregoing is if you found yourself pouring from a vessel which appeared to be empty, in which case the dream predicts unexpected gains.

Emu. This strange animal in a dream represents a well-meaning friend who is, nevertheless, giving you stupid advice. Don't be influenced.

Enamel. To dream of this glossy top paint, or of enameled pots or decorative ware indicates that you are cultivating a new relationship which will turn out to be a hindrance instead of the help you anticipate. Back off before you get let down.

Enchantment. See *Bewitched*.

Encore. A dream featuring an artist responding with an encore predicts satisfying rewards for work well done; however, if the artist refuses the request, you can expect some joy but not much reward.

Encourage. Whether the encouragement was given or received, it is a dream of contrary, signifying a period of unhappiness due to quarrels and/or disagreement arising from your own jealousy or that of people around you. Try to reflect before you react for the time being.

Encyclopedia. See *Book*.

End. The end of anything, featured in a dream, is another contrary symbol signifying new beginnings, unless it was a dead end or cul-de-sac, in which case the symbolism is straightforward and your dream is trying to awaken you to the possibility that you are following a road to nowhere. See also *World*.

Endive. A new and interesting experience with a foreigner or in a foreign place is predicted in a dream of eating endive.

Enema. To observe, give, or see the equipment for an enema signifies an unhappy or unfortunate short-lived affair which will prove to have a long-term benefit. A dream of being given, or taking an enema predicts a sudden unexpected drain on your resources,

but it will be temporary.

Enemy. A dream of contrary. You can rely on having loyal and helpful friends if you dreamed of someone you knew, or suspected, was an enemy. See also *Hostility*.

Energy. A feeling of unusual pep or abnormal energy in a dream is a warning that you are in danger of "walking in where angels fear to tread." Try to control your impulses. However, if your dream concerned an abnormal lack of energy, you are probably pushing yourself and a medical checkup is suggested.

Engagement. A dream of an engagement (made or broken) is a forecast of family and/or romantic troubles. Try to cultivate a philosophical attitude; it's not really what happens to you, but how you react to it that counts. See also *Ring* and *Appointment*.

Engine. A dream of contrary. The harder or faster the machinery in your dream was working, the more the setbacks you must expect along your chosen path; however, if the engine was stopped, it forecasts certain success in your endeavors, although you may have a few obstacles along the way. An engine which is broken down or damaged predicts delays in reaching your objective through interference from treacherous associates; but their efforts will be ineffective; you'll get there in the end.

Engineering. Whether civil, electrical, mechanical, chemical, or what have you, you'll have happy happenings aplenty if your dream involved engineering work or engineers at work.

England. A dream of England or English people is a forerunner of difficult situations involving lack of cooperation which will require great tact and patient effort to overcome. Unless, of course, you are English or live in England, in which case the national aspects of the dream have no significance and only the other details should be considered.

Engrave. You are in for a season of all-around improvement if your dream featured engraving or engraved articles.

Enigma. You may expect a period of confusion and disorganization to follow a dream of this type of riddle, but if you make a determined effort to roll with the ups and downs, you'll find, in retrospect, that the bumps were beneficial.

Enjoyment. A general feeling of enjoyment without an apparent reason is a forerunner of minor disappointments probably of a personal or social nature, but other aspects (if any) of the dream should be considered. See also *Party, Wedding, Entertainment,* etc.

Enlistment. This kind of a dream suggests a basic reluctance to settle down and/or to accept the discipline that is required to progress in the ordinary drama of life, so you will probably succumb to the siren song of the open road and become a rolling stone for a while. Might as well get it over with, as it's better sooner than later.

Enterprise. See *Business*.

Entertainment. Usually an omen of very good luck, unless the performance embarrassed you in any way, in which case it is a warning that you could lose a useful contact through careless gossip.

Entrails. A definite warning to slow down. Try to avoid any situations which cause you undue anxiety for the time being and get a medical checkup as soon as you can.

Entrance. An imposing or ornate entrance to a building signifies an underlying desire for greater security. Take steps to achieve it by increasing your skills and/ or your knowledge.

Envelope. An obstacle dream. Closed envelopes represent frustrations which can be overcome if you help yourself by cultivating a harmonious mental attitude. Open envelopes signify trivial troubles which you can overcome by an application of patient good humor.

Envy. The meaning of this dream alters according to the circumstances. A dream of envying someone's material possessions predicts an increase in your own, but to dream of envying another's good looks or personal beauty presages marital or romantic discord. On the other hand a dream of being envied signifies that you will soon be in an enviable position.

Epaulets. For a woman, they predict a new and exciting love affair; for a man, they signify professional advancement or business improvement, whichever applies.

Epicure. A warning to restrain your selfish overindulgence. Taking is easy, now try giving.

Epidemic. This dream signifies some mental disturbance probably arising from an organic malfunction; see your doctor.

Epilepsy. See *Convulsion*.

Epitaph. If you could read the epitaph(s), the dream means that you can solve whatever problems are facing you much more easily than you think; if the epitaph(s) were not legible, you can expect news of a happy family event.

Equator. If you crossed this imaginary division of poles in your dream, you will soon make a complete change of all the circumstances now around you; if you were aware of but did not cross the equator in your dream, it signifies indecision concerning a new venture or offer. Don't be

139

faint-hearted; a step into the unknown can frequently be a voyage of splendid discovery.

Equestrian. See *Horse.*

Erase. Whether on paper or blackboard, the use of an eraser forecasts a possible (and possibly severe) social embarrassment, so don't repeat any idle rumors because you might be faced with the irate subject of gossip when and where you least expect it.

Ermine. Oddly enough, this noble and elegant fur in a dream signifies a reduction of status and/or income, unless you gave it away, in which case the reverse is indicated and you can expect a sudden rise in status.

Errand. A straightforward obstacle dream. If you completed the errand, you can expect a satisfactory conclusion to your problems; if not, you'll have to continue the struggle. However, you should remember that bashing your head against a stone wall seldom produces anything more useful than a headache; try to find a way around it.

Error. See *Mistake.*

Eruption. The eruption of a volcano or other natural phenomena such as a geyser forecasts a sudden change for the better. See also *Skin,* etc.

Escalator. This dream symbol follows the general rule that up is an omen of success and down is not; however, in this particular instance the downward motion indicates a defeat which could be reversible by the application of intelligent determination.

Escape. A straightforward obstacle dream. The interpretation depends on the details, but as a general guide:

From prison or similar type of confinement means a rapid rise in the world.

From fire or water indicates success but preceded by a period of anxiety.

From an animal suggests you must seek to uncover a false friend in your sphere. See also under name of animal.

From an unidentifiable danger or threat predicts social and/or romantic success.

If, in your dream, you couldn't escape, you must be prepared to fight your way through a discouraging phase; and if you tried but were caught in the act, the dream is telling you that you could end up being your own worst enemy through careless talk and/or indiscreet behavior.

Escort. See Accompany.

Eskimo. Eskimos forecast financial difficulties which can be overcome by ordinary methods of retrenchment, but if you dreamed of these natives of the frozen north, you can forget about help from friends or relatives and get a tight grip on your spending.

Estate. A dream of contrary. A large, impressive, elaborate estate in your dream suggests that you are approaching a danger point in your effort to "keep up with the Joneses"; unpleasant aftermath can be avoided if you adjust now to a more realistic budget. A small or modest estate in your dream predicts a slow but steady rise in life.

Etchings. This type of artwork featured in a dream predicts a widening of cultural pursuits and/or contacts.

Ether. To notice a smell of

ether in a dream forecasts an important change in life. See also *Unconscious* and *Sleep.*

Etiquette. Emphasis on precise behavior in your dream suggests a social rebuff, probably caused by either overaggression or lack of confidence due to an underlying inferiority complex. Try to be more relaxed in company. See also *Manners.*

Eulogy. To dream of the eulogy of another person signifies an embarrassment due to your own insincerity; to dream of your own eulogy predicts a valuable surprise gift. See also *Funeral,* etc.

Eunuch. See under *Castrate.*

Europe. See *Foreign.*

Evacuate. Whether your own or that of others, a forced move in your dream is a strong warning against gambling, risky ventures, or speculation of any kind at the present time.

Evaporate. To be aware, in your dream, of something evaporating signifies disappointment in an acquaintance. See also *Odor, Perfume, Steam,* etc.

Eve. See under *Adam* and *Eve*.

Evening. A fine evening is a forecast of increasing contentment through middle and old age.

Everglades. See *Jungle* or *Swamp*.

Evergreens. A very fortunate omen for both personal and· business affairs.

Eviction. See *Evacuate*.

Evidence. To give evidence in court signifies a request for help from a friend; to hear someone else giving evidence predicts that you will need help in protecting your reputation.

Evil. A dream involving an evil atmosphere or evil spirits predicts unaccountable obstacles to your current ambitions; you would do well to consider a change of direction and/or objectives.

Ewe. See *Lamb*.

Ewer. See *Jug*.

Examination. The classic daddy of obstacle dreams with a classic simplicity of meaning. If you failed the examination, the dream is telling you that your ambitions are beyond your ability and you would benefit from a change of goal. However, if you passed the exam easily or it presented no major problem to you, it predicts comfortable achievement of all your hopes.

Exchange. A dream of exchanging things is a forerunner of business difficulties. Exchanging money, however, signifies an unexpected trip.

Excrement. See *Bowel Movement* or *Feces*.

Execution. To see or be aware of an execution in your dream suggests that the success of some current undertaking is doubtful and if achieved will take more money, effort, and/or time (whichever applies) than you anticipated. To be condemned to execution signifies good news concerning a health problem. To dream of an execution forecasts some disturbing news of a friend or associate.

Executor. Any dream involving this legal functionary predicts upcoming events of a fortunate nature.

Exercise. An omen of good luck if you enjoyed it, but

if it tired you, it is a warning to guard your credit and/or avoid forcing any issues for a few weeks' time.

Exhaust. The sound of an engine or motor exhaust in your dream forecasts an upcoming period of power in your life.

Exhaustion. The same meaning as the tired aspect of exercise only more so.

Exhibition. An exhibition in your dream represents numerous, but small, obstacles in your path. You need only have patience and they will gradually disappear.

Exile. A dream of being banished from your own country is a warning to guard against hasty speech and/or impulsive actions which, if seriously misinterpreted, could make you the subject of damaging gossip.

Expedition. An "errand" dream in a different form but with the same basic meaning; however, the details should also be considered.

Expert. Whether the expert in your dream was yourself or someone else, the forecast is of a return of something you thought lost or an unexpected reward for a past favor you had forgotten.

Explore. See *Expedition,* unless the dream featured an explorer, in which case it signifies family quarrels.

Explosion. The blast of high explosives in a dream is a forerunner of lasting improvement in all aspects of your life.

Express. To observe one passing signifies a possible missed opportunity—better pay closer attention to business; but if you were riding one, the dream is telling you to be more discreet in the company of those whose good opinion you value.

Extinguish. The interpretation here depends on the details of what was extinguished and how; but generally this action pertains to affairs with the opposite sex and indicates boredom. See *Flame, Fire, Water, Blanket,* etc.

Extravagance. Oddly enough, this is not a dream of contrary but predicts domestic happiness and an abundance of all the good things in life.

Eyebrows. Heavy eyebrows signify distinction as well as success; exaggeratedly arched eyebrows predict a surprise; thin eyebrows forecast disappointment in business or love, whichever concerns you most. A dream in which you were worried about your eyebrows or they fell out is telling you that you are probably being deceived in love, but if you were pleased with their condition and appearance, you may expect some small but important gain shortly.

Eyeglasses. The interpretation here varies greatly depending on the circumstances. In your dream, to notice glasses on someone who normally doesn't wear them signifies a need on your part to take firm action in ending a relationship you no longer want. To find spectacles or try them on predicts unexpected profit through a friend or a successful gamble. Dark (or sun) glasses in a dream indicate a need for a change from routine; try a new hobby.

Eyelashes. Long, beautiful eyelashes predict happy love affairs and/or enjoyable social events, unless they are false ones, in which case the dream signifies discovery of a secret which would be best shared with some competent adviser. To be without lashes or see someone else minus lashes indicates some treachery around you; be cautious about confidences.

Eyelids. Eyelids featured in a dream are thought to symbolize troubles, other than your own, which will soon be revealed to you. Give tangible assistance, if possible; otherwise lend a sympathetic ear.

Eyes. Strange or disembodied eyes in a dream are considered a prediction of a very beneficial change of events soon to come. To injure your eyes, get something in them, or be otherwise worried about them is a warning that someone is trying to trick you in a business affair. If the main feature of your dream was the beauty of the eyes, the dream is telling you that you can count on the sincere love of those who matter to you. Crossed eyes are a lucky omen for money matters, but a squint, cast, or other defect is a warning against an illicit love affair. Animal eyes are a sign of hidden rivalry or jealousy in your close circle. Exceptionally large and/or wide-open eyes in a dream signify an inheritance. Blue or light eyes mean a new friendship; dark eyes, a new love affair.

R

Fable. Whether the dream involved reading, hearing, or telling fables, it pertains to impulsive actions. Don't be overconfident.

Face. This is a straightforward dream in which its interpretation is in line with its aspect. If the face was smiling, it signifies pleasant new friends, experiences, and/or financial gains. Unpleasant or grotesque (unless amusingly so) faces portend loss. To dream you are washing your face denotes a necessity to atone for some past indiscretion; better make amends! To see the faces of strangers signifies an approaching change of residence. If the main feature of your dream was a facial blemish, you will have a variety of new opportunities to risk your reputation; if you can't re-

sist at least be very selective.

Factory. If you dreamed of a busy factory, you will succeed after a hard struggle. If you were working in the factory, you can expect some important and beneficial change in your life.

Failure. A dream of contrary. Stick to it, you'll succeed.

Fairy. Whether the form in your dream was of pixies, gnomes, or just plain garden-variety fairies, these charming creatures, promise the materialization of your dearest wish when you least expect it. See also *Elf*.

Fake. Something that is not what it seems is a warning against gambling of any kind. Whether it concerns business or love affairs, hesitate, think it over, and then don't do it.

Fall. A very common dream action generally symbolic of some basic fear in the dreamer's life, such as fear of a moral lapse, job failure, sexual inadequacy, loss of status, etc.; however, the prophetic meaning of this dream is, strangely, very similar in that it indicates setbacks but modified by the details of its action. If, in your dream, you fell a long distance, you can expect the reverses to be general and fairly severe; however, if you landed without hurting yourself, they will be upsetting but quite temporary. If you hurt yourself, you should be prepared to endure some real hardships for a time. To fall from a medium height signifies a loss of prestige; to fall to the floor (as from a standing or sitting position) is a warning of danger from false friends. If your dream involved others falling, it indicates triumph over enemies; and if you fell but got up again, you will overcome the obstacles in your path. To fall into water means financial stress, but the water factor and condition must also be considered.

Falsehood. A dream of contrary. No matter whether you tell the lie or someone tells it to you, it indicates true friends and general good luck.

Fame. To dream of achieving fame yourself is a sort of dream of contrary and suggests you are trying to grasp something which is beyond your reach; high aims are commendable but it's healthier to keep them within reasonable bounds. However if your dream involved a famous person, keep trying, because you'll get help from some unexpected source.

Family. A dream of a large and/or happy family, whether human or animal, predicts a general upswing in all your interests.

Fan. This dream pertains to love affairs. To fan yourself predicts an embarrassing entanglement; to see others fanning is a warning that you're playing too wide a field; to lose a fan is a sure sign that you're in danger of losing true love through fickle behavior; cool it! See also *Electricity*.

Fang. Animal fangs in a dream are a warning of serious family troubles brewing, likely, but not necessarily, with inlaws. It would be wise to avoid any controversy (or better still, contact) with such relatives for as long as possible following this dream.

Fantasy. A fairy-tale type of fantasy atmosphere in your dream is a forecast of favorable tides for your current undertakings.

Farewell. The omen depends on the circumstances. If you said good-bye to someone known to you, it signifies a coming break in a close relationship; if you said it to a stranger, it predicts a new friend; if someone said it to you, the forecast is of a change of residence or position.

Farm. A prosperous-looking, well-kept farm in your dream predicts a life of abundance, simple pleasures, and good health; a derelict, neglected, or poor-appearing farm signifies a small loss of money, expected gain, or property.

Fashion. To dream of looking at fashions in shop windows, magazines, or on models signifies all work and no play, unless you make some active effort to mix socially.

Fasting. A dream of fasting suggests that you need to make amends for some past injustice; get on with it; the sooner it's done the quicker you'll be able to forget it.

Fat. Although some of the ancient prophets believed this dream to be a forerunner to an illness, the more modern ones agree that it predicts a happy life of few worries and many pleasures and that the fatter you (or others) were in your dream the better is the omen. Eating fat signifies success in love affairs; cooking fat indicates business profits.

Fate. A dream of contrary. If the feature of your dream was that fate played you a dirty trick, you can rest assured that a lucky break will follow; but if the feeling in your dream was that fate dealt you a winning hand, you will have to plod on. A dream concerning the Fates or Norns of mythology signifies a new chance at something you thought lost.

Father. See *Parents*.

Father-in-Law. See *Parents*.

147

Fatigue. Sufficient money for necessary and modest social enjoyment are forecast in a dream of being pleasantly fatigued. See also *Tire*.

Faucet. A dripping faucet is a strong warning to resist the efforts of someone who is trying to persuade you to divulge a secret. No matter how strong the temptation, don't do it, as the breach of confidence would have much broader consequences than you can imagine and would be to your everlasting regret. A dream featuring a shiny new faucet predicts an unexpected satisfaction.

Favor. A straightforward status symbol. To ask or receive a favor signifies a slight loss of status, whereas to do a favor predicts an increase in prestige.

Fawn. See *Deer*.

Fear. The meaning of this dream can vary greatly according to the details, action, and circumstances of the dreamer; therefore all those factors should be carefully considered and correlated. As a general guide if you conquered the cause of your dreamed fear and/or the sensation disappeared during the dream, the forecast is that you will overcome your difficulties; however, if the feeling persisted and/or the cause was indefinable, you should expect to have to cope with problems arising from the deceit or dishonesty of someone you trusted. To dream of calming the fears of others indicates the clearing up of a misunderstanding and/or removal of a threat to your peace of mind.

Feast. A feast, of the harvest or thanksgiving type (as differentiated from a formal banquet) has, oddly, a meaning which varies according to the age of the dreamer; for the young to early middle-aged it is a happy omen of abundance, but for the elderly or old it is a dream of contrary and signifies some unexpected financial difficulty.

Feathers. If your dream featured many small feathers, or a cloud of them, as from a pillow fight, it signifies an exceptional stroke of luck which will enhance your prestige as well as your income. Ornamental feathers, or articles made of them, such as ostrich feather fans, boas, or feathered hats, indicate an increase in social popularity for a woman or personal power for a man. To dream of gathering or sweeping feathers up or picking them off clothes or furniture predicts a life of many small joys. Other than the foregoing, a dream of feathers can have as many meanings as there are varieties of feathers, or it must be interpreted by correlating its action and other factors to the color of the feather(s).

Feces. All sources pretty well agree that excrement (whether human or animal) in a dream represents money, wealth, profits, or tangible value and is a lucky omen pertaining to material gain. See also *Bowel Movement*.

Feeding. To dream of feeding children or animals is an omen of prosperity, but if your dream featured others doing the feeding, it is a reminder of the old adage, "trust everyone, but cut the cards!"

Feet. The interpretation depends on the circumstances of the dream but as a general guide:

Itching feet predict travel.
To bathe the feet indicates release from anxiety.

Strange feet signify new acquaintances.
Aching feet mean family troubles.
Stocking feet forecast an annoying mystery.
Bare feet suggest new experiences with the opposite sex.
Dirty feet are a warning to guard your credit.
Burning feet signify jealousy.
Cold feet augur a disappointment in love
A broken foot suggests reverses through carelessness.
Loss of feet indicates unexpected obstacles.
Having your feet stepped on is a warning against indiscreet actions and/or talk.
Children's feet represent small disappointments.
Many feet walking on a sidewalk predict a financial loss or loss of an expected gain.
Very large feet promise good health.
Very small feet signify needless worry.
Pain from bunions or sore feet forecasts comfort in old age.
Treatment by a chiropodist predicts a change for the better.

Fence. An obstacle dream signifying difficulties ahead; the interpretation depends on the results of the dream action.

Fencing. See *Duel*.

Fender. A dented or smashed car fender suggests you are doing something you suspect might damage your social image; better give it up. A fireplace fixture in your dream predicts a happy family event.

Ferns. To see fresh, healthy ferns growing in natural surroundings is an augury of a benign atmosphere surrounding you and your undertakings. However, if the plants are dead or wilting, it is an omen of trouble. Ferns in pots forecast a misunderstanding, which you should make an effort to clear up before it grows into a permanent rift. To buy, pick, sit, or lie on ferns predicts a new and thrilling experience.

Ferret. A dream featuring this shrewd little animal is a warning not to repeat gossip, even to your immediate family.

Ferry. Suitable rewards for your efforts are predicted in a dream of being ferried across water, or of watching a ferry ply to and fro.

Fertilizer. An auspicious

dream signifying new sources of income.

Festival. See *Feast* and *Music*.

Feud. A dream of contrary. You can look forward to a long period of good fellowship and happy times.

Fever. If the feature of the dream was your own fever, the dream is telling you that the things you worry about most may never happen and that your futile anxiety is compromising your ability to enjoy today. A dream involving high temperatures in others suggests some coming excitement which could be either of a happy or troublesome nature depending on the side action of the dream. If your dream concerned fever in children, it is an augury of success in your current desires.

Fiasco. See *Failure*.

Field. This dream can have many meanings, and its details must be carefully correlated, but as a general guide:

Green and/or pleasant fields signify great prosperity and happy circumstances in both personal and business affairs.

Withered or dry fields suggest coming reverses.

A newly plowed field indicates that you can attain your goal, but it will entail very hard work and possibly some sacrifice.

See also *Clover, Barley, Hay,* and *Wheat.*

Fiend. This type of character in your dream emanates (if not from something you ate) from a prickly conscience. If it is a past misdeed or an injustice that is worrying you, try to find a way to put it right. If it's some guilty knowledge, perhaps it's time to share it with a competent adviser.

Fife. To hear or play a fife indicates a disappointment in a friend or in a love affair; however, if it is accompanied by the sound of drums, it signifies news from a distance, probably (though not necessarily) from or of someone in the Armed Forces. See also *Music* and *Musical Instruments.*

Fig. Fresh figs predict a deeply embarrassing situation with someone of the opposite sex; dry figs signify a financial difficulty.

Fight. The basic meaning in a dream of fighting is change. For a business person, it signifies a change of enterprise; for an employed person, a change of job, etc. The degree of success or failure you may expect from the change was forecast in the outcome of your dreamed fight. If your dream concerned others fighting, it is a warning against waste of time and money in idle pleasure.

Figures. To dream of a multitude of unrelated figures is a forerunner to the discovery of some previously hidden rivalry or opposition; however, you will be better able to combat it in the open. A dream of a woman's or man's figure indicates a period of pleasant diversions. See also *Numbers, Accounts,* etc.

Filberts. These nuts in a dream predict a troublesome trip, or perhaps it should be designated as trouble-shooting travel; in any case, the trouble concerning which you will travel will be someone else's.

File. To dream of using a rasp-type file on wood is a warning against actions which, if misunderstood, could cause unpleasant gossip. A dream which involved filing metal signifies a reconciliation. See also *Fingernails*.

Filing. New opportunities are predicted in a dream of filing papers in a filing cabinet, but to look for papers you cannot find indicates an awkward business misunderstanding. A closed filing cabinet signifies a legal entanglement which could be with the tax man, so be sure to keep your records straight.

Filling Station. See *Gas Station*.

Films. A dream of handling film, whether movie or still, signifies a gratifying gift or unexpected bonus; if you were making prints from film, you can expect to see new faces in new places fairly soon.

Fin. See *Fish*.

Fingernails. Long fingernails signify difficulties with the opposite sex; short ones predict an unexpected gift; to polish (or varnish) your nails is a warning against impulsive behavior which could lead to a scandal; to (painfully) bend back or damage a nail indicates a rather long season of dis-

content; to cut your fingernails signifies achievement in prestige; to file your nails signifies achievement through your own efforts; if you dreamed of biting your nails or of nails bitten to the quick, a medical checkup would be advisable.

Fingerprints. A dream of fingerprints on furniture or woodwork predicts minor financial stress; to dream of being fingerprinted for any official purpose signifies help from a friend.

Fingers. The interpretation of this dream varies greatly according to its details but as a general guide:

To point a finger or see one pointing predicts a complete change of environment.

A bandaged finger suggests you will escape lightly from a situation which could have been disastrous.

A hurt finger indicates difficulties of your own making.

A cut finger means some unusually hard work ahead.

A lost (or missing) finger predicts legal troubles concerning money matters.

An unusually long finger predicts a romantic upset.

A very short or stubby finger signifies new friends.

A hand with extra fingers is a sure forecast of an inheritance.

If, in your dream, you were specifically aware that the finger involved was a left-hand one, you are being warned that any illicit affair (whether business or love) could have a very unpleasant backlash.

Finland. See *Foreign.*

Fiord. To dream of a narrow bay between mountains is a promise of a contented life in a happy home.

Fir. If your dream involved cutting down a fir tree, it is warning you that your undisciplined spending habits could seriously inhibit your chances of getting ahead; but to dream of a forest of fir trees is an omen of extraordinary good luck, especially if you were aware of their aroma.

Fire. The portent of this dream varies greatly according to its details and action, so all aspects should be carefully correlated, but as a general guide:

A fire is an omen of impending trouble if it burned you; good news if it didn't.

To observe a house or building that is on fire forecasts an urgent appeal for help from a close friend or relative.

You can expect an exciting romantic adventure if you built a fire or stirred one with a poker.

To dream of putting out a fire or escaping from one predicts ultimate success over all obstacles.

A small cheerful fire in a fireplace indicates contentment.

A dream of setting fire to a house, building, or anything of value is telling you to control your temper or be prepared for serious consequences.

A roaring big fire (contained in a grate) signifies new hope after a time of discouragement.

Firearms. See *Guns.*

Firecracker. Whether you saw them, heard them, or lighted them, firecrackers in your dream are a forecast of irritations and disappointments; however, the former will be petty and the latter minor.

Fire Engine. Any type of fire-fighting apparatus on its way to a fire portends an important stroke of money luck, especially if you saw it leaving its station;

however, if it was returning from a fire, you may be somewhat disappointed concerning the size of an awaited payment, bonus or dividend. To dream of driving a fire engine predicts a lucky escape from an embarrassing predicament.

A dream of using protective fireproof clothing is a forerunner of family quarrels.

Fire Escape. To dream of being on, or using, a fire escape is a warning to guard against stretching your credit too far.

Firefly. These amusing insects in a dream are a warning that uninhibited behavior will be discovered, so if you are contemplating anything you wouldn't want known, better reconsider; better yet, don't do it!

Fireplace. Peace and contentment are forecast in a dream of a fireplace in which an appropriate-sized fire was burning, but you can expect an upset in love affairs if the hearth was cold.

Firewood. Sawing or splitting firewood predicts a happy change of residence or important home improvement; to gather, carry, or transport firewood signifies gratifying success in community affairs.

Fireworks. A sort of dream of contrary, as it forecasts obstacles to the accomplishment of some cherished plan, and the more spectacular the display was in your dream, the longer will be your season of frustration.

First Aid. An increase in personal prestige is predicted in a dream of administering emergency medical aid.

Fish. To see fish swimming freely in clear water is an omen of wealth and personal power. If you were fishing in clear water and could see the fish bite, it indicates that you will discover or acquire some knowledge which can be used very advantageously. Dead fish either in their natural habitat or in a market are an omen of disappointment or discouragement. To dream of catching a fish is an augury of success, and the bigger the fish the bigger the success; and if you saw a fish moving its fins, you can expect to be freed of any worrying responsibilities. If your dream featured carp, it is a warning against subjecting yourself to criticism by ill-considered actions. Eating or cooking fish (except carp) is considered a general good omen for your current undertakings. If your dream involved a fishnet, it means reverses if the net was empty, success if it was full, and disappointment if it was torn, unless it was torn but still had fish in it, in which case it signifies success of a limited nature. Tropical or goldfish in tanks, bowls, or pools indicate ephemeral pleasures. Baiting a fishhook in a dream is a prediction of a passionate new love affair—and if you're not eligible, it will be someone close enough to share the excitement with you; but to get a fishhook stuck in any part of the body is a warning against deceitful acquaintances. To dream of seeing a variety of food fish (live) of rather uncommon species, such as salmon, trout, etc., indicates an increase in social activity and prestige. A dream of trying to hold a fish which wriggles out of your grasp has the obvious meaning, and you must be prepared to lower your sights or find a new liaison. Oddly enough, really rotten fish are an exception to the dead fish rule and are a sign of a sudden large increase in income.

Fist. A dream of contrary. Gratifying events in both personal and business affairs will follow a dream of clenching or shaking a fist.

Fit. To dream of seeing a dog, cat, or other animal having a fit is an indication that you may encounter frustrations in your career (or avocation) due to hidden opposition. It would be wise to consider a change of position or approach. If your dream involved a person having a fit, see *Convulsion*.

Fizz. See *Drink*.

Flags. A dream featuring the flag of your own country waving in the breeze is a forecast of pleasant social engagements. To dream of raising or carrying a flag predicts an important increase in material wealth; to lower a flag at an appropriate time (such as at sunset) is a forerunner of money luck, but to lower it at any other time suggests a small loss or a disappointment in a friend. A gala display of brightly colored flags signifies satisfying achievement and/or admiration from the opposite sex. See also *Colors*.

Flakes. Whether your dream concerned paint flakes, snowflakes, cereal flakes, or any other kind of flakes, it is a warning that you will have to use more than ordinary diplomacy to escape an embarrassing entanglement.

Flame. A flickering or diminishing flame signifies a disappointment which will probably be in the nature of a limited success; a definitely red flame warns against uncontrolled temper; a very steady, strong, vertical flame predicts unqualified success; and a very bright flame promises great happiness. See also *Fire*.

Flamingo. This exotic bird promises new experiences in strange, exciting places if it was flying, but if it was on the ground, it indicates unexpected worries.

Flash. Whatever the source, a sudden flash of light in your dream is a forerunner of a momentous change in your life due to the success of an invention or creative idea.

Flashlight. A dream featuring the use of a flashlight out of doors is a forecast of help from a new influential friend; a flashlight used inside is a warning against impulsive behavior in the face of strong temptation.

Flask. The flask itself has no significance, unless you broke or damaged it, in which case it forecasts a minor loss of money or a personal item of no great value. See also *Drink, Wine, Brandy,* etc.

Flattery. Whether you gave or received it in your dream, it is a caution against insincere companions.

Flatulence. A dream of being flatulent in the presence of other people is a warning against allowing your energy to be directed into the wrong channel; however, if the flatulence was suffered by someone else, an unexpected trip is forecast.

Flavor. To taste an unidentifiable flavor is a good omen if you liked it; if not, it signifies petty arguments.

Flaws. To dream of noticing a flaw in something supposed to be perfect is a warning that you could be suffering the consequences of someone else's mistake or misdeed; if someone else pointed out the flaw, the dream is a warning to steer clear of controversial subjects or serious clashes could develop with friends and/or associates.

Flax. Whether growing, harvested, or being worked, flax in a dream is a symbol of sexual satisfaction.

Fleas. To be annoyed in your dream by these revolting pests is a straightforward omen of deceit and malice around you; but if you managed to kill them or get rid of them, you will triumph over your enemies.

Fleece. This type of woolly material in a dream signifies a season of discontent.

Fleet. The meaning here varies according to the action and the kind of ships. A fishing fleet in harbor or coming in signifies peace of mind, but putting out to sea it indicates worries. A naval fleet riding at anchor augurs a release from a burdensome responsibility, but moving along in formation it predicts extended travel. Sailing ships or sailboats, especially in clear weather, are an omen of renewed hope.

Flesh. A dream of human flesh in the carnal sense is a warning that you had better unsnarl your love life before it causes you real distress.

Flies. Petty annoyances and minor irritations arising from the jealousy and envy of those around you; if you killed the flies or got rid of them, you will soon sort out the troublemakers in your circle.

Flirt. An omen of social success if kept within the bounds of good taste, but if done with malicious intent, it signifies trouble brewing in domestic affairs.

Floating. A marvelous symbol of success, prosperity, and all that you desire if you had no trouble staying afloat, and even if there was some difficulty, it only delays the success slightly by reason of obstacles which you can easily overcome. To use a rubber or plastic float is a sign of reconciliation.

Flood. A variation of the obstacle dream, and for an accurate interpretation all its details should be correlated, but as a general guide:

If the flood was gentle and the water clear, your

troubles will be short-lived.

If the water was muddy and/or the flood a raging destructive force, you can expect to have to hoe a long hard row.

If you were swept away in the flood, it is a warning that someone of the opposite sex whom you trust is actually trying to use you.

If you escaped from the flood, you will be helped to overcome your obstacles.

Floor. Whether you were painting, polishing, sweeping, scrubbing, or what have you, any dream which featured cleaning or improving the appearance of a floor, or laying a new floor, foretells profitable business activities. Personal good luck will be yours if you dreamed of sitting, lying, or lounging on the floor.

Flophouse. You will soon be faced with a decision regarding a change of residence if you dreamed of one of these downbeat hostels.

Florist. The meaning of this dream depends on your domestic status; if you are married or involved, it presages a serious rift; if you are uncommitted, it predicts a serious new romance.

Floss. This type of embroidery thread seen or handled in a dream is a warning against harmful gossip from insincere acquaintances.

Flounder. See *Fish*.

Flour. Buying flour in a dream signifies news of an illness, but using flour for cooking or baking is an omen of domestic contentment modified by the following specifics:

Barley flour pertains to happy family events.
Potato flour suggests difficulties with young people or children.
Rice flour indicates an increase in the family.
Wheat flour predicts prosperity and abundance.
Corn flour indicates successful speculation.

Flow. See *Water, River, Flood,* etc.

Flowers. Fresh, brightly colored flowers featured in your dream, whether growing out of doors or arranged indoors, are an auspicious omen of great personal happiness. If the flowers were dead or wilted or if you threw them away, the dream is warning you that overconfidence and/or carelessness also goes before a fall. Artificial flowers predict a situation where you will be under pressure to act against your principles; don't allow yourself to be influenced. Wild flowers signify a happy, exciting adventure. See also *Colors, Roses, Daffodils,* etc.

Fluke. A dream of a serendipitous achievement is a forecast of an unexpected increase in income or a small inheritance.

Flute. To hear the sound of this high-pitched woodwind being played by someone else signifies a happy domestic event, but to play it yourself predicts embarrassment in your personal relationships. See also *Music.*

Flying. This is one dream symbol on which practically every source from Artemidorus on down agrees. It represents the dreamer's basic ambition, but the interpretation of flying (like a bird) is modified by the details of the flight and its conditions, so the surroundings, weather, etc., must be correlated with the action, but as a general guide:

If you successfully maintained your flight at a low to medium height, you can expect to achieve your goal without much difficulty.

If you were trying (or straining) to reach a high altitude, the dream is telling you that your grasp is greater than your reach and you would be wise to alter your course.

See also *Water, Mountain, Airplane, Balloon, Clouds, Sky,* etc.

Foal. See *Horse.*

Foam. Whatever its source, foam featured in your dream is a forecast of gay social activities.

Fog. An obstacle dream the meaning of which alters according to its location. A fog at sea predicts seriously doubtful issues in love or domestic affairs. A fog on land indicates a sudden business or financial dilemma which will require great patience and ingenuity to handle. In either case a successful outcome is forecast if the fog dispersed during the dream, and if it dispersed into sunshine, you may expect an ultimate benefit. The sound of a foghorn in your dream is an omen of contrary and signifies a swift release from worry.

Foliage. This dream pertains to affairs of the heart and/or sex relations. If the foliage was fresh and pleasantly healthy, it is an augury of improving (or continuing) pleasant experience; however, if the foliage was wormy, faded, or wilted, it presages quarrels, dissatisfaction, and possible separation.

Food. As a general guide, seeing or preparing food is an auspicious omen, providing the food was fresh and sufficient for the occasion; but if it was spoiled in any way or you were short of it, you can expect some reverses which will require careful planning to overcome. Selling food is a dream of contrary and signifies a stroke of money luck; buying food predicts a happy family celebration. but tasting food indicates a minor loss of money or personal property. See also under separate items of food.

Fool. A sort of dream of contrary. If the feature of your dream was the feeling of playing the fool, you can expect to have some gay experiences with new and amusing acquaintances.

Football. If you dreamed of playing football, a money windfall of some kind should soon come your way. Could be a lucky gamble, an unexpected bonus, extra dividends, or even a legacy, but whatever it is it will be an interesting size. A dream of watching a football game is a warning to be more selective in making new friends.

Footlights. See *Light*.

Footprints. A woman's footprints forecast success in a new venture; a man's suggest extra caution in considering a change; children's are a sign of disappearing worries. To see your own footprints indicates success in your current undertakings; a conglomeration of mixed footprints signifies help from an unexpected source.

Footsteps. If you heard footsteps in your dream, you can expect to learn something to your great advantage.

Forehead. A dream of your own forehead is a prediction that some expected help will not materialize, and you will have to (and be able to) solve your problems through your own efforts. If your dream involved smoothing someone's forehead, it signifies a happy love affair. A wrinkled forehead featured in a dream is an omen of contrary; you will soon have nothing to worry you.

Foreign. To dream of a foreign place or country indicates that the realization of your heart's desire is closer than you imagine; persevere and have patience. A foreigner in your dream, whatever the nationality, is an auspicious omen if he or she was friendly.

Forest. The interpretation of a forest dream depends on the action, the circumstances of the dreamer, and other features of the dream, all of which should be correlated, but as a general guide:

If you were alone and/or frightened, you can expect to be let down by someone on whom you rely.

If you were lost in the forest, the dream signifies gain if you are in modest circumstances but loss if you are well off.

If the main feature of the dream was the green of the trees, the dream promises a release from worry; if it was the height of the trees, the prediction is of success but only after a time of trial.

A forest fire forecasts happy news.

Hiding in a forest suggests that some difficulty you are now undergoing will have an eventual benefit.

See also *Fir, Foliage,* etc.

Forge. A dream of a blacksmith working at a forge is a prediction of steady progress in your ambitions; a cold forge signifies disappointment. If you were working at the forge yourself, it indicates some money troubles which you can overcome by a little extra effort; however, if the main feature of your dream was the glow of the fire and/or the sparks rising from the forge, it is a warning of domestic and/or lovers' quarrels on the horizon, so try to control your temper.

Forgery. A warning against making friends too easily is contained in a dream of having had your name forged on a check or document; if your dream featured committing a forgery, expect money from an unusual source.

Forget-Me-Not. These charming little blooms are an assurance that you are surrounded by love and loyalty. See also *Flowers*.

Forgive. Whether you forgave or were forgiven, this dream promises an extended period of comfort and peace of mind.

Fork. To dream of a fork in a road is a straightforward sign that you will soon be faced with a decision which will be important to your future. A dream of an eating fork signifies a release from present worries; a cooking fork is a forecast of gay social times; a garden fork indicates that it is a significant time for clearing out the time-consuming clingers in your circle; to stab or see something or someone stabbed with a fork predicts a possible loss of status, so guard your tongue.

Form. Unidentifiable or vague forms in a dream are telling you that if you concentrate, you can solve a mystery which has been troubling you. See also *Figures*.

Formula. A dream of anything prepared from a formula is a happy omen in regard to your love and/ or sex life.

Fornication. See *Intercourse, Adultery,* or *Rape*.

Forsythia. Peace of mind is the message in a dream featuring this lovely bush in bloom; to see its yellow blossoms in an indoor arrangement predicts a happy new love affair.

Fortitude. If your dream featured strength of character (as opposed to physical bravery), it is a sign that yours will soon be put to the test. See also *Bravery*.

Fortune. A dream of contrary in that, although it signifies ultimate success, the greater the dreamed inheritance or gain the more limited will be the reality.

Fortune-telling. To have your fortune told in a dream is considered a good omen for personal affairs but a poor one for business matters. However, if you were doing the fortune-telling, you can expect all your plans to flourish.

Fountain. A happy fulfilled life is predicted by a well-functioning fountain, but if it was dry or just trickling, you must be prepared for a period of transition.

Fowl. A variety (or mixed flock) of fowl seen in a dream signifies an impressive rise in status, especially auspicious if there were some wild species among them. See also *Hen, Pheasant, Ducks,* etc.

Fox. No matter what the action, a fox in a dream is a strong warning of danger around you from wily rivals or hidden enmity, unless you killed the animal or it was dead, in which case you will outwit the plotters.

Fractions. To dream of figuring in fractions is a prediction of petty annoyances. Try to be philosophical; they will pass.

Frame. A dream featuring a frame or the framing of anything forecasts the happy accomplishment of a project or undertaking.

France. See *Foreign.*

Fraud. A modified dream of contrary. If you were the victim in your dream, it is a straightforward warning to guard against a loss due to treachery around you; however, if you perpetrated the fraud, prosperity is just around the corner.

Freckles. To dream of having freckles or noticing them on others is a sure sign of popularity with the opposite sex—whatever your age may be.

Freedom. If you experienced a sensation of freedom in your dream, you can count on being content with the partner of your choice.

Freemason. Anything to do with Freemasonry in a dream forecasts an expanding social life.

Freeze. See *Cold* or *Frost.*

Freight. Whether your dream featured freight standing in a yard, being handled, being transported by train or truck, or even if you only observed a freight train passing, you may expect an improvement in your working or business conditions.

Friends. Any demonstration of true friendship in a dream is a straightforward prediction of happy social times with good companions. Dreaming of distant friends is generally a forerunner of unexpected news, good or sad depending on whether or not they were in trouble in your dream.

Fright. The augury of this emotion depends on the action. If you had a sudden fright, it indicates an unexpected success in some current activity; if your feeling of fright was general and/or steady, it indicates that whatever your current fears are they will not materialize; however, if you dreamed of deliberately frightening another person, you can expect reverses due to your lack of judgment.

Frogs. A good dream whether you saw them, heard them, or ate them; they signify personal contentment, success within your sphere of activity, and sincere friends.

Frost. The meaning varies according to the details. If you saw frost patterns on a window or building, you can expect to have an interesting and unusual experience; but if you dreamed of being frostbitten or of seeing the effects of frostbite on plants or vegetation, it is a warning that you will have to be extra cautious in the near future if you want to avoid great difficulties in either your personal or business life.

Frosting. A dream which especially features the frosting and not the cake is a reminder that you can lose out on some of the basic satisfactions if you concentrate on grasping at the transitory pleasures.

Froth. See *Foam.*

Frown. This dream pertains only to matters of friendship, and if, in your dream, a friend was frowning, you may expect to hear a surprising confidence from that friend; if you observed a frown on the face of a stranger, you will soon make a new friend. See also *Face* and *Forehead.*

Frozen Food. Eating or preparing frozen food in a dream is a forecast of pleasant celebration and/or an exciting trip.

Fruit. As a general rule cultivated fruit in a dream is a favorable omen if it is ripe but an unfavorable one if unripe, bitter, or spoiled. Wild fruit signifies a life of reasonable comfort but no luxury. A variety of fruit, such as a bowl or decorative arrangement of mixed fruits, predicts material wealth of unanticipated proportions. See also under individual listings.

Fry. A dream of frying anything indicates unhappiness in love, unless you burned it, in which case you will soon be consoled.

Fuchsia. This charming flower is a warning that nervous tension gives rise to temper and temper to mistakes. Try to relax more.

Fudge. A dream of making or eating fudge is a warning against extravagance. Try to conserve your funds. Buying or being given a gift of fudge in your dream predicts some ups and downs in your love affairs.

Fugitive. This dream signals upcoming troubles; if you dreamed of being a fugitive, you are probably in for a rather violent family row, but on the positive side, if you keep your temper within bounds. the argument may serve to clear the air. However, if your dream involved seeing or helping a fugitive, you could be in for a bit of a shock concerning finances.

Fun. Good-natured clean fun is a forecast of general good times ahead, but boisterous hilarity or fun at someone else's expense

is a forerunner of business difficulties.

Funeral. A dream of contrary. To see or attend a funeral in your dream signifies cause for a happy celebration, probably news of an engagement or wedding; to dream of attending your own funeral indicates a relief from worry.

Fungus. Observing fungus on anything is a warning that you have hostile competition which you can overcome if you just refuse to be intimidated.

Funnel. If your dream featured the use of a funnel, it signifies a period of confusion during which you will have to sort out your future aims. The funnel of a ship indicates satisfaction and recognition for a job well done.

Fur. The meaning of this dream is modified to some degree by the type of fur, but as a general guide:

To wear or possess luxurious furs in good condition signifies a change for the better.

If the furs appeared to be worn or shabby, the change will affect status but not income.

See also under individual animal.

Furnace. A cold furnace presages fortunate financial transactions; a furnace with a brightly burning fire signifies an increase in social activities; to stoke or tend a furnace predicts recognition for community or charitable efforts. See also *Coal, Heat,* etc.

Furniture. Shabby and/or dilapidated furniture signifies marital or love troubles; otherwise, the meaning of the dream depends on the circumstances of the dreamer in relation to the quality of the dreamed furnishings. To dream of furniture somewhat better than that you actually live with is a fortunate omen for your future contentment, but furniture which by your standards appeared very grand or elaborate signals a need to reevaluate your aims and perhaps trim your ambitions to fit your abilities. To dream of a full bookcase predicts advancement through your own efforts, but an empty bookcase signifies setbacks through lack of diligence. If your dream featured buying furniture, you must be prepared to adjust to a change which may not be entirely to your liking; selling furniture forecasts some minor financial problems. See also under separate heading as *Chair, Table, Couch,* etc.

Furrow. A crooked furrow predicts new, troublesome, but not insoluble problems; a straight furrow forecasts difficult work ahead, but it will be rewarding. See also *Plow.*

Fury. If your dream involved your own fury, it is warning you against indiscriminate sex relations or other impulsive behavior; a dream of someone else being furious predicts a reconciliation or recovery of something you thought lost.

Fuse. A dream featuring a faulty or blown fuse is telling you that you are wasting time and energy on some unproductive project.

Future. Any dream that looks into the future or in which you are projected into or see yourself in the future predicts a sudden unexpected change in your life.

Gable. You will have some exciting and unusual experiences, possibly in far-away places, if you dreamed of a gabled house.

Gag. This follows the pattern of most obstacle dreams; if you got rid of the gag or managed to speak in spite of it, you will overcome your difficulties. If your dream involved gagging someone else, or others who were gagged, it is a warning that if you are not more discreet, you may have to defend yourself against damaging gossip.

Gaiety. See *Fun*.

Gain. A very contrary dream of warning. The greater the profit or gain was in your dream the more carefully must you guard your resources, unless you made the profit by taking an un-fair advantage or by dishonest means, in which case the dream prophesies a successful business deal or recovery of a loss.

Gaiters. A dream of wearing gaiters is a warning against extravagance; try to budget your spending. To dream of gaiters on someone else indicates sexual vigor, but to see them in a shop window suggests you need to relax and recharge your battery. To dream of wearing one gaiter predicts a change of position.

Gala. The interpretation depends on the general atmosphere and the action, but the omen is pretty straightforward; if you enjoyed the festivities, you may expect to enjoy a happy social occasion soon; but if you did not join in the gaiety, you are likely to hear some sort of distressing news.

Gale. You may be buffeted by your current difficulties, but you will eventually emerge unbowed. See also *Wind*.

Gallery. The meaning of this dream varies according to its details; if your dream featured paintings and they were of the old master variety, you can expect the renewal of a bygone relationship; but if they were contemporary, the prediction is of interesting new additions to your social circle. If the gallery featured sculpture, it indicates an unprofitable speculation. If the gallery involved was the observation type, as in a building, theater, or church, and you looked down from it, the dream signifies a happy outcome to your current project; but if you fell from it, you can expect domestic and/or lover's quarrels.

Gallop. See *Horse*.

Gallows. Most sources agree that this is a dream of contrary and will be followed by a period of general good luck, as in the hanging rhyme:

To see someone hanged, or to be hung yourself,
Is absolute promise of increase in pelf,
And however uncomfortable may be the sensation,
One cannot have doubt of a just elevation.

Gambling. This dream can have as many interpretations as there are ways to gamble, so you must try to correlate all the contributing factors and remember that the meaning will be modified by the relation of the sums involved to your own financial status; but as a general guide it is considered a dream of contrary; therefore, if you dreamed of winning a significant amount, the dream is warning you not to risk anything it would hurt you to lose. On the other hand if your dream featured an unpleasant or distressing loss, it indicates that a very profitable opportunity will soon come your way; latch on to it. See also *Dice, Cards,* etc.

Games. The meaning of this dream is fairly well expressed by the old axiom: "It's not whether you won or lost, but how you played the game." If you enjoyed the game in your dream, you can anticipate pleasant sailing ahead; however, if you were bored or annoyed by it, you can expect a spell of petty vexations. See also *Sports*.

Gander. This web-footed fellow in your dream predicts a happy surprise, especially joyous if you caught or held him.

Gang. To dream of being a member of a gang suggests a tendency to drift with the tide; to be the leader of a gang indicates stagnation through lack of initiative; to be frightened or threatened by a gang signifies a period of depression—pull up your socks and try some positive action. To be mugged or beaten by a gang is a warning that you are on the verge of financial embarrassment; put a tight rein on the spending.

Gangrene. See *Infection*.

Gangway. This passageway in your dream represents a period of transition in your life, and if the surroundings were gay and happy (as for instance a cruise or holiday atmosphere), you can expect the future to be much easier than the past; however, if the general atmosphere was one of worry or distress (as with emigrants), you can expect some difficulties in making the change. If you walked the gangway, up is, of course, better than down, and if it was a level one you crossed, progress is indicated, but you will first have to cope with some reactivated enmity from the past.

Garage. A public garage signifies an upturn in your general affairs; an empty private garage is a warning that you are in danger of being cheated by someone you trust; to put your car in your own garage predicts security through your own efforts.

Garbage. Oddly enough, and contrary to other dreams of similar content, a dream of garbage, as such, is an omen of contrary and predicts a future success beyond what you now believe possible.

Garden. A well-kept neat garden but without flowers signifies an occasional brief disturbance but on the whole a comfortable life; a neglected, overgrown garden indicates adversity, but according to old Franximus, a dream of a garden in bloom is the absolute best and foretells spiritual satisfaction, domestic love, and financial security. What more is there!

Gardenia. A passionate new love affair or renewal of a past romantic attachment is forecast in a dream of this strongly scented flower.

Gargle. You are in for a period of awkward changes if your dream featured gargling; be as flexible as you can and in retrospect you will realize that the trials were beneficial.

Gargoyle. An unexpected (but amusing) embarrassment due to your own mischievous behavior is indicated in a dream of one of these bizarre figures.

Garland. To wear a garland of flowers in your dream predicts that you will turn defeat into victory by "thinking" your way out of a difficult situation. To receive a garland signifies progress toward your goal, but to give a garland is a warning against unscrupulous friends or associates. See also *Flowers*.

Garlic. This pungent seasoning is considered an omen of general welfare and protection, unless you are one of the people who loathe it, in which case it must be considered a sign of some brief but annoying unpleasantness.

Garret. See *Attic*.

Garter. The meaning of a dream featuring garters depends entirely on the action and is as follows:

If your garters were unfastened, it is a warning of danger from bad companions.

To lose a garter indicates coming trouble, but if someone picked it up and gave it back to you, you can expect help from a friend; however, if it was not returned, your problems will be compounded by unexpected treachery.

To dream of finding a garter is a warning that you are currently skating on thin ice and you would be wise to alter your course before you go through.

Gas. The smell of gas in your dream was a warning to keep your nose out of other people's affairs; seeing someone overcome by gas predicts news of a scandal; lighting a gas stove or other appliance is a suggestion to economize and avoid overextension of your credit; to

170

see a gas fire burning in a fireplace or furnace indicates a pleasing social invitation; financial difficulties are forecast by a dream of anyone wearing a gas mask, and if you were wearing one yourself, you'd be wise to try to pacify your creditors before they cause you some real hardship.

To dream of a gasman reading your meter is a warning that you could be embarrassed by someone (probably a relative) making unauthorized or unwarranted use of your credit, so don't be careless about such facilities. A lighted gas lamp in your dream indicates a stroke of money luck; turning off a gas lamp or seeing one suddenly go out is a sign of coming disenchantment with a personal relationship.

Gas Station. Buying gas at a gas station predicts an interesting increase in income, but buying anything else there is a warning against dishonest associates. Selling gasoline suggests a period of lack of business progress if not actual reverses; plenty of patience will be needed. To use the washroom in a gas station signifies a release from some current worries.

To run out of gas in your dream is an omen of opposite; you will be inspired and imbued with initiative and constructive energy.

Gate. This is a form of our old friend the obstacle dream, and of course all the contributing (if any) factors should be correlated, but as a general guide:

An open gate signifies opportunities ahead.

A closed gate indicates obstacles which can be overcome if you succeeded in opening it.

A locked gate predicts insurmountable obstacles, unless you climbed over it or found a way around it, in which case your frustration will be transitory.

Gather. A dream of gathering a variety of things signifies satisfaction with all your concerns; otherwise: wood pertains to friendships; flowers, to joy; money, to money; papers, to speculation (don't!); books, to profits; and a dream of others gathering signifies pleasant family relations.

Gauze. The use of medical gauze in a dream is a forecast of relief from worry;

but a dream featuring gauze curtains, draperies, or garments warns of repressed resentment which you would be wise to get off your chest.

Gavel. Seen or used in your dream a gavel forecasts the correction of an injustice.

Gaze. See *Stare*.

Gazelle. See *Antelope*.

Geese. To see them, whether swimming, flying, or on the ground, is a forecast of improving conditions; but if you heard them cackling, you are being warned that someone is trying to con you with sweet talk.

Gems. See *Jewelry*.

Generosity. You are assured of more than a fair share of material wealth if you dreamed of being generous in either thought or deed.

Genii. See *Fairy*.

Genitals. This is a rather straightforward indication of your sexual attitudes and/or feelings, as follows:

To dream of your own or other sex organs being healthily normal signifies a satisfactory love life.

A dream of diseased sex organs is telling you that you are either overdoing it or being dangerously promiscuous.

Deformed sex organs in a dream are another form of warning against overindulgence.

Unusual sex organs are a sign of underindulgence and a little initiative might be a good idea.

A dream which featured exposing the sex organs indicates that you are on the verge of being dangerously sex-starved and professional advice would be useful.

To dream of pain in the genitals suggests you should see your doctor.

Gentian. Wearing one of these beautiful blue flowers is a sign that you have attracted and will continue to attract true love and sincere friends. To see them growing or arranged indoors is a forecast of a future filled with simple but satisfying pleasures. See also *Colors* and *Flowers*.

Geography. Any dream to do with geography is a straightforward forecast of an early opportunity to travel.

Geranium. Geraniums in

bloom predict unexpected wealth or unexpected recognition, and if you smelled their pungent aroma, the omen is strengthened. See also *Plant(s)*, *Flowers*, and *Colors*.

Germany. See *Foreign*.

Germs. A dream of contrary. Whether you saw them, worried about them, or were simply aware of them, the dream signifies renewed energy generated by new interest.

Geyser. A geyser spurting in your dream forecasts a change of direction in your life which will entail some ups and downs but will ultimately give you much happiness.

Ghetto. A ghetto type of dwelling, atmosphere, or location featured in your dream is a warning against living beyond your means; that inevitable rainy day can occur when you least expect it, and even a small umbrella is better than none.

Ghost. The meaning of this dream varies according to the action. If the ghost simply appeared in your dream, it is an omen of general good luck; however, if you were frightened by it or it spoke to you, it is a warning that some powerful pressure will be brought to bear on you to join in a scheme or activity which is against your principles. Resist the temptation with all the strength you can muster, and if necessary get help from a trusted friend or adviser.

Ghoul. Active ghouls in your dream are a forecast of disappointment and vain hope; however, if you did not join in the ghoulish activities, there is a slight possibility that you might be able to recover the situation, but abandoning it would really be better.

Giant. A dream of being a giant yourself is warning you against any speculative ventures for the time being. Meeting a giant boldly is a promise of future success; killing a giant signifies an increase in material wealth; to see a giant trampling over others or pushing them aside indicates obstacles which you can overcome through determination and perseverance.

Giddiness. See *Dizziness*.

Gift. A "beware the Greeks bearing gifts" message is

contained in a dream of receiving or being offered a gift; but to give or offer a gift has a similar meaning to "generosity" and predicts happy news.

Giggle. To dream of giggling yourself suggests that you could be financially embarrassed if you are not more prudent; a dream of others giggling forecasts a pleasing upswing in your social life.

Gimlet. A dream of using this tool is a promise of new interests and/or increased sexual vigor which will bring you great contentment.

Gin. Other people drinking gin in your dream is a forecast of confusion in your affairs due to sudden changes; a dream of drinking gin yourself or of buying it signifies a pleasant surprise. See also *Bar*.

Ginger. Tasting or smelling this spicy flavor in a dream predicts a passionate but fleeting love affair; eating or baking gingerbread forecasts a family celebration.

Giraffe. This long-necked creature in your dream is warning you not to meddle in other people's affairs.

Girder. Trouble ahead is signaled in a dream featuring the girders of a construction; someone is waiting to catch you in a mistake. Be diligent.

Girdle. You will accomplish your current aims with ease if your dream featured a girdle, unless it was shabby or torn, in which case you will still achieve what you set out to do but perhaps not so quickly as you hoped.

Girl. To dream of a young girl whom you recognize is a sign of encouraging prospects; if she is a stranger, the dream forecasts some sudden surprising news. For a man to dream of being a girl indicates a latent sexual problem and a visit to a psychologist might be helpful.

Glacier. Important news from a distance or alternatively news that will take you on a long journey is forecast in a dream of seeing, or being on, a glacier. A dream of looking or falling into a crevasse in a glacier is a warning that some change you are contemplating could be extremely dangerous; don't do it—or at least put it off until you've had really competent advice. To dream of crossing safely over a crevasse in a glacier signifies that the obstacles facing you are not as great as you think.

Glade. All your worries will soon fade and your secret fears will prove groundless if your dream featured a verdant, green glade. See also *Grass, Foliage, Mountain,* etc.

Gladiola. These majestic flowers predict an advancement or improvement within your present sphere of activity. See also *Colors* and *Flowers.*

Glamor. This quality is such a subjective matter that only a general guide to its meaning can be suggested, to wit: Any thing, personage, or action which seems to you to be undeniably glamorous is a warning against impulsive or ostentatious behavior.

Glands. You are foolishly depleting your energy with unnecessary worry if you dreamed of swollen or painful glands.

Glass. Clean glassware signifies general good luck, dirty glassware indicates domestic trouble or personal squabbles, broken glass predicts changing conditions, putting a new pane of glass in a window signifies satisfaction, polishing or cleaning glass panes is a warning against complacency or overconfidence. If your dream featured decorative glass, or glass blowing or molding, it predicts a rise in status and/or an increase in income. See also *Eyeglasses, Mirror,* etc.

Glider. Riding the wind in a glider predicts a surprising proposition from a friend or acquaintance; listen to advice before you act on it.

Globe. A globe (or ball) of any material predicts new interests; a globe-type map of the world indicates interesting new adventures.

Gloom. Whether your dream featured an atmosphere of gloom or a gloomy feeling, it's an omen of contrary, and you will soon be uplifted by a change for the better.

Gloves. The meaning of this dream varies according to the details, but as a general rule gloves worn in a dream signify emotional security, and brand-new gloves portend financial security. Losing gloves indicates that some expected help will not materialize, whereas finding gloves predicts help from an unexpected source. Shabby, soiled, or torn gloves are an omen of disappointments, but they will be temporary. Long or gauntlet-type gloves pertain to love matters, and if they were in good condition, so will be your love affairs. See also *Colors*.

Glow. Any dream which features a bright and/or pleasant glow predicts a swift improvement in all that deeply concerns you.

Glue. You are being warned to guard your capital and recheck on any recent investments if your dream featured the use of glue to mend anything; to get glue on your fingers or clothes is an assurance of loyal friends; the use of glue to stick things together (as opposed to mending) predicts advancement and/or recognition within your profession, business, or main sphere of activity.

Glutton. Observing a glutton in your dream indicates business advances through social contacts; however, a dream of being a glutton indicates business success without social acceptance.

Gnats. Petty but troublesome annoyances from jealous friends or associates are forecast in a dream concerning these irritating pests, unless you managed to elude or get rid of them, in which case the problems will clear up without any effort on your part.

Gnome. See *Fairy*.

Goal. To dream of scoring a goal or seeing one scored predicts new friends and new opportunities.

Goat. A dream concerning goats is a warning against involving yourself in any venture or activity which is not strictly on the up and up; the warning is especially strong if the dream featured milking a goat. If you were chased, frightened, or butted by a goat, the message pertains specifically to gambling—don't!

Goatee. If your dream featured this type of chin decoration, it was warning you not to take chances with your health and/or reputation. See also *Beard*.

Goblet. As a general rule a dream featuring a goblet made of metal signifies good news, but if you were drinking from the vessel, the meaning would be modified by the type and/or taste of the liquid, and this detail as well as the kind of metal should be looked up under separate headings. See also *Glass*.

God. You can expect to achieve rare contentment and peace of mind through intelligent adjustment to circumstances and acceptance of your lot in life if you had the rare experience of seeing, hearing, or being aware of God in your dream. Graven images, totems, or carved idols signify personal pleasures.

Godparent. A dream of godparents (seeing, being, or whatever) indicates a coming opportunity to serve the community or engage in a constructive activity which will give you great satisfaction.

Goggles. See *Eyeglasses*.

Goiter. Whether you dreamed of having it yourself or of others so afflicted, the dream is telling you that you are inhibiting your enjoyment of today by worrying needlessly about tomorrow. Try a dose of positive thinking.

Gold. Easy come, easy go is the message contained in a dream featuring the precious stuff as such, i.e., in bars or nuggets, etc. However, there are many variations dependent on the action and details. Gold cloth, garments, embroidery, or trimmings signify honors and/or recognition; looking for gold indicates that a successful change of unsatisfactory conditions can be made through your own initiative. Finding and/or mining, melting or working with it is a reminder that "all is not gold that glitters," and you must guard against a tendency to be too easily taken in by appearances. Hiding it suggests that you are not aggressive enough about protecting your own interests; take positive action. Stealing or counting gold is a warning that "the love of money" is truly a root of evil and can be very costly. Items made of gold, such as tableware, jewelry, medals, coins, etc., or gold-plated items, are a forerunner of steady financial gain. See also under separate listings: *Coins, Medal, Buttons*, etc.

Goldenrod. If your dream featured it growing, you are being cautioned against interfering in the personal affairs of others; however, if you picked it or it was indoors in a vase or floral arrangement, it predicts a new influential friend. See also *Colors, Flowers, Foliage,* etc.

Goldfish. See *Fish.*

Golf. Whether you played yourself, or observed others playing, this dream pertains to affairs with the opposite sex, and its meaning depends on the circumstances. If the game, general atmosphere, and condition of the course was pleasant, your heart interests should flourish; however, if the game was a strain and/or the links not well-kept, you can expect a siege of heartburn.

Gondola. This classic symbol of gay romance is, unhappily, a dream of contrary and signifies romantic boredom; you could do with either a change of partner or a vacation.

Gong. Hearing the sound of a gong in your dream predicts an exciting event in the offing. The importance of the event will be in ratio to the volume of the sound. If you saw but did not hear a gong, you will hear news of a change in the life of someone close to you.

Goose. The meaning of a goose in your dream depends on the circumstances and the action. If it was in a barnyard, it is a suggestion to alter your diet; if your weight doesn't need to be increased or decreased, then check on your blood pressure and/or blood sugar. A flying goose signifies an unexpected trip; a swimming goose indicates an unexpected visitor; a quacking goose is a warning against repeating gossip; eating goose is a forerunner of a happy social occasion; plucking and/or cooking a goose is a sign of improving circumstances; and catching a goose predicts sad news. See also *Geese.*

Gooseberries. A dream which featured gooseberries, whether eaten, picked, cooked, or served, is a warning of impending embarrassment through indiscreet behavior or foolish companions.

Gooseflesh. If you broke out in goose bumps in your dream, the message is that you are jeopardizing a valued relationship by taking it too much for granted; remember the straw that broke the camel's back and mend your ways.

Gopher. These sneaky little burrowers are a signal of trouble brewing in your vicinity; could be either business or family type. It will be upsetting but not really serious.

Gorilla. To dream of this frightening big ape portends a painful misunderstanding, unless the animal was very docile or definitely friendly, in which case the dream forecasts a very unusual new friend.

Gospel. A dream of reading, or listening to, the gospel predicts a request for help which it will please as well as benefit you to give.

Gossip. The interpretation of this dream varies with the action. If you were the subject of the gossip, it's a dream of contrary and predicts pleasant news; to dream of engaging in, or listening to, gossip about others signifies family disagreements over property or domestic quarrels. A dream of being accused of gossip or being caught at it is a warning that you could be humiliated by repeating confidences, so guard your tongue.

Goulash. Eating or serving this type of spicy stew is a forecast of gay social times ahead.

Gourd. Used or seen in a dream, a gourd is a sign of happy companionship.

Gout. To suffer this painful condition in a dream suggests that a medical checkup would be wise.

Government. A dream of being involved with government, whether local or national, indicates a period of uncertainty.

Gown. An academic gown featured in a dream is a sort of contrary omen in that it signifies achievement although of a lower order than anticipated. Otherwise, see *Clothes, Colors,* and *Dress.*

Grace. You can expect a valuable gift or a small but pleasing legacy if you dreamed of saying or hearing grace before a meal.

Graduation. Whether you were a participant or a spectator, a dream of being present at a graduation ceremony predicts a substantial rise in business and/or social status.

Grain. No matter what the action, grain in a dream

is a most fortunate omen of prosperity, unless it was spoiled or on fire, in which case it is a warning that your business affairs need closer attention if you want to avoid hardship.

Grammar. You'll be lucky if someone corrected your grammar in your dream, but you can expect to get the worst of any current controversy if you did the correcting.

Grandparents. Grandparents in a dream are a symbol of protection and security.

Grapefruit. This yellow citrus in your dream forecasts a period of confusion due to a conflict between your business and love life; listen to advice but rely on your own intuition to resolve the matter. See also *Fruit* and *Colors*.

Grapes. You are being warned against preoccupation with sensuous pleasures if you dreamed of picking or eating grapes; but if you saw them harvested or growing on the vines, they are an omen of future comfort and plenty. See also *Fruit* and *Colors*.

Grass. Sunburned, neglected, or bad grass indicates that you will have to work hard for what you get; but green

and well-tended grass predicts success in all your undertakings. To cut or mow grass forecasts sad news; to eat it signifies sensual pleasures; to sow, roll, or plant it portends future security against rainy days but no luxury.

Grasshopper. These green jumpers signify confusion and complexities ahead. Issues hanging in the balance will require very careful handling. Don't try to cope alone; get all the competent advice you can muster from friends and associates.

Grate. See *Fireplace*.

Gratitude. If you were grateful in your dream, you can expect some minor but pleasing good luck; if someone was grateful to you, an unexpected visitor is forecast.

Grave. No matter what the circumstances, this is not a happy dream omen. A new grave banked with flowers is a forecast of a broken promise; a neglected grave signifies heartache; an open grave predicts sad news from a distance; to fall into a grave is a sign of lost friendship; to dig a grave or to be aware of your own grave is a warning that you are being thwarted by secret enmity. See also *Epitaph, Funeral,* etc.

Gravel. Gravel in a dream represents obstacles, and if you walked on it, you will have to expend some effort to overcome the difficulties; but if you drove over it, the problem will be quickly solved. If you were spreading the gravel, your dream was telling you that the trouble is of your own making and you would be wise to reconsider your attitudes.

Gravestone. Oddly enough a new gravestone seen in a dream is an omen of contrary and signifies a new opportunity; old gravestones forecast a renewed friendship. See also *Epitaph.*

Gravy. Eating or serving gravy is a warning that you are concentrating on meaningless activities and are in danger of overlooking a good opportunity, but making gravy signifies a favorable time for a speculative venture or even a modest bit of gambling.

Gray. See *Colors.*

Grease. You are contemplating something which would turn out to be a great mistake if you dreamed of grease on yourself or on your clothes; think things over again and don't be influenced by outside pressure. To dream of greasy pots, dishes, or other articles is a warning not to interfere in the affairs of others—even if asked to do so. Stay neutral.

Great Lakes. See *Lake.*

Greece. A dream of ancient Greece is a sign of success in your current undertakings. Otherwise, see *Foreign.*

Green. See *Colors.*

Greenhouse. Love, success, and an altogether bright future is promised in a dream of being in a greenhouse, unless there was something unpleasant about it, in which case the interpretation must be modified by, or correlated with, whatever the disagreeable factor was. See also *Foliage, Plants, Odor,* etc.

Greyhound. Strangely, a greyhound is a symbol of triumph if it was not running, but to dream of a running greyhound is a warning that you have bitten off more than you can chew and an alteration in your future plans would be advisable.

Griddle Cakes. See *Pancakes*.

Grief. A dream of contrary. You will soon be rejoicing.

Grill. A window grill or other decorative grillwork featured in your dream suggests you are contemplating a back-street affair; think it over well, and then be careful. If your dream involved a cooking grill, see *Barbecue*.

Grin. To see someone else grin is an augury of an unexpected and pleasing social invitation; but if you did the grinning, you can stop fretting about the fancy maneuver that worries you; you'll get away with it!

Grind. Grinding grain, corn, cocoa, coffee, or any form of foodstuff is a forecast of increasing material wealth through prudence, but grinding stones or any hard material predicts limited rewards for hard work.

Grindstone. To dream of turning a grindstone is a warning that you must give closer attention to details if you wish to succeed.

Grit. If you dreamed of having grit in your food, or on yourself, you are being warned against repeating questionable rumors.

Groan. To groan in your dream signifies some kind of financial embarrassment; make sure your tax accounts are in good order. If in your dream you heard someone else groan, it indicates a period of petty annoyances.

Groceries. A dream of shopping for groceries is a forecast of luck and prosperity. See also *Market*.

Groom. To dream of an animal being groomed signifies news of a legal nature.

Grope. A dream of contrary. Your affairs will soon take a turn for the better. See also *Darkness* and *Light*.

Grotto. A religious grotto in your dream predicts a lightening of your burdens —whatever they may be.

Ground. You are being warned against getting drawn into pastimes you can ill afford if your dream featured lying on the ground. Otherwise, See *Fall, Furrow, Dry*, etc.

Ground Hog. If you dreamed of this funny animal, you

can expect to have an unusual and interesting romantic experience.

Grove. See *Forest* and *Trees*.

Grow. To be aware of things of nature flourishing is an omen of advancement, but other factors of the dream should be correlated. See also *Colors, Trees, Shrubs, Plant(s), Grass, Flowers,* etc.

Growl. See under separate headings of *Dog, Bears, Animals,* etc.

Grunt. Hearing an animal grunt predicts a choice of opportunities to change your job, the kind of work you do, or your life-style; to dream of grunting yourself signifies an embarrassing or troublesome experience with the opposite sex.

Guard. If your dream concerned observing something being protected by guards, it portends a loss through carelessness or theft, so be sure your insurance is in order. To dream of being on guard predicts a rise in income.

Guardian. You can expect to be worried by financial problems connected with a friend if you dreamed of

being made the legal guardian of another person.

Guess. A dream of contrary. If you were doing the guessing, you will soon hear a confidence or the solution to a puzzling situation; but if someone else was doing the guessing, it's a warning that you've got a potential Judas in your social circle.

Guest. See *Visitor*.

Guide. Whether your dream featured acting as a guide, being guided, seeing others guided, or consulting a guide or guidebook, it is an augury of an interesting new opportunity through an influential friend which you would do well to consider.

Guillotine. You are in danger of losing a valued friend by being childishly contentious if your dream featured an execution-type guillotine; if it was the paper-cutting type, you are being warned to be more diligent concerning your responsibilities if you want to avoid a humiliating loss.

Guilt. A dream of others being guilty signifies untrustworthy friends; to be guilty or be aware of a personal sense of guilt indicates a

183

need to make amends for some past injustice.

Guitar. See *Banjo*.

Gulf. A dream which featured a gulf of water signifies a sudden sad parting; however, if you were in a boat on the gulf, or landed at a gulf port or cove, it indicates the sudden forging of a new link in your life. If your dream concerned a land-type gulf, see *Abyss*.

Gum. Whatever the action, chewing gum featured in your dream is a warning against confiding in new acquaintances and/or against casual sex affairs.

Gum Drops. See *Candy*.

Gums. Sore or inflamed gums predict family or personal problems; if you were undergoing treatment in your dream, it indicates a disturbing rift or painful quarrel. See also *Teeth*.

Guns. Whether you saw it, heard it, or used it, any type of gun featured in your dream forecasts an injustice, either to you or to someone in your close circle, which you will have to fight hard to overcome. To dream of loading a gun is a strong caution against

giving way to temper. A dream of gunpowder indicates a sudden change of occupation for a man; for a woman, it means an unexpected change of residence.

Guru. An enjoyable and worthwhile new friend is forecast in a dream featuring this philosopher-mystic.

Gutter. To dream of cleansing out a gutter is an omen of success in your current undertakings; if you found anything of value in a gutter, it predicts an increase in status without a commensurate increase in income; a dream of falling into or lying in a gutter is a warning of possible loss of status and/or hardships through your own foolish actions.

Gymnasium. A dream of being in a gymnasium warns against impulsive behavior which could cause you social embarrassment. See also *Exercise*.

Gypsy. The meaning of a gypsy dream varies according to the action, so all the factors should be carefully correlated, but as a general guide:

If you observed them in

a camp or a caravan, it predicts a period of restlessness and uncertainties.

If you bought anything from them, it signifies good luck, but only after some trials and tribulations.

If your dream featured only one gypsy—female—it indicates news from a distance or a sudden trip; male forecasts lighthearted amorous adventures.

See also *Fortune-telling, Colors,* etc.

Habit. You can expect to have some difficulty in regard to a useful social contact if your dream featured a personal habit such as smoking, drinking, chewing, etc. A riding or religious-type habit suggests that you will have to be firm about breaking off a relationship which has become a drag.

Haddock. See *Fish*.

Hag. See *Witch*.

Haggis. To see or eat this Scotch concoction in a dream is an omen of prosperity; but if you cut and/ or served it, you are being warned against indiscreet behavior.

Hail. Whatever your current high hope is fastened on, this dream forewarns of a disappointment. However, you should remember that most endings generate new beginnings.

Hair. All details of the dream should be carefully correlated to determine its meaning, but as a general guide: if your hair was luxuriant and you were pleased with its appearance and/or condition, it is a sign of good health, progress, and contentment; but if it was thin, falling out, or worrying you in any way, it forecasts difficulties ahead. A dream of combing (or brushing) your hair signifies a solution to an annoying situation which has been plaguing you for some time; to dream of combing (or brushing) someone else's hair predicts a request for help from a friend. To comb or arrange the hair of anyone of the opposite sex indicates a happy outcome to your current sex problems. To cut your own hair, or have it cut, is a sign of success in a new venture or sphere of activity. To cut someone else's hair is a warning of hidden jealousy around you. A dream of braiding your hair predicts the forging of a new link of friendship, but to braid someone else's hair portends an unhappy argument. Curling or setting your hair pertains to emotional affairs and promises either an improvement in your marital relations or a new romance. Bleaching your hair suggests you would be wise to be somewhat less flirtatious, and dyeing it suggests that you are allowing vanity to overcome your common sense. Having your hair pulled indicates untrustworthy friends or colleagues, and gray or white hair predicts sad (but not grievous) news. To put brilliantine (or similar treatment) on your hair to slick it down smoothly is a forerunner of brightening prospects and/or advancement in status; to have your hair done by a hairdresser is a warning against repeating gossip. Eating or chewing hair signifies that you would be well advised to give more attention to your own affairs and less to the affairs of others. To find hair on some unusual part of your body promises a steady increase in material wealth. See also *Beard* and *Wig(s)*.

Hairpin. A dream featuring hairpins is an omen of happy future prospects.

Half Dollar. See *Coins*.

Half-mast. See *Flags*.

Halibut. See *Fish*.

Halitosis. See *Breath*.

Hall. The portent of the dream varies according to the aspect of the hall. A long narrow hall predicts a long period of worry; an average normal entrance hall signifies petty vexations; an elegant and/or impressive hall indicates coming changes; a public (or meeting) hall suggests that you have been delaying an important decision on which you would be wise to act.

Hallmark. To be aware, in your dream, of a missing or false hallmark, is a warning of treachery among your associates, but to observe a hallmark where expected is a promise of success in your current interests.

Halloween. A dream featuring the decorations or celebration of All Saints' Eve (out of season) predicts recognition in community affairs.

Hallucination. If your dream involved hallucinations, you can expect to be asked to help a friend who will not be entirely truthful regarding the nature of his or her difficulty. Help if you can do so without getting personally involved.

Halo. To see someone wearing a halo in your dream indicates sad news; if you were wearing the halo, it predicts foreign travel; if you dreamed of taking off a halo, you can expect some kind of improvement in business or financial matters. A halo of lights seen around an object signifies a praiseworthy accomplishment. See also *Sun* and *Moon.*

Halter. A halter seen in your dream is a symbol of obstacles ahead. If you succeeded in putting it on a horse, you can rest assured that you will be able to overcome the forces that seem, at present, to be working against you.

Ham. No matter what the action was, ham in a dream is a good omen. Smoking it signifies a prosperous year ahead; baking it indicates that your current difficulties will result in ultimate good fortune; and eating it in any form predicts business luck.

Hamlet. See *Village.*

Hammer. To hear or see a hammer being used is a fortunate dream; if you used it yourself, it predicts a satisfying achievement.

Hammock. An empty hammock suggests a minor loss; if you were in it alone, the dream is warning you that your selfishness in personal affairs could drive off a friend you value; if you were in the hammock with someone of the opposite sex, you can expect a pleasing upturn in your social life. If you fell out of the hammock, it is a warning not to take your mate (or partner) for granted; make a little effort.

Hamper. A laundry hamper, if empty, signifies an emotional upset; if full, good progress is indicated. A picnic or food hamper forecasts pleasant family unity.

Hand. The meaning of a dream featuring a hand, or hands, varies greatly according to the action and other aspects, but as a general guide:

If the hands were dirty and/or their appearance unpleasant, it is a warning to guard against behavior which could bring you into ill-repute.

Beautiful, clean, and well-groomed hands forecast satisfaction in life.

Busy and/or skillful hands predict well-earned rewards.

Bent or gnarled hands signify an easement of financial worries.

Waving hands indicate separations.

Caressing hands are a sign of sincere love.

Bloody hands are an omen of family quarrels.

Washing your hands suggests you should make an effort to rectify some past injustice.

Swollen hands predict an unexpected gain.

Hairy hands forecast a stroke of business luck.

Tied hands indicate frustrating obstacles which in turn suggest a change of plans.

A broken hand or the loss of a hand is a warning that you need to pay closer attention to your own personal affairs.

A bandaged hand signifies temporary setbacks.

The right hand predicts carefree joy.

The left hand predicts irritation and minor difficulties.

Very small hands portend infidelity.

Very large hands are an omen of sexual satisfaction.

Children's hands are a promise of happiness.

Shaking hands is a sign of reconciliation or renewed friendship.

Handbag. The significance depends on the action. If you lost your handbag, it is an obstacle dream, and the outcome of your problem depends on whether or not you found your bag. Finding a handbag is a dream of contrary and predicts gain if the bag was empty, loss if it was full. A dream which featured yourself, or someone else, opening and rummaging in a handbag forecasts the opening of new doors in your life. Buying a handbag predicts moderate gains.

Handball. A rather long period of ups and downs but followed by eventual success is predicted in a dream of playing handball.

Handcuffs. Unlike tied hands, a dream of being handcuffed is an omen of contrary and promises a release from worry. To see others handcuffed signifies security and protection, and to snap them on someone in your dream predicts an unexpected improvement in your lifestyle.

Hand Grenade. You can expect to suffer a painful humiliation brought on by your own impulsive behavior if you dreamed of throwing a hand grenade. Any other aspect of a hand-grenade dream is a warning against being persuaded to act contrary to your own best judgment.

Handkerchief. A soiled or blood-stained handkerchief indicates a quarrel; a cotton one is a suggestion that you could benefit from asserting yourself more; a linen one is a warning of hidden hostility; a silk one is a good omen in regard to your general interests; a torn handkerchief signifies a business embarrassment; a lost one indicates a broken relationship; buying one is a caution against new ventures or gambling; and receiving one predicts a happy surprise. Blowing your nose in a handkerchief portends an improvement in social status; wiping your face or forehead with it augurs a lightening of responsibilities; waving it prophesies an interesting new friendship; and washing it is a warning against extravagance.

Handwriting. See *Writing*.

Hangar. An empty hangar signifies a disappointment, but if there were planes in it, you can expect a speedy rise in status.

Hanger. Putting anything on a hanger portends freedom from care.

Hanging. A dream of contrary. A season of good luck will follow if you dreamed of being hanged or seeing another hanged. However, to dream of performing the function of a hangman is a strong warning to refrain from criticizing lest you be criticized yourself.

Hangover. For single people this dream is a warning against promiscuous sex relations; for married ones it portends a relief from family worries.

Happiness. The meaning of this dream is similar to

that of Fun and depends on the quality of the sensation. A normal degree is a good omen, an excess is not.

Harbor. To dream of coming into a harbor signifies future security; a dream of leaving a harbor predicts the discovery of a false friend.

Hardware. Bits and pieces of hardware featured in a dream are an omen of general good luck.

Hare. If your dream involved killing one, it predicts some temporary upsets; if you saw one running, it indicates a change of position and/or residence; eating it signifies prosperity, and cooking it forecasts pleasant family events.

Harem. Whether you are a woman and dreamed of being in one, or a man and dreamed of keeping one, the symbol is a straightforward one of busy times ahead with the opposite sex. Don't overdo it.

Harlequin. See *Masquerade* and *Costume*.

Harlot. See *Prostitute*.

Harmonica. Satisfying social

pleasures are forecast in a dream of tuneful harmonica playing. See also *Music*.

Harmony. This is one of the rare dreams that means exactly what it says; harmony in all things will be yours.

Harness. See *Halter*.

Harp. All pleasant musical sounds are favorable dreams; however if a string broke or there was a sudden discord or stoppage, it signifies that you will have to demonstrate your ability to ride out a period of difficult times.

Harpoon. A dream of a harpoon being used on a large fish or a whale predicts an improvement in living conditions and an increase in income; but to be injured by a harpoon or see it go astray is a warning of serious financial distress; don't overextend your credit.

Harpsichord. Classical music played on this instrument predicts happy love affairs, but swing, jazz, or pop tunes played on it signifies an interesting new experience in the offing. See also *Music*.

Harrow. Hard work ahead

191

but it will be rewarding.

Harvest. If the harvest was a good one, you couldn't have a better dream, it forecasts success in all your deepest concerns; however, if it was a poor harvest, the dream is warning you against friends or associates who are trying to exploit you. Don't be passive.

Hash. This mixed dish in a dream represents confusion, puzzles, or mysteries, and its meaning varies with the action. If you merely observed the hash, you will soon be faced with a puzzling situation which will require your utmost tact and patience to sort out; if you made the hash, it predicts minor troubles precipitated by your own hasty action in some matter on which you would be wise to backtrack; and if you ate the hash, it signifies a confusing mystery which will be vexing for a time, but will eventually be solved in a most surprising manner.

Hassock. Sitting on a hassock forecasts peace after a period of strife; kneeling on one predicts that you'll soon be rid of some hostile influences now around

you; putting your feet on a hassock indicates a favorable wind of change blowing in your direction.

Haste. "Less haste, less waste" is the warning message contained in a dream of doing anything in a hurry. Anxiety and worry can be avoided if you take the trouble to plan ahead.

Hat. The significance varies according to the action and other factors, so all details should be correlated, but as a general guide:

A new hat is a sign of good luck.

A hat which was too small for you predicts a disappointment.

A hat too large for you signifies an embarrassment.

Tipping your hat or holding it in your hand forecasts a humiliation.

Losing your hat or having it blow away indicates money trouble.

An old, shabby, or soiled hat portends business irritations.

A top hat (silk) predicts a rise in status.

A cotton hat is a caution against a calculating friend.

An elaborate hat suggests social popularity.

Hate. To feel hatred in a dream suggests that you should beware of misjudging someone; but to be hated is a dream of contrary and predicts an improvement in your affairs through the influence of sincere friends.

Hawk. Bright prospects are forecast if the hawk was flying; otherwise you must be prepared to sit out a period of gloomy boredom.

Hawthorn. As with most spring flowers, these are an omen of hope and better times ahead. See also sudden relief from worry. See also *Colors*.

Hatbox. A hatbox in your dream predicts a pleasant surprise, unless it was empty, in which case it signifies a social disappointment.

Hatchet. You can expect a period of disturbing predicaments, domestic and /or business, if your dream involved using a hatchet to chop any thing, unless is was used to split kindling wood, in which case it forecasts a reconciliation. To sharpen a hatchet signifies an increased income. See also *Ax*.

Hay. Oddly enough, a dream of hay in the sunshine is a warning that you are on the verge of serious financial strain `and should take measures to cut your debts; but in cloudy or dull weather hay predicts unexpected money. A haymow augurs successful love affairs, and a haystack (or stacks) indicates a profit where loss was expected. A dream of suffering hay fever (if you don't) suggests a medical checkup. To dream of a hay cart forecasts a change, and if your dream featured mowing or cutting hay, you must expect a period of uncertainties.

Hazelnut. See *Filberts*.

Head. The significance of a dream featuring the head must be determined by correlating its details, but as a general guide:

A living head (your own or someone else's) is an excellent omen for all that deeply concerns you.

A disembodied head predicts a new situation in which you will have to use your head rather than lose it!

A small, narrow, or

pointed head indicates more work and less profit than expected, whereas a very large, wide, or round head means the reverse.

A swollen head is a warning against overconfidence.

To dream of yourself (or another) having more than one head signifies a sudden gratifying rise in status.

A dream of suffering pains in the head or headache is telling you to keep your private affairs to yourself.

To see yourself (or anyone else) with the head of an animal is a warning against overemphasis on material or sensual pleasures. Remember that an ounce of restraint can frequently prevent a pound of regret.

Strangely enough, in a dream half a head is better than a whole one as it forecasts achievement beyond your ambition.

An accident or blow to the head suggests tension and/or overwork; try to take it easy for a time or have a change of scenery if possible.

If your dream involved beheading, see *Behead.*

Headlights. Headlights moving toward you in a dream are a warning that a situation you have allowed to drift is a potential danger unless you take quick action.

Headstone. See *Gravestone* and *Epitaph.*

Health. Good health featured in a dream signifies the same for the dreamer, but a dream of a breakdown in health is a warning against speculation.

Hearse. If you only saw the hearse in your dream, it predicts a lightening of your burdens; if you rode with the driver (or were the driver), the dream indicates an increase in responsibilities, but if you were inside the hearse, you can expect to soon make a change which will be important to your future.

Heart. To be pleasantly aware of a heart, as for example a heart-shaped frame or object, is a favorable dream pertaining to love affairs or personal relations. But to dream of having a heart attack, or pain or difficulty with the beat is an omen of contrary and predicts a long and active life. A dream of having a heartache (regardless of the cause) signifies the reverse, and you can confidently expect your fears and/or worries to evaporate.

Heartburn. This unpleasant sensation experienced in your dream is telling you to cut down on high living in low places.

Hearth. See *Fireplace, Fire, Ashes,* etc.

Heat. A dream of heat on your face has the same meaning as blushing, but a dream of suffering from heat is a warning to keep a strong control on your passion and/or temper if you want to avoid getting into an awkward situation.

Heater. See *Furnace.*

Heather. An especially auspicious dream for everything that closely concerns you, and if it happened to be white heather, it's almost the luckiest dream you could have. See also *Plant(s), Foliage,* and *Bush.*

Heaven. To dream of heaven predicts a change which may not suit you at the time but will prove, in the long run, to be very beneficial. See also *Angel, Saint,* etc., or *Sky.*

Heavy. Obviously the object, material, and action must be correlated to interpret the meaning of the dream, but anything heavy (package, bundle, or whatever) is a symbol of wealth.

Heckling. Whether you did it yourself or someone else was the culprit, the dream is telling you that you would benefit from shifting the chip off your shoulder and using it to strengthen your backbone.

Hedge. A dream of strangely contrasting meanings depending on the action and other factors. If you clipped the hedge, it is a lucky omen, but if you jumped over one, it signifies that you will get something you have been wanting but it will not come up to your expectations. To dream of going through an opening in a hedge is a forecast of social chagrin. Green and/or blooming hedges are a symbol of happiness and success in love; however, thorny and/or prickly hedges predict that you will have determined and hostile rivalry to overcome. See also *Plant(s), Colors,* and *Foliage.*

Hedgehog. You'll have a prickly choice to make if you dreamed of this little animal; you'll be able to make either a gain or some

195

progress but at the expense of a friend.

Heels. Blisters, pains, sores, or any discomfort of the heels is a warning that you are in danger of being exploited by unscrupulous friends, associates, or even family connections. Losing or breaking a heel off your shoe predicts a sudden break in a long association; to dream of nailing or fastening a heel on a shoe indicates a social embarrassment. A dream featuring rubber or plastic heels signifies danger from a cuckoo in your nest of friends; take off the blinkers and open your ears.

Height. The sensation, in a dream, of being taller than you actually are is telling you that your problems are not as knotty as you like to make them out and that you can solve them through your own efforts if you really try. Otherwise, see *Altitude*.

Heirloom. An heirloom featured in your dream signifies dignity in your personal relations, recognition in your social circle, and/or honor in your business associations.

Heliotrope. This charming purple flower forecasts a quiet but satisfactory love life and a modest but secure future. See also *Flowers, Colors,* and *Perfume.*

Helium. Any dream featuring this gas is a prediction that both your time and money will be prudently invested.

Hell. A dream featuring the classic concept of hell is a forecast of an increase in income and/or material wealth but a decrease in social popularity; to dream of returning from hell indicates that you will face a terrific temptation to do something contrary to your principles.

Helmet. To see others wearing helmets indicates that you could run into problems created by your own lack of organization; but to wear a helmet yourself signifies that there are protective forces around you.

Help. See *Assist.*

Hem. To repair a hem or put one in a garment or other article predicts the satisfactory conclusion of pending affairs.

Hemorrhage. Whether it was your own or someone else's, any type of hemorrhage in a dream is telling you that you are on the verge of either mental or physical exhaustion, possibly both. Try to get more relaxation.

Hemorrhoids. A dream of this painful affliction usually has its origin in an internal disturbance. See your doctor.

Hemp. See *Rope*.

Hen. A black hen signifies sad news, a white one glad news, a brown one promises money luck, a fat one prophesies gain, a lean one mediocrity, a clucking one exciting gossip, and a pecking hen means you may have to back up and start again. A laying hen indicates prosperity; killing a hen forecasts ups and downs; and plucking one warns of an unexpected demand on your finances.

Herbs. Peace and contentment with your lot in life are forecast by a dream of herbs growing in a garden, especially auspicious if they were flowering. To smell the aroma of herbs predicts new and exciting adventures, possibly foreign travel.

Herd. See under separate animal listings or *Cattle*.

Hermaphrodite. Whether you dreamed of being one or seeing one, the dream is a warning to cut down your indulgence in the fleshpots!

Hermit. If you dreamed of seeing one, you are being reminded that nothing ventured may lead you not only to nothing gained, but also to boring stagnation; be a little adventuresome. On the other hand, if you dreamed of being a hermit, you can expect to have ups and downs but eventual peace of mind.

Hernia. See *Rupture*.

Hero. A sort of dream of contrary in that if you played the hero's part in your dream, you can expect to come in for some sharp criticism from your associates or from someone whose opinion you value; but if the hero in your dream was someone else, it predicts a profitable new offer.

Heroin. The use of this hard drug by yourself, or others, in a dream, signifies a serious loss of prestige through ill-considered behavior. A change of companions seems advisable.

Heron. You can expect some losses, but you will regain them and more if you dreamed of these exotic birds.

Herring. See *Fish*.

Hiccough. This dream usually has a physical (or organic) origin and is a warning against overindulgence in alcohol.

Hickory. Hickory wood in a dream forecasts hard work and not much joy, but hickory nuts are a sign of success in your current undertakings. See also *Trees, Nut(s)*, etc.

Hide. If you dreamed you were hiding, you are contemplating some action which you suspect (or know) you may later regret; don't be hasty. To dream of hiding some object or article suggests you are being secretive concerning a problem on which you could do with advice; confide in a trusted friend. If your dream featured animal hides, see *Animals*.

Hieroglyphics. See *Code*.

High School. See *School*.

Highway. To dream of a busy highway is an ob-

stacle dream and indicates an increase in present difficulties; however, if you crossed it, the omen is that things will get worse only before they get better, and the worries will suddenly disappear.

Hills. Another obstacle dream. The higher the hill, the greater the obstacle, but other factors must be correlated. See *Climb, Colors, Trees, Foliage*, etc.

Hindu. See *Foreign*.

Hinge. A rusty hinge predicts difficulties in connection with family or personal affairs; a squeaky hinge signifies that you will have to combat some malicious gossip. Otherwise, see *Hardware*.

Hippopotamus. This clumsy animal in its native habitat signifies a dangerous rival or hostile competitor; in captivity (or in a zoo) it forecasts a period of frustration or boredom which will require real initiative and energy to overcome.

Hips. Painful, injured, or sore hips in your dream indicate deception within your close circle; be careful where you place your confidence. To dream of the hips of the opposite sex is a warning against casual love affairs; very large hips predict unexpected gains.

Hiss. To hear or see a snake hiss in your dream is a warning that you will have to control your temper and/or your impulsive actions in order to avoid antagonizing someone whose respect you value. Human hissing is a dream of contrary. If you did it, you can expect to be caught in an embarrassing boo-boo; but if you were hissed at, your progress toward your goal may be slow but it will be steady.

History. If your dream featured historic occasions, it is alerting you to be prepared for a sudden opportunity to improve your circumstances which will present itself in the near future.

Hit. See *Blows, Fight, Slap,* etc.

Hitchhiking. A dream of hitchhiking is a suggestion to try to develop your self-reliance; if your dream involved picking up a hitchhiker, it is a warning of financial embarrassment; guard your credit.

Hive. A beehive is a symbol of prosperity and freedom from worry, unless you upset it or let the bees out, in which case it signifies troubles of your own making which will only become serious if you allow them to.

Hives. See *Allergy* or *Skin.*

Hoarse. There are discordant influences around you and you will soon have to make a decision to protect your resources if you dreamed of yourself or anyone else being hoarse.

Hoax. To be aware of a hoax, even a harmless one, in your dream indicates that you will be obligated to explain some past action which you assumed had been either unnoticed or forgotten.

Hobby. Any kind of hobby featured in a dream predicts annoying but basically unimportant changes.

Hobo. See *Tramp.*

Hockey. A game of hockey, whether on ice or field, augurs success through your own diligence. See also *Games* and *Sports.*

Hoe. Momentary frustration but improved future prospects are indicated in a dream featuring a hoe or hoeing.

Hog. A clean hog predicts unusual success through your own competence; a dirty hog or one in a wallow signifies a new profitable business offer; a wild hog is a warning of malicious gossip by a jealous acquaintance. Watch your step!

Hold. Holding something in your hand predicts recognition in community affairs; holding someone in your arms indicates coming personal happiness.

Hole. To step or fall into a hole is a warning against undesirable companions; reassess your relationships. A hole in a garment forecasts improving luck in financial matters. A dream of digging a hole predicts a sudden trip, and to observe holes made by others indicates easier times ahead.

Holiday. You will have to work hard but your efforts will be productive if you dreamed of a holiday.

Holland. See *Foreign*.

Holly. You'll be lucky with both money and friends if your dream featured holly, unless it pricked you, in which case it is a warning to avoid getting involved in some petty intrigue which could backfire to your great chagrin. See also *Bush, Foliage,* etc.

Hollyhock. See *Flowers* and *Colors*.

Holy. See *Church, Religion,* etc.

Home. If your dream featured a general atmosphere of homelife, it predicts small satisfactions and an adjustment to whatever your circumstances might be. Otherwise, see *House*.

Homesick. A dream of contrary. You will receive useful information through or from an absent friend.

Hominy. Be prepared to sit out a rather extended period of boredom if you dreamed of this dull boiled cereal.

Homosexual. Assuming that the dreamer is heterosexual, dreams of this nature suggest feelings of basic insecurity in relations with the opposite sex, and, perhaps, professional psychological advice would be beneficial.

Honey. Most ancient as well as modern sources agree that this is an unusually favorable dream predicting domestic, social, and temporal sweetness which is manifestly as lucky as anyone can get.

Honeymoon. There is some disagreement on the interpretation of this dream, but the consensus appears to be that whether it was your own or someone else's honeymoon, it is a dream of contrary and signifies disappointment in love or a personal relationship.

Honeysuckle. Whatever your status, this sweet scented flower is an auspicious omen promising love to the uncommitted, domestic bliss to the committed, and interesting new opportunities to those whose main concern is business.

Honor. Whether you were being honored or the recognition concerned others, this is a dream of contrary and is a warning to restrain your tendency to take people at face value.

Hood. To dream of yourself or others wearing a hood is a warning of deception by someone you trust. Be more selective about where you place your confidence.

Hoodlum. See *Gang*.

Hoof. An animal hoof featured in a dream pertains to financial matters and is a warning that you are in danger of being cheated, unless it was a cloven hoof, in which case it refers to affairs with the opposite sex and signifies embarrassing complications. See also *Animals*.

Hook. The significance here depends on the action. To be caught on a hook forecasts vexing difficulties, but if you were able to free yourself, your concern will be temporary. If, in your dream, you were using a hook to catch something, it predicts the solution of a long-term mystery; others using hooks signify an unexpected gain or surprise gift.

Hoop. Hoops of any kind are a happy dream omen for your current hopes.

Hop. See *Jumping* or *Skip*.

Hope. A dream which produced a feeling of hope in spite of difficulties can be considered as just that; a hopeful omen for the future.

Hops. To see them growing or harvested predicts coming prosperity, but to pick them forecasts a sudden passionate but short-lived love affair. See also *Grain*.

Horehound. To dream of horehound candy predicts a long period of peace of mind. If it was the plant, see *Herbs*.

Horizon. A sort of dream of contrary in that a far horizon to your dream signifies early success, but a near one predicts delays.

Horn. The sound of a horn heard in your dream signifies good news; if you blew a horn, you can expect increased social activity. An automobile horn is a warning against taking risks. Regarding animal horns see under separate heading of animal involved.

Hornet. Oddly enough a dream of suffering the sting of these nasty creatures is an omen of success in your current undertakings; otherwise they must be considered a warning against hostile associates.

Horoscope. A dream featuring your horoscope predicts the eventual achievement of contentment and security through your own patient efforts.

Horror. This element in a dream must be correlated with the features that figured in its cause in order to determine its meaning, therefore it need not, necessarily, be seen as an unfortunate omen.

Horse. The meaning of a dream featuring a horse or horses varies greatly with the details and the action so all the elements should be looked up, but as a general guide:

A dream of seeing horses predicts a period of all-around ease.

If your dream involved fear of the animal, it signifies worry over the loss or misplacement of an important document or article of value.

To dream of riding (or sitting on) a horse indicates a coming rise in status, but if you were thrown (or fell off) you will have to cope with a rival who is out to thwart you.

A bucking horse is an augury of unexpected resistance to some current plan.

To be kicked by a horse is a warning against complacency.

A dream of horses fighting is a forerunner to disturbing news concerning a friend.

To dream of a horse being shod is an omen of unexpected money.

Trading horses is a warning of deceit by someone you trust.

Cleaning or grooming a horse foretells a lucky speculation.

Advantageous news is forecast in a dream of seeing a foal, especially auspicious if seen with the mare.

Galloping or racing horses predict swift success.

Seeing a horseshoe in your dream is an omen of general good luck; finding one predicts wealth and/or success beyond your wildest expectations.

Color must also be considered in interpreting a horse dream and the meaning modified as follows: Black signifies delays. White intensifies the positive. Gray indicates preceding difficulties. Sorrel or Piebald pertains to confusion. Brown concerns mental pursuits, and Tan or Palomino relates to love affairs.

If your dream featured a game of horseshoes see *Quoits*. See also *Bridle* and *Saddle*.

Horseradish. You can expect some vexations in regard to the petty actions of friends or neighbors if your dream featured this hot-tasting root.

Hose. Changes of an adventurous nature are forecast in a dream of a squirting hose; however, if it was used on a fire, it indicates sexual satisfaction and/or an exciting new love affair. A sprinkler or hose sprayed on a lawn or garden predicts pleasant new friends and/or social occasions. See also *Stockings*.

Hospital. If you dreamed that you were taken to a hospital or were a patient in one, the dream is telling you that you are in imminent danger of being overwhelmed by some load you are trying to carry alone; don't be a proud fool—ask for help. A dream of visiting a hospital or helping in one predicts surprising news. See also *Nurse*.

Host(ess). A dream of being a gracious host or hostess is a forecast of improving conditions; however, if you played this part reluctantly you can expect some setbacks or delays in your plans.

Hostility. Directed at you in a dream, this element must be regarded as the needling of your conscience for a past unworthy action or injustice; try to make amends. If, in your dream, you demonstrated (or felt) hostility to others, you can expect to find yourself in an uncomfortable situation unless you control your impulsive reactions.

Hot Dog. See *Sausage(s)* and *Eating*.

Hotel. If you were alone in the hotel, the dream pertains to your business or financial interests; if you were with one of the opposite sex, it relates to your love life or domestic affairs, and the omen is one of contrary depending on the general atmosphere. If the hotel was, by your usual standards, ostentatious, or even very luxurious, it predicts failure or disappointment in the outcome of an important issue; but if it was the same type (or more modest than) you normally patronize, the forecast is one of satisfying achievement. However, the action and other elements of the dream should also be considered.

Hothouse. A well-kept hothouse is, as a rule, a good omen, signifying happiness in affairs of love or friendship and general stability; however other elements must be considered, such as the condition of the plants and/or flowers, etc. See also *Flowers, Plant(s), Fruit, Vegetable(s)*.

Hounds. To dream of being chased by bloodhounds suggests you should use more restraint regarding your indulgence in sensual pleasures. Otherwise, see *Dog*.

Hour. A dream in which you heard a clock strike or were otherwise made aware of the hour suggests that you are exerting your energy in the right direction; but to dream of sand running through an hourglass is a warning against wasting your time in meaningless pursuits.

House. An old house signifies a reunion or renewal of an old association. A new house predicts financial security. Building a house or seeing one under construction forecasts unexpected gain, possibly through a legacy; buying a house indicates a short but exciting love affair; selling a house augurs a release from pressing responsibilities. A dream which featured a house being demolished or being in an empty one suggests you are grieving over a recent loss, broken rela-

tionship, or missed opportunity; don't despair, time really DOES heal all things.

Housekeeper. See *Servant(s)*.

Hovel. See *Hut*.

Howl. The sound of either human or animal howling in a dream is a forecast of sad news.

Huckleberries. Any dream featuring huckleberries is a warning against general carelessness in the way you conduct either your personal or business affairs (or both!).

Hug. A friendly hug signifies relief from worry, but a passionate hug predicts an important change.

Hula. Exciting romantic adventures are forecast in a dream featuring this undulating dance form.

Hum. The sound of humming in a dream signifies news from a distance; if it seemed to stop for no particular reason, the news will be startling. To dream of humming yourself augurs a social uplift.

Humidity. Personal chagrin over a hasty misjudgment is forecast in a dream of discomfort due to humidity.

Humility. A dream of contrary. Humility in a dream is warning you to be less arrogant and more tolerant when dealing with others.

Humor. See *Fun*.

Hunchback. A hunchback in a dream is a symbol of luck similar to that of a horseshoe.

Hunger. A dream of being hungry may be regarded as a promise of better times ahead; to dream of others being hungry predicts money luck, possibly through an unexpected legacy.

Hunting. An obstacle dream. Whether you were looking for something that was lost, or hunting for game, the significance depends on the outcome of the quest. If you were successful in the dream, you will soon overcome your difficulties; if not, you will have to struggle yet awhile.

Hurdles. Another obstacle dream, but this one pertains to personal behavior and is a warning that you should try to avoid giving false impressions which could rebound to your discredit.

Hurricane. See *Cyclone*.

Hurry. The meaning of the dream depends on the reason for the hurry. If it was purely on your own account, the dream predicts personal worries; but if the hurry was for someone else's sake, you can expect a pleasant upturn in your affairs.

Hurt. A dream of contrary. If you dreamed of being hurt, you can expect a financial improvement; but if your dream involved others being hurt, it is a warning that you are in danger of being hurt by someone who is pretending to be other than they are.

Husband. An omen of contrary regarding love affairs. If you dreamed of being married when you aren't, it signifies a serious lovers' quarrel and/or a broken relationship.

Husking. A dream featuring this type of harvesting activity is auspicious for affairs with the opposite sex.

Hut. This dream is as contrary as they can get. The lowlier the hut the more secure will be your future.

Hyacinth. Growing out of doors, these heavily scented flowers forecast unexpected events; in pots they are a sign of improving circumstances. See also *Flowers, Plant(s)* and *Colors*.

Hydrant. A flowing hydrant is a forecast of fading worries; a burst hydrant predicts great wealth in the future; a dream of a fireman fastening a hose on a hydrant indicates a lucky escape from potential danger.

Hydroplane. Whether floating, taking off, or landing, a hydroplane in your dream signifies a satisfactory solution to a troublesome situation.

Hymn. See *Music* and *Singing.*

Hypnotism. A dream of being hypnotized is a warning to let sleeping dogs lie in regard to a past mistake. Confession may be good for your soul, but one must also remember that as far as others are concerned ignorance is frequently beneficial bliss. If your dream involved hypnotizing someone else, you'd better start economizing because you'll soon be under some delayed financial strain.

Hypocrite. If the element of hypocrisy in your dream was attached to someone else, you are being warned against making hasty decisions or judgments; but if you were guilty of the hypocrisy, it is a warning to guard your health.

Hysteria. To see someone else have hysterics indicates that you should resist outside pressure to act contrary to your own judgment; to dream of having hysterics yourself suggests that you could profit from the advice of trustworthy friends.

I

Ice. Some aspects of an ice dream are contrary omens and some are not. To sit on ice forecasts comfortable living conditions, but to walk on ice is a warning of loss through speculation. To slip, slide, or fall on ice indicates coming difficulties, whereas if you broke through the ice, it signifies that your greatest anxieties are groundless. Ice seen floating in clear water (as in a brook, stream, or lake) is a sign that you will overcome jealous opposition. Putting ice into drinks is a caution to stop wasting time, money, and energy on meaningless temporary pleasures. Ice skating by yourself signifies recognition for work well done, but skating with a partner is a warning against indiscreet behavior or indiscriminate sex relations. To see ice-laden trees or bushes indicates success after inexplicable delays, so don't get discouraged, persevere!

Iceberg. A pretty straightforward symbol of hidden opposition and/or obstacles which are more formidable than you realize; however, with determination and careful handling you can circumnavigate them.

Ice Cream. Whether your dream featured eating, making, buying, selling, or serving ice cream, it predicts important advantages and/or major success.

Icicles. Whatever your most distressing anxiety may be it will soon vanish if your dream featured icicles, unless they were dripping, in which case the dream is telling you that you should conserve your financial resources for the next few months.

Icon. A dream featuring an icon is telling you to accept changes calmly. Your anxieties are unnecessary; in the final analysis all will be well.

Idea. Getting a great idea in a dream predicts frustration, unless you recalled the idea when you woke up, in which case you can expect a stroke of unusual luck.

Idiot. Whether you dreamed of being an idiot yourself, or of others who were so afflicted, it is a dream of contrary and signifies success in all your undertakings through your own intelligent competence.

Idleness. If, in your dream, you were idle by contrast to others around you, it signifies that you will be obliged to make an embarrassing confidence or explanation.

Idol. Any dream featuring idols predicts that you are about to discover a secret or to learn the reason behind a perplexing situation. Keep the knowledge to yourself.

Ignorance. If the element of ignorance in your dream attached to others, you are in for a shock concerning someone you have trusted; however, if it was your own ignorance you were aware of, it is a dream of contrary and you can expect some well-deserved praise.

Iguana. This strange animal signifies an unusual social event and/or interesting new friends.

Illness. Disturbing dilemmas are predicted in a dream of being ill; if your dream involved others being ill, you can expect to be upset by a broken promise.

Illiteracy. To be aware in your dream of an illiterate person, or persons, indicates a growth of your responsibilities but the increase will give you great satisfaction.

Illumination. Any bright illumination in a dream, by whatever means, is an omen of great good fortune in that which concerns you most deeply.

Illusion. If you were aware in your dream that what you dreamed was an illusion, you can expect to receive some extremely valuable information which you must use judiciously.

Image. See *Pictures* or *Statue(s)*.

Imitation. See *Fake*.

Immodesty. A dream featuring immodest dress, actions, or language, whether your own or someone else's is a warning to guard your temper.

Immorality. Any action or atmosphere of this nature in a dream is a reminder that we all have failings and people who throw stones are apt to be hit by a ricochet; don't criticize unless you are above reproach.

Imp. See *Devil* or *Elf*.

Impale. A dream of this nature has the same significance as Hook.

Impatience. This trait in a dream, whether displayed by yourself or someone else, is a forerunner to confusion and disturbance within your close circle. Be on guard against making a hasty judgment.

Impersonation. If you dreamed of impersonating another, you can expect to be brought to account for some past act of omission or commission; but if you were taken in by an impersonation, you will probably make an interesting new friend very soon.

Impostor. To dream of being cheated by an impostor is a caution to prepare for a period of hard plodding.

Impotence. A dream of contrary. Success in your love life, as well as your other interests, will follow as surely as the wheels of the cart follow the heels of the ox.

Impudence. To dream of impudence, whether on your own part or that of others, predicts an unexpected rise in status.

Impurity. Another dream of contrary. Impurities which would normally constitute a hazard, discovered in your dream, signify happiness in personal and/or domestic life.

Inauguration. It is a favorable omen to dream of being present at an inauguration ceremony.

Incantation. Exciting new experiences are forecast in a dream of hearing strange incantations.

Incense. The burning or smell of incense in a dream predicts a lightening of your burdens, unless you found the odor unpleasant or the incense was in a church, in which case you must expect your worries to increase before they decrease.

Incest. A dream of incest is a warning that you are contemplating some discreditable action; resist the temptation no matter how strong the pressure or how promising the proposition. It will turn out to be a matter of lasting regret, if not remorse, if you give way.

Incision. Obviously, this dream has no significance for a surgeon, but if you are not one and dream of acting in this capacity, you are likely to have legal troubles. Make certain your records are in good order. See also *Scar(s)*.

Incoherence. If your dream featured unintelligible talk, you are likely to be embarrassed by the exposition of something you would prefer to keep hidden.

Income. A dream of opposite import. If it was comfortably large, it indicates a period of preoccupation with financial problems; but if it was low or insufficient in your dream, you can expect an increase or a relief from some financial burden.

Income Tax. Chagrin due to failure of an expected payment or alternatively to inability to assist a friend is likely to follow any dream concerning tax matters.

Incubator. Seen in a dream, incubators are a symbol of unnecessary anxiety. Relax; you'll be able to meet your obligations nicely.

Incubus. See *Nightmare*.

Indecency. See *Immodesty*.

Index. Improved relations with the opposite sex will follow a dream of looking in an index; a dream of compiling an index signifies social and/or business advancement.

India. See *Foreign*.

Indians. North American, South American, or Mexican Indians in a dream may be considered as good omens if they were friendly, but if they seemed hostile, the dream is a warning of treachery among your associates.

211

Indigestion. This dream generally arises from over-indulgence and has the obvious meaning—slow down. If the dream recurs, see your doctor.

Infant. See *Baby*.

Infection. A warning against possible losses through poor advice from friends is contained in a dream featuring even a small infection. If the contemplated speculation or investment is of an important size, get professional advice before you commit yourself.

Inferiority. An amusing contrast of meaning, for if your dream featured a feeling of inferiority, you can expect recognition for some superior achievement.

Infidelity. A dream of being unfaithful in any way is warning you to be more discriminating in regard to your choice of playmates.

Infirmary. See *Hospital*.

Infirmity. See *Weakness*.

Influence. If your dream was pervaded by an atmosphere of outside influence over your actions, you are being warned that mischievous plotting is going against you. Open your eyes—you

can discover the source.

Ingratitude. A dream of contrary. If you suffered from it, the omen is a happy one, but if you were guilty of it in your dream, your conscience is being gnawed by the worm of remorse. Try to make amends.

Inheritance. Receiving one in a dream is usually a straightforward prediction of a legacy to come.

Initiation. Happy social times are forecast in a dream featuring an initiation ceremony.

Injury. If the injury was to your reputation, it is a dream of contrary and signifies pleasing recognition; but if the feature of your dream was physical injury, it is a warning that you are surrounded by hostile forces and you must proceed very carefully in order to expose and thwart them.

Ink. Strangely enough, the spilling of ink in a dream signifies a satisfactory solution to a perplexing problem or difficult situation. To dream of making an ink blot while using a pen is a forerunner to a period of sadness. If the use of a blotter figured in your dream, you are in danger of being betrayed by a friend; be sure the ear into which you whisper your secrets is a trustworthy one. To pour ink into an inkstand predicts unexpected travel. See also *Writing* and *Colors*.

Inn. See *Hotel*.

Inoculation. Though money may be in short supply for the time being, you can be sure your creditors will be sympathetic and cooperative if you dreamed of being protected from disease by inoculation.

Inquest. New, but gratifying, responsibilities are forecast in a dream featuring an inquest.

Insanity. A sort of dream of contrary, as good news is predicted if you dreamed of being insane, but if your dream featured others so afflicted, you can expect an unpleasant surprise.

Inscription. See *Epitaph*.

Insects. An obstacle dream. If you succeeded in killing them or otherwise getting rid of them, or if they didn't annoy you, it signifies that your difficulties will be easier to overcome than you anticipate. If the insects were identifiable, see also under separate headings, as *Bees, Flies,* etc.

Insignia. A dream of seeing this type of identification signifies progress in spite of hostile competition; to dream of wearing insignia forecasts an exciting new love affair.

Insolence. See *Impudence*.

Insolvency. See *Bankrupt*.

Instruments. Medical instruments indicate family quarrels; other types of instruments signify family unity. For *Musical Instruments* see under that heading or under separate listing, as *Piano, Violin,* etc.

Insult. This is a classic example of a contrary omen; whether you took it or dished it out, it signifies loyalty from your friends and/or esteem from your associates.

Insurance. A peculiar omen of contrast in one aspect, and that is if you dreamed of collecting an indemnity, you are likely to have to cope with a setback; but if your dream involved buying insurance, you can rest assured that your plans for the future are sound.

Intemperance. See *Drink, Drunk,* and *Glutton.*

Intercourse. The interpretation of this dream depends on the details. If you were personally involved and you enjoyed the experience, it is, obviously, an omen of happy adjustment to your circumstances. If your dream featured others having intercourse, the meaning relates to whether or not your reactions were unpleasant. If they were, it is likely you are repressing an emotional problem and some psychological counseling might prove beneficial; if they were not, contentment and success will soon be yours. See also *Immodesty, Adultery,* etc.

Interest. To dream of paying it signals a warning to curb your extravagance; a dream of receiving it forecasts important changes in the offing.

Interpret. Money problems are predicted by a dream of either acting as an interpreter or having to use one.

Interruption. A serious disturbance in marital relations or a broken love affair is indicated in a dream of being interrupted while working or speaking.

Intestines. To dream of your own intestines is a sign of physical strain; get more rest. If the dream involved severe pain, see your doctor as soon as possible. A dream of human intestines other than your own signifies a period of worry concerning a close friend or a relative. Animal intestines featured in a dream predict an impressive improvement in your lifestyle.

Intolerance. If you dreamed of being intolerant, you will be disappointed in a friend; but if your dream concerned the intolerance of others, it predicts an unexpected gift of considerable value or a small legacy.

Intrigue. An element of intrigue in your dream suggests that you will be embarrassed by having your private affairs bandied about due to a breach of confidence by someone you trusted. Turn the bad experience to good account and be more discreet in the future.

Invalid. Delayed success is the message contained in a dream of being an invalid; if your dream concerned other invalids, you can expect an appeal for help from a friend or relation.

Invention. You are likely to achieve your dearest wish or highest hope if you dreamed of a new invention or of being or meeting an inventor.

Invisibility. A dream featuring the rare element of invisibility signifies swift and unexpected changes for the better.

Invitations. Written or printed these are an omen of contrary and indicate a period of depression or boredom, but given by word of mouth they forecast an increase in social activity.

Invulnerability. A dream of being impervious to danger is a warning to avoid any risks to your health for the time being.

Iodine. Whether white or brown, this chemical in your dream indicates that your troubles are of your own making and you can easily overcome them with a little constructive effort.

Ipecac. To take or give this emetic in a dream is a

sign of a sudden release from worry.

Ireland. See *Foreign*.

Iris. Whether indoors or out, these beautiful blooms seen in a dream predict contentment and prosperity. See also *Flowers*, *Colors*, and *Garden*.

Iron. Many of the ancient oracles believed that metal in a dream was a symbol of difficulties, but others preferred to regard them as a sign of strength. A consensus leads to the conclusion that iron in any form or color predicts slow but steady advancement toward the dreamer's ultimate goal.

Ironing. For a woman, the performance of this household chore in a dream signifies a joyous relief from some onerous burden; for a man, it predicts an unexpected profit or increased income.

Island. An obstacle dream if you were a castaway on one, and the outcome of your problem depends on whether or not you were rescued or succeeded in getting safely away. However, if your dream featured living on or visiting an island, you can expect to have a new and exciting experience shortly.

Israel. See *Foreign*.

Italy. See *Foreign*.

Itch. This dream indicates that you are a worrywart and you could be your own best friend if you'd give up nourishing yourself on gloom and start emphasizing the positive.

Ivory. Any form of ivory in a dream is a favorable omen for all that concerns you deeply.

Ivy. Growing out of doors ivy signifies faithful friends; indoors in pots it presages personal happiness; growing on a house it predicts future wealth; and twining around a tree it promises health and vigor. See also *Plant(s)* and *Foliage*.

Jab. A rather straightforward dream symbol which takes its meaning from the action or sensation involved. If, in your dream, you felt (or were given) a jab, it is telling you that you are standing in your own way by underestimating yourself. Try to be more forthcoming. However, if you dreamed of jabbing others, you must guard against a tendency to be overaggressive. Remember that you can catch more flies with honey than with vinegar.

Jabot. See *Collar*.

Jacaranda. This fragrant tropical tree is a sign of growing contentment.

Jack. An automobile (or mechanical) jack predicts a sudden relief from a heavy burden or an unexpected favorable change of conditions. If your dream concerned the card, see *Cards*.

Jackal. This wild dog in your dream is telling you that you need to protect yourself from overpersuasive friends with overambitious plans.

Jackass. See *Donkey*.

Jacket. See *Clothes* and *Colors*.

Jackknife. See *Knife, Blade, Cut*, etc.

Jackpot. An omen of contrary if you won it yourself; be prepared for a period of hard work with small reward; however, if you saw someone else win it, you can expect to gain something you want with less effort than you anticipate.

Jade. This lovely semiprecious stone featured in your dream predicts prosperity and/or protection against adverse influences.

Jaguar. See *Animals* or *Fur*.

Jail. An obstacle dream. Your difficulties will be short term if you escaped or were released; otherwise expect a long tough struggle. If your dream featured others in jail, it signifies freedom from worry.

Jam. This is another obstacle dream. Whether it was a logjam, traffic jam, subway jam, or whatever, it signifies delays, but have patience—all jams eventually give way to intelligent effort.

To make, eat, or serve jam in your dream forecasts happy domestic times ahead.

Janitor. To dream of being or seeing a janitor portends additional responsibilities which may seem onerous but will prove ultimately beneficial.

January. A dream of January when it isn't suggests that you will soon find the solution to a perplexing problem.

Japan. See *Foreign*.

Jars. Jars, featured in a dream, predict pleasant social affairs in the offing.

Jasmine. This flower in a dream is an omen of success in romantic or personal affairs.

Jaundice. See *Illness* or *Disease*.

Javelin. See *Spear*.

Jaws. Any dream concerning your own jaws, such as lockjaw, pain, injury, or whatever is a warning that you will have to cope with some malicious gossip which could damage your standing among those whose esteem you value. Don't rely on passive resistance, combat it actively. A dream featuring the jaws of others signifies financial gain through outside help. To dream that you see, or are in the grip of, the jaws of a monster portends a misunderstanding which could lead to a broken friendship. Don't be too quick to judge.

Jay. See *Birds* and *Colors*.

Jaywalk. If your dream featured others crossing against the signals, it's your conscience reminding you that you could be humiliated by the discovery of some foolish action you are contemplating; better forget it! However, if you did the jaywalking, you can expect some difficulty of a legal nature.

Jazz. Hearing this type of syncopated music in your dream is a warning against getting involved in social or community affairs which are beyond your means; better a slight social chagrin now than a financial embarrassment later. Of course, if you are a jazz aficionado, the dream has no special significance. See also *Music*.

Jealousy. You can expect to be heavily involved in a series of problems concerning your romantic (or marital) affairs, your profession (or job), and/or your important friendships if you dreamed of being jealous; however, if the element of jealousy was directed at you, it signifies that some overt hostility from which you now suffer will eventually turn out to your advantage.

Jeers. Another dream of contrary. If you were the subject of the dreamed derision, you will triumph over those who are pulling against you; but if you did the jeering or were

aware of it in connection with others, it is a warning to be less controversial or your lack of diplomacy could result in serious quarrels.

Jelly (or Jell-O). A dream featuring jelly, Jell-O, or gelatin signifies a period of gloom (or depression) due either to loss of a friend or to the exposition of something you'd have preferred stayed hidden— unless you ate it, in which case the augury is reversed.

Jellyfish. This squishy marine animal in your dream is a symbol of problems arising from false pretenses; be yourself; it's the only part you can effectively sustain over a long run.

Jeopardy. See *Danger*.

Jerusalem. To dream of this Holy City suggests loneliness; remember that to have a friend you must also be one.

Jessamine. All the best things in life are forecast in a dream featuring this beautiful and fragrant blossom. See also *Flowers*.

Jesus. Fortitude and consolation in adversity are forecast in a dream of Jesus, and if you spoke or prayed

219

with Him, or He touched you or you Him, you will be blessed with true peace of mind and contentment.

Jet. This black stone portends sad news, though not necessarily of a grievous nature. Concerning a jet of water, see *Fountain* and *Hose*.

Jetty. See *Quay*.

Jewelry. A display of real jewelry featured in your dream is a fortunate augury for your current interests, but a display of costume jewelry is a warning that you are in danger of being led astray through foolish vanity. A dream of stealing jewelry is a signal that extra caution is needed in regard to business affairs; to lose jewelry is an obstacle dream and the meaning depends on whether or not you recovered it. To give or receive jewelry, buy, or sell it pertains to love or domestic affairs and is considered a fortunate omen, whereas to wear it is a warning against impulsive behavior or shady transactions. The meaning of any jewelry dream must also be correlated to the details, such as the type of the pieces, i.e., ring, necklace, earring, bracelet, etc., as well

as the color and kind of the jewels. See *Amethyst*, *Diamonds*, *Emerald*, etc.

Jew's Harp. If you played it, it signifies foreign travel or foreign visitors in the near future; however, if you only saw one or heard it, it predicts good business news or a welcome change of circumstances.

Jig. To dream of dancing a jig alone predicts that you will soon have cause to feel lighthearted, but if you were doing this dance with a partner, it is a warning against overindulgence in sexual activity. To see others jigging indicates that you are too easy (or careless) regarding money and are in danger of having your generosity abused. Conserve your funds for the time being.

Jigsaw. See *Puzzle* or *Saw*.

Jilted. A dream of contrary signifying success in your love affairs or constancy in your marriage, whichever applies.

Jingle. To dream of reciting a jingle or hearing one repeated signifies the enjoyment of a harmless flirtation. The jingle of small bells of any kind forecasts gay social times ahead;

however, the jingle of money is a dream of contrary and predicts a financial loss, but so small as to be all but inconsequential.

Job. A sort of dream of contrary. If you were seeking a job or lost one, you can expect a promotion or other beneficial event; but if you dreamed of being offered a job, it is a warning to pay closer attention to your responsibilities.

Jockey. The significance of this dream varies according to the sex of the dreamer. For a woman, it predicts a surprise proposal (or proposition); for a man, it is a warning to control his passion.

Joints. Oddly enough, a dream of painful joints predicts an increase in material wealth, unless you actually suffer from such trouble, in which case the dream obviously has no significance.

Joke. The meaning of a joke dream depends on the action and reaction. If you heard a joke and were amused, it indicates a disagreement with a friend or an embarrassing social predicament in the offing; to dream of telling a success-ful joke is an omen of business success, but if it was a dud, it predicts a personal disappointment. Dirty or offensive jokes forecast large profits.

Joker. A dream featuring this card is warning you that your idleness could make someone else richer. Get busy.

Jonah. Money disputes are forecast in a dream featuring this Old Testament character.

Jonquil. An unusually happy and successful sex life is promised in a dream of these lovely spring blooms. See also *Flowers* and *Colors.*

Joss. See *Incense.*

Journey. Changes are predicted in a dream of a journey, but whether for better or worse depends on the details which should be carefully considered. As a general guide pleasant journeys indicate favorable changes, disagreeable ones the reverse; however, the meaning will be modified by such things as the weather, the scenery, the mode of transportation, etc. See also *Travel.*

Jowls. You will have to cope

with a relative or close associate who will try to ride roughshod over you if your dream featured heavy or pendulous jowls. Be firm about protecting your own interests.

Joy. To dream of an atmosphere or feeling of joy on a proper occasion is a promise of domestic happiness; however, if the joy was of a vindictive nature or at an unseemly time, you can expect to be called to account for a past indiscretion.

Judas. A dream of this betrayer is a warning to be cautious in accepting new friends; no matter how attractive they may appear, go slow and let them prove themselves first.

Judge. A time of trials, troubles, and thankless tasks is forecast in a dream which features a judge, being a judge, or being judged. However, you can console yourself with the assurance that the troubles will be temporary.

Jug. Full jugs indicate good friends, and to drink from a jug predicts happiness through vigorous health and an optimistic outlook. A broken jug signifies an influential new friend or

an exciting new romance.

Juggler. You will be dubious concerning an opportunity for quick and easy profit or alternatively an offer of advancement if you dreamed of this kind of art, but don't hesitate; just latch on and count your blessings.

Juice. To dream of drinking juice of any kind signifies that financial help will be forthcoming when you need it. To dream of serving juice indicates you will have a surprise request for a loan.

Jujitsu. See *Karate*.

July. A dream of July when it isn't is a warning to be cautious about accepting new offers no matter how attractive they seem. Investigate thoroughly.

Jumping. This dream has a similar meaning to that of climbing. You will overcome your trials and tribulations through patience and perseverance.

June. To dream of June when it isn't signifies an exciting new romance, and if you are not eligible, you'll be close enough to share the excitement.

Jungle. You are being warned to guard your resources and avoid getting involved in someone else's financial problems if your dream featured a jungle, unless you were walking in it, in which case it indicates a foolish romantic entanglement which you would be wise to cut before it becomes a serious problem.

Juniper. This tree is a symbol of danger from treachery; be very circumspect in all your actions, words, and dealings for a few months following a dream in which it was featured, unless you cut it down or it was in poor condition, in which case it is an omen of good luck. To dream of picking or eating its berries is a caution against undesirable companions who could cause you serious concern.

Junk. A dream of anything which struck you as junk, whether in a shop or elsewhere, predicts that you will soon be faced with a perplexing choice. Don't try to make it alone; get a friendly opinion.

Junket. You are wasting your time and energy on meaningless pleasures.

Jury. To dream of seeing a jury signifies recognition and prestige among those whose opinion you value; but a dream of serving on a jury is telling you to rely more on your own intuition and less on the opinion of others when it comes to making important decisions.

Justice. You may, from time to time, have to suffer some injustice in the form of undue criticism, but a successful future will surely be yours if you dreamed of the lady with the scales.

Kaleidoscope. You can expect a period of swiftly changing patterns and new interests in your life if your dream featured one of these fascinating instruments.

Kangaroo. If the kangaroo was jumping and had a young one in her pouch, it signifies an unexpected and exciting trip. Otherwise, see *Animals*.

Karate. If your dream involved others demonstrating or using this system of self-defense, you should be prepared for a surprise obstacle to your long-range ambition or plans; but if you were learning or engaging in the art yourself, you can expect your current affairs to flourish.

Katydid. To hear its song predicts the renewal of an old friendship; otherwise, see *Grasshopper*.

Keepsake. It is an omen of good luck to dream of giving a keepsake, but if you dreamed of being given one, it is a warning against allowing a trivial family argument to be magnified into a serious quarrel. Don't be stubborn.

Keg. A symbol of contrast in meaning. Full, it signifies reverses, whereas an empty keg predicts prosperity. If you had no indication as to contents, the dream forecasts a gay social occasion.

Kelp. You can cheer up if you dreamed of this useful sea plant. It's a sign of better times ahead.

Kennel. A dream concerning a kennel suggests that you are frustrated regarding an influential person who refuses to be friendly. Forget it; you can't win them all, and you will find that this one is not so important as you imagined.

Kernels. Whether you gathered them, bought them, planted them, scattered them to the birds, or whatever, kernels of grain or corn predict a valuable gift or unexpected reward.

Kerosine. The smell or use of this fuel in your dream indicates the dawn of new interests after a period of boredom.

Ketchup. An intriguing new friend of the opposite sex is predicted in a dream featuring this national weakness.

Kettle. If it was bright and/ or bubbling merrily away, it signifies domestic contentment; but if it was dull or dry, it indicates that some unexpected expense is looming over you. Hold on to your money; you're going to need it.

Kettledrum. A dream of this big boomer is a warning to cut down on your favorite vice—whatever it may be—overindulgence will lead to anxiety, if not actual illness.

Key(s). The meaning of a dream featuring keys varies according to the action, but as a general guide:

To find keys signifies a happy solution to any pressing problems you may now have.
To lose keys indicates some unexpected unpleasantness, or disappointment in a friend.
To give someone a key forecasts an improvement in home conditions.
To be given a key is a sign of help from influential friends.
To fit a key in a lock pertains to satisfaction in sex and/or romantic relations.
To turn the key in a lock predicts the opening of new doors.
A broken key portends a lost opportunity.
To dream of being a keeper of the keys augurs a position of authority.

Keyhole. If your dream featured a keyhole without a key in it, you are being warned against a treacherous friend; and if you dreamed of peeping through a keyhole or observing someone else looking through one, you are being cautioned against impulsive behavior which

225

could be misinterpreted to your great chagrin.

Khaki. See *Colors* or *Uniform.*

Kick. A pretty straightforward dream symbol. To be kicked, by man or beast, portends anxiety caused by strong competition, but if you did the kicking, you can expect an improvement in your conditions and/or position.

Kid. A new friend who walks in the corridors of power is forecast in a dream featuring a young goat.

Kidnap. If you were kidnapped in your dream, you are likely to be embarrassed by the company you have been keeping; a change of companions would probably be beneficial. However, if you did the kidnapping, you are being warned to guard your valuables against theft or loss, and if you can't do that, then be sure your insurance is in order. To dream of a kidnapping in which you were not personally involved is a sign of sudden important changes in the offing.

Kidney. To dream of your own kidneys suggests that a medical checkup might be advisable. A dream of eating, cooking, or serving kidneys is a warning against speculative ventures.

Killing. If you dreamed of killing someone, whether intentionally or by accident, it signifies a period of severe emotional stress during which you must make a heroic effort to control your temper. To dream of being a witness to a killing portends a change which will not be entirely to your liking. A dream of seeing others kill insects or animals prophesies help from friendly sources, but to dream of killing them yourself predicts that you will overcome your obstacles through your own efforts.

Kilt. You are likely to take an unexpected trip if your dream featured a Highlander in his native dress; otherwise the kilt itself has no special significance and must be related to other factors of the dream. See *Clothes, Colors,* etc.

Kindergarten. The action in the dream must be analyzed for an accurate interpretation, but anything to do with children of this age is considered to be a generally good omen.

Kindling. See *Fire, Gas,* etc.

King. Happiness, prestige, and prosperity are forecast in a dream of being, seeing, or meeting royalty, unless the dream had some embarrassing or unpleasant element in it, in which case it is a warning that you could be victimized by underhanded gossip, so keep your private affairs to yourself. If your dream concerned the playing cards of this denomination, see *Cards.*

Kingfisher. This beautiful blue fellow takes his meaning from his lovely color and is a symbol of great good luck.

Kiss. The meaning of a dream kiss depends on the circumstances involved. If the kissing was pleasant, proper, and a sincere token of affection, it predicts happiness and contentment; but if it was of a perfunctory, meaningless, insincere, or illicit nature, it signifies a false friend or disappointment in a love affair. A dream of kissing babies or small children forecasts success in a difficult undertaking. To dream of trying to avoid a kiss from someone you dislike portends a minor illness or a vexing experience.

Kitchen. Another dream which depends, for its meaning, on the general atmosphere. If the kitchen was modern and/or attractive and well-kept, it predicts good news or happy social events; if it was messy, run down, or bare, it indicates that your health may be a bit under par and a medical checkup might be in order.

Kite. An obstacle dream. Whether you flew it yourself or observed others doing it, you can expect to achieve your highest hopes if the kite flew easily, and the happy omen is intensified if children were involved; however, if the string broke or the kite was damaged or blew away, you should be prepared for disappointment due to careless management of your affairs.

Kitten. For a woman, a dream of playful kittens predicts a pleasant but unimportant romantic affair; for a man, it signifies a disappointment in love.

Kleptomania. To dream you have this uncontrollable

urge to steal things you don't need, or to see others so afflicted, is a warning to curb impulsive actions which could be deliberately misinterpreted to your disadvantage.

Knapsack. A full or heavy knapsack (or rucksack) predicts a pleasant trip or vacation; an empty one suggests an upcoming period of financial strain.

Knave. See *Jack*.

Kneading. If your dream featured the kneading of dough or clay, it is telling you that it's time you stopped being putty in other people's hands. Assert yourself more and you will find that the results will be beneficial.

Knee. To dream that your knees were shaky is an indication that you are contemplating an illicit liaison or a shady deal. Don't do it; it will develop into a large-sized headache.

Kneel. Whether your dream concerned yourself or others kneeling for any reason except prayer, the dream is warning you that you are in danger of being cheated; curb your tendency to be overgenerous.

Kneeling in prayer predicts reasons for thanksgiving.

Knell. An omen of contrary. Exciting new opportunities for advancement will soon come your way.

Knife. A sharp knife signifies personal strife; a rusty knife means family troubles; a broken knife indicates failure in love; an open switchblade knife or penknife predicts legal troubles, a closed one suggests financial reverses; a dull knife portends hard work with little reward. To cut yourself with a knife is a warning that you could be embarrassed by a neglected creditor; don't stretch goodwill too far. See also *Cut* and *Blade*.

Knight. Knights in armor are straightforward symbols of security and protection, so lucky you if you saw one (or more) in your dream.

Knit. You will be blessed with peace of mind and a contented homelife if you dreamed of knitting, unless you dropped stitches or had to unravel, in which case a spell of domestic strife is indicated. A dream of very fancy knitting such as argyle or intarsia patterns predicts the renewal of an old friendship or the acquisition of a new, unusually interesting one. Of course if you are in fact a habitual or very skilled knitter, the dream has no significance.

Knob. You can expect a stroke of unusual luck if you dreamed of a knob, and if it was a doorknob, it might be a propitious time for a little speculation or even a gamble if you are so inclined.

Knock. If you were doing the knocking, the dream is warning you against loose talk and/or companions; however, if you merely heard the knocking (or saw others doing it), it represents the sound of approaching money.

Knot. An obstacle dream signifying serious differences with someone close to you. If you succeed in untying the knot, you are likely to reach a satisfactory compromise, but if you cut it, a break is forecast.

Knuckle. Whether the knuckles featured in your dream were your own or someone else's, they indicate that you are wasting time and energy on an exercise in futility; reassess your goals.

Ku Klux Klan. These hooded figures in a dream are a reminder that no lasting good can come of sacrificing your ethics or principles for the sake of material gain. Resist the temptation.

Label. A dream in which you were specifically aware of the label on a container of any kind, or in a garment, is a forecast of profit from a business venture or an investment. If your dream concerned labels on boxes, trunks, baggage, or just unattached labels, it predicts a surprise, most probably in the form of an unexpected trip or a visitor from a distance.

Labor. Steady and satisfying progress is predicted by a dream concerning construction labor; however, if the workmen were idle, or there was an unpleasant atmosphere or aspect in the dream, it indicates an emotional upset. To dream of having labor pains is a forecast of achievement but only after hard work. A dream concerning labor politics signifies a coming improvement in your cir-

cumstances.

Laboratory. A dream concerning a laboratory signifies a successful risk, unless you actually work in one, in which case the dream has to be interpreted in terms of the action rather than the place.

Laburnum. This tree in bloom predicts that you will overcome the adverse influences around you by vigorous application of intelligent effort. See also *Trees* and *Foliage*.

Labyrinth. Obviously another obstacle dream. If you found your way out or were not worried by the maze in your dream you can expect to solve your problems with a minimum of effort; however, if you were lost or frightened in your dream, you can expect to be frustrated by some puzzling opposition and a change of direction might be advisable.

Lace. A dream of lace or garments made of lace signifies unusual popularity with the opposite sex and/or success in love affairs. To dream of making lace indicates profits acquired through questionable dealings. Lace curtains warn against a tendency toward preoccupation with passing pleasures, and paper lace is a caution not to put too much confidence in appearances.

Lacquer. See *Paint*.

Ladder. Although a ladder dream follows the general rule that up is good and down is not, its meaning is greatly modified by the other elements, details, and action. For instance if, in your dream, you were climbing a very high ladder and reached the top, the predicted achievement will be greater than if the ladder was of medium height or low. If a rung of the ladder broke under you, you may not attain your greatest ambition but you will achieve financial security. The disappointment signified in a dream of descending a ladder is mitigated if you used the ladder to escape from danger. If a ladder fell on you, it portends trouble ahead due to quarrels or malicious gossip; if you fell from it, you are being warned that your grasp is greater than your reach. To walk under a ladder in your dream is, contrary to the popular superstition, a sign of good luck. If you saw a ladder break or fall, you can expect to have to contend with some unanticipated obstacles in your path. To dream of carrying a ladder indicates that you will have to come to the rescue of a relative or close friend. A dream featuring the use of a rope ladder signifies success in some activity or business venture of an unusual type. To dream of feeling dizzy on a ladder is a reminder that arrogance or overconfidence frequently goes before a fall. A dream of entering a house or other structure by way of a ladder indicates misdirected efforts; reassess your plans.

Ladybug. These amusing creatures in a dream are a sign of easy success in modest endeavors.

Lair. A lair in a dream is a symbol of a coming struggle. If the animal was in the den, you will overcome

231

the obstacle, but if not, you must either be prepared to find a way around it or to back up and start again.

Lake. The interpretation of this dream depends on its various aspects, such as the condition of the water, the weather, etc., but as a general guide:

A stormy lake predicts a failure which, if you refuse to let it depress you, will lead to an important benefit. To dream of a calm lake in good weather signifies smooth sailing on the sea of life. A moonlit lake augurs a happy love life. A dream of traveling around a lake or observing one from the air is a sign of passive stagnation; try to find some new interests. To dream of wading into a lake indicates unnecessary anxieties; take life more calmly.

Lamb. If you dreamed of carrying a lamb, you can expect a period of solid satisfaction; baby lambs predict an uplifting experience; to see lambs gamboling in a field signifies happy domestic occasions; a dream of eating, serving, or cooking lamb indicates an increase in material wealth; to find a lost lamb forecasts the re-

newal of a valued friendship; to hear lambs bleating indicates new, but pleasant, responsibilities.

Lame. See *Cripple*.

Lament. See *Sorrow*.

Lamp. Whether the lamps were oil, gas, or electric, lighted ones signify success, and if you were carrying one, your success will be crowned by distinction and prestige. To light a lamp predicts an unexpected reward for a past kindness; to put out a lamp suggests a holiday or a well-earned rest. An unlit lamp indicates a disappointment; a dim or flickering lamp forecasts news of an illness; to hang a guide lamp outdoors or in a window augurs a stroke of good luck; to break a lamp portends difficulties through lack of trust; many bright or decorative lamps are a sign of coming festive occasions, and red lamps are exactly what you'd expect—a warning of danger due to uncontrolled passion or temper. A lamppost in your dream is an omen of family troubles.

Land. If you dreamed of owning land, you can expect an important improvement in your circumstances, unless you actually own some, in which case the dream predicts temporary reverses.

Landing. Whether in connection with a plane, boat, or ship, a safe landing signifies a solid and satisfying achievement.

Landscape. The meaning of this dream depends on your reaction to the landscape; if it struck you as being beautiful or pleasing, it signifies bright future prospects; but if it was ugly or unpleasant in any way, you must be prepared to sit out a season of dissatisfaction.

Lane. A dream featuring a narrow or country lane is a caution to be more discreet in your affairs with the opposite sex.

Lantern. A swinging lantern is a warning of danger through indiscriminate sex relations; cool it! If your dream featured a lantern blown out by the wind, you are likely to have some minor legal troubles.

Lap. Sitting on the lap of one of the opposite sex forecasts an exciting new love affair; a dream of slipping or falling off someone's lap predicts a loss of status

through foolish behavior.

Lapis Lazuli. This beautiful blue gemstone featured in your dream is a sign of peace of mind through a happy adjustment to your lot in life.

Lard. If lard was the main feature of your dream, you are being warned against dealing or associating with people of questionable character; be firm, no matter how persuasive or plausible they seem.

Larder. See *Pantry*.

Lark. A lark in flight predicts quick success; to hear the song of a lark signifies joyful news; a caged, injured, or dead lark is a warning that your grasping attitude could cause you a loss; try to give others more consideration.

Laryngitis. To dream of losing your voice is a warning not to gamble or take any unnecessary risk for the next few weeks. Otherwise, see *Hoarse*.

Lasso. Swinging a lasso in your dream is a happy omen for love or domestic affairs, providing it was done with reasonable skill; but if the rope got tangled, or you were caught in the

233

loop, you are in for an embarrassing experience.

Late. If you dreamed of being late, it's your conscience telling you to refrain from making promises you can't keep; if your dream featured others being late, it's a warning that you need to curb your extravagance to avoid financial difficulties.

Lathe. See *Machinery*.

Lather. Regardless of what it was on, lather featured in your dream signifies the solution to a pressing problem, probably through news from a distance.

Latin. A dream of seeing something written in Latin, or hearing it spoken, portends a rather long period of frustration; but if you can find the patience to stick it out, things will eventually change to your advantage.

Latrine. See *Toilet*.

Laughter. There is some difference among authoritative sources, but the consensus seems to be that this should, in the main, be interpreted as a dream of contrary, unless the dreamed laughter was that of children, in which case

it predicts a stroke of money luck. Otherwise, if you were laughing in your dream, it signifies approaching unhappiness or disappointment in love, and if you heard others laughing, it portends a broken friendship.

Laundry. A dream of doing your own laundry predicts that you will receive unexpected benefits (either social or financial) through an acquaintance on whom you made a strong impression. To dream of being in a laundry is a sign of approaching festivity. If your dream concerned sending laundry out, it is a warning against repeating gossip.

Laurel. If your dream concerned laurel growing out of doors, it predicts success and contentment; if you picked laurel in your dream, the forecast is of triumph over enemies or obstacles; if you dreamed of being crowned with laurel, the dream is reminding you that pride often goes before a fall, so don't let good luck go to your head.

Lava. Molten rock, seen in a dream, coming from a volcano, is a sign that your social life will become more exciting, but you may have to juggle your budget to keep up; however, you should find the effort worthwhile.

Lavatory. Any business affairs or important issues now hanging in the balance will come to a satisfactory conclusion if you dreamed of going to the lavatory.

Lavender. To see lavender growing or to smell its aroma in a dream predicts pleasant affairs with the opposite sex. See also *Colors, Flowers, Plant(s), Garden,* etc.

Law (and Lawyers). To dream of being involved with the law predicts some disagreeable business experiences. If you retained a lawyer in your dream, you are being warned against carelessness in money matters. To dream of winning a lawsuit is an omen of contrary; you are likely to be on the losing side of a serious difference of opinion. A dream of being sued is a warning against casual love affairs. To dream of being a lawyer augurs unexpected good news.

Lawn. A lovely, green, well-kept lawn is a forecast of domestic or personal contentment, but a neglected, weedy, or discolored lawn signifies that there are hostile influences around you at the moment and you would be well advised to avoid any changes for the time being. To dream of mowing or watering a lawn predicts a long happy life.

Laxative. To dream that you had to take a laxative predicts that you will be called on to perform a difficult duty which will, however, be to your eventual credit, but if your dream concerned administering a laxative, it signifies a gain where you expected a loss. See also *Constipation, Bowel Movement,* and *Feces.*

Laziness. Popularity and social success are forecast in a dream of being pleasantly lazy, but if the laziness was of the neglected-duties variety, you can expect some family or business disagreements.

Lead. Lead featured in a dream is a symbol of unhappiness, signifying domestic quarrels, disappointment in love, or business troubles. Don't do anything hasty for the time being.

Leaf (or Leaves). Green leaves signify abundance, good health, and happiness, but wilted or dry leaves are a warning that you will have to cope with malicious competition. Falling leaves predict a parting from friends; leaves blowing in the wind forecast family squabbles; leaves on a stem with fruit or blossoms are a sign of approaching money. See also *Foliage* and *Trees*.

Leak. A leak, as such, is a symbol of wasted energy in the form of futile efforts, but a more specific meaning can be determined by correlating the other details of the dream with the source and type of the leak. See *Faucet, Water, Pipe(s), Hose, Gas, Boat,* etc.

Lean. A dream of contrary. If you were leaning on someone or something in your dream, it predicts independence, but if someone was leaning on you, it signifies that you will need help to support an unexpected burden. Don't try to go it alone; there are times when we all need help of one kind or another.

Leap. See *Jumping.*

Learn. If, in your dream, you were seriously trying to learn a new skill, language, or subject which you found difficult, the dream is telling you that you may have bitten off more than you can chew and you had better rethink your situation. On the other hand if the dreamed learning came easy, it predicts a rise in prestige through your own diligent efforts.

Lease. A lease featured in a dream is a fortunate omen for whatever concerns you most.

Leather. Anything made of leather is, as a general rule, a lucky omen, but the meaning will be modified by the type of leather, the action, and the article involved. See *Buying, Handbag, Purse, Halter, Animals,* etc.

Lecture. To dream of listening to a lecture is a sign of limited success; to dream of giving a lecture predicts a pleasant change of surroundings.

Ledger. See *Accounts.*

Leech. A dream featuring this repulsive bloodsucker predicts that you are likely to have an unexpected demand on your resources, but don't get depressed, the strain will be temporary.

Leek. To see the plant growing in a garden signifies slow progress, but a dream of eating, cooking, or serving this type of onion predicts a quick rise in status.

Left. If your dream featured the left side of anything, or a left turn or direction, it is telling you not to be discouraged by a temporary setback; persevere and you will ultimately attain your goal. A dream of being left-handed if you are not indicates an awkward personal situation or a dangerous rival; but if you are actually left-handed, the dream predicts better times ahead.

Leg. A dream concerning any injury, deformity, swelling, bruising, or blemish of the legs signifies financial difficulties the degree of which will be in ratio to the seriousness of the leg troubles. A dream of skinny legs is a warning of embarrassment due to an ill-advised romance, but a dream of beautiful legs forecasts a happy change of circumstances. See also *Calf.*

Legacy. This is considered to be a very lucky dream, unless the source of the legacy was a member of your immediate family, in which case it indicates a season of vexing annoyances.

Lemon. Not a particularly auspicious omen, but its portent is modified by the action in your dream. If the lemon was sucked, it portends social difficulties or embarrassment; if it was being squeezed, it indicates upcoming money problems and a need for economy; however, to dream of making, serving, or drinking lemonade predicts an increase in personal popularity. See also *Fruit, Trees,* and *Leaf.*

Leopard. These spotted cats are a symbol of dangerous enemies or rivals, but their meaning in your dream can be determined by reference to the other details. See *Animals.*

Leper. You are likely to be in for a period of hardship and frustration if your dream concerned leprosy.

Lessons. See *Learn.*

Letter. In a dream concerning letters the meaning depends on the content. If you dreamed of receiving good news in a letter, your prospects are very bright indeed; but if the letter contained anything of a disappointing or upsetting nature, it portends an approaching struggle. Unimportant or routine letters signify financial difficulties due to overstretched credit. To dream of writing a love letter is a sign of regret over a foolish love affair. If your dream concerned destroying an unopened letter, it signals a need to make amends for a past injustice. To dream of reading a letter addressed to someone else portends a money loss, but a dream of mailing a letter predicts unexpected good news, and a chain letter indicates an unusual new experience in the offing. A bundle of love letters featured in your dream suggests that you would benefit from relieving your conscience of a guilty secret; filing letters or looking for letters in a file augurs an improvement in your circumstances. A letter delivered by messenger rather than by post indicates discord in small matters; letters written in brightly colored ink signify domestic problems; and to dream of hiding a letter or finding a hidden letter is a warning against an unfaithful friend or lover.

Lettuce. See *Vegetable(s)* and *Eating*.

Lewdness. Lewd behavior in a dream signifies a tempting offer to participate in a profitable but slightly unethical venture; let your conscience be your guide.

Library. A generally fortunate omen but particularly auspicious for those engaged in artistic or creative activities.

Lice. These nasty creatures signify petty annoyances and frustrations due to the stupidity or stubborness of others, unless you killed the lice or otherwise got rid of them in your dream, in which case the dream augurs a period of good luck.

Lick. To dream of being licked by an animal predicts that you will shortly be asked to advise a friend or relative in a serious matter; be as helpful as possible but avoid getting personally involved. A dream of being licked by a baby forecasts a happy outcome to your current problems. If your dream concerned licking something yourself, it indicates satisfaction in passing small matters.

Lie. If you dreamed that you told lies, you can expect to have trouble due to your own foolish behavior; but if your dream featured others telling whoppers, it predicts help from an unexpected source. See also *Perjury*.

Lift. A dream of lifting someone or being lifted by another person predicts happiness and personal prestige. See also *Carry, Burden,* etc.

Light. Daylight featured in your dream is promise of renewed hope. A beam of light, as from a spotlight or arc light, signifies the sudden solution to a longstanding problem. Otherwise, see *Candle, Electricity, Lamp, Lantern, Fire, Gas, Searchlight,* etc.

Lighthouse. A lighthouse seen at night is a sign of good luck in both love and business affairs; seen in daylight it predicts a long journey, likely to be abroad; however, the condition of the water should also be taken into account for an accurate interpretation.

Lightning. Luck like a bolt from the blue will surely follow a dream of this electrical phenomenon of nature, unless it was accompanied by rain and thunder, in which case it is still an omen of good luck, but in this case it will be preceded by a period of anxiety. Heat lightning forecasts exciting social events; a lightning rod featured in your dream indicates possible interference in your current plans due to hidden jealousy. Be careful about where you place your confidence.

Lilac. Whether in bloom out of doors or inside a vase, these fragrant blossoms predict a broken friendship which will cause you heartache at the time but will subsequently prove to have been a blessing in disguise. See also *Flowers* and *Colors*.

Lily. Easter lilies or calla lilies in a dream predict a sudden rise in status, but lilies of the valley signify happiness in love affairs and/or contentment in homelife.

Lime. A dream concerning chemical lime predicts an upturn in money matters. For the fruit or trees, see *Lemon*.

Limp. See *Cripple*.

Linen. See *Cloth*.

Lint. The meaning of a dream concerning lint is similar to that of dust. Otherwise, See *Bandage* or *Gauze*.

Lion. A lion featured in your dream is a symbol of social distinction and/or business leadership. If you heard the lion roar, you are likely to have to cope with jealousy from someone close to you. A friendly lion cub is a forecast of a new and valuable friendship. See also *Animals*.

Lips. Thin or cruel lips in a dream are a warning against making hasty judgment of others. Beautiful lips signify a successful sex life and happiness in love. Thick, overly sensual, or ugly lips forecast failure in love but success in business. Chapped, dry, or sore lips indicate a loss of status or business reverses. Children's or a baby's lips are a sign of true friendship where you least expected it.

Lipstick. See *Cosmetics*.

Liver. To dream of having liver trouble is a sign of improving conditions. Improving health is forecast in a dream of eating, cook-ing, or serving liver. Taking or giving liver oil in a dream predicts a passing but pleasant romance.

Lizard. This reptile in a dream is a warning that you have false friends in your close circle. A dead lizard signifies a successful battle to protect your reputation. Shoes, bags, or other items made of lizard skin predict an increase in income.

Llama. A dream featuring this native of the Andes, or of the superfine cloth made from its wool, predicts a high order of success in your current undertakings.

Load. See *Burden*.

Loan. See *Borrow*.

Lobster. Live lobsters in a dream signify approaching difficulties, but of an annoying rather than limiting nature. To eat, cook, or serve lobster predicts the recovery of something you thought lost, repayment of a forgotten loan, or receipt of an overdue sum of money.

Lock. To dream of picking a lock predicts an embarrassment due to involvement in someone else's affairs. If your dream fea-

tured a padlock, it signifies a probable need for legal advice or legal services to sort out some family or personal matters. See also under *Key(s)* and *Bolts*.

Lockjaw. A straightforward warning that your tendency to indiscreet talk could involve you in serious trouble. Try to remember that discretion is more admirable than momentary popularity.

Locomotive. The meaning of a dream featuring a locomotive depends on the action. If you were driving it, the augury is one of solid achievement; if you were riding in it, you can expect a significant rise in status and/or income. If, in your dream, you merely observed a locomotive, it forecasts either travel or arrival of visitors from a distance.

Locust. If your dream concerned the white-flowered tree of this name, it signifies general good luck, but a dream featuring the destructive leaping locust insect is a strong warning against risky ventures.

Log. To dream of sawing logs signifies an improvement in home conditions. To see stacks of logs, or fallen

trees in a wood, is a generally favorable omen for whatever concerns you most; logs floating in water predict a new opportunity which should not be overlooked; a logjam portends obstacles likely to be in the form of inexplicable delays; plenty of patience will be required. A brightly burning log augurs family joy; to sit on a log is a sign of personal contentment, and a log cabin is a symbol of satisfaction through diligent hard work. See also *Lumber*.

Loneliness. An omen of contrary. To dream of being lonely is a sign that you won't be.

Looking. A dream of looking must be interpreted according to the object, subject, or direction of the action. For up or down see under chapter on general guides for interpretation. And for left or right see those entries. Otherwise see under separate listings, as *Landscape*, *Eyes*, *Flowers*, or whatever.

Loom. Whether you used the loom or just observed it in your dream, it indicates that you will soon have to take a step backward, but don't get discouraged; you

241

will subsequently be able to take two steps forward.

Loss. This is generally a form of obstacle dream, and its meaning must be related to the article lost and whether or not you eventually found it. If you lost something of great · value, the dream is warning you that if you try to be too sharp you can end up by cutting yourself.

Lottery. Family troubles are forecast in any dream concerning a lottery or lottery tickets.

Lotus. These beautiful blossoms predict love and romance, and if you smelled their aroma, you can expect to be ecstatically happy.

Loudspeaker. An unpleasantly high volume of sound signifies approaching worries, but if you adjusted the volume, the dream indicates recognition for useful social or charity work.

Love. Dreams of sincere love are a forecast of happiness and contentment through a healthy and intelligent adjustment to the conditions of life; but a dream of illicit love or sheer lust has a portent of disappoint-

ment or failure due to your own greed. To dream of observing the lovemaking of others predicts success in your current undertakings.

Luck. This dream is a classic example of the "good news-bad news" joke; the good news is that if you dreamed of being lucky you will be, and the bad news is that the dream also contains a warning that if you let the luck go to your head, you are likely to reverse it. To dream of being unlucky is a caution against overconfidence.

Luggage. See *Baggage*.

Lumber. Neat stacks of lumber seen in a dream signify increasing prosperity; but if the lumber was scattered around or in poor condition, it portends a need for careful planning to protect your interests. See also *Log*, etc.

Lunatic. See *Insanity*.

Lunch. See *Picnic, Eating, Food, Restaurant,* etc.

Lungs. To dream of suffering any form of upper respiratory discomfort is a warning to see your doctor, unless you actually have a chest complaint, in which case the dream has no special significance. See also *Breath, Choke,* etc.

Lust. See under *Love.*

Lute. This romantic, sweet-toned instrument featured in a dream augurs happy, lighthearted love affairs or good news from absent friends. See also *Music* and *Musical Instruments.*

Luxury. A dream of contrary containing a warning that your indolence may make someone else richer, and the greater the dreamed luxury, the more serious the warning.

Lye. You can expect to have your honesty and/or integrity challenged if your dream featured this alkaline solution.

Lynx. This unusual creature is a symbol of hidden hostility. See also *Animals* and *Fur.*

Lyre. See *Lute.*

m

Macaroni. Unexpected guests or an impromptu party are predicted in a dream of eating, cooking, or serving macaroni.

Mace. To use or smell this subtle spice in your dream signifies recognition in community affairs.

Machinery. Smoothly running machinery in good condition is a sign of success in your current efforts, but if the machinery is idle or derelict, it indicates approaching family or employment problems.

Mackerel. See *Fish*.

Madness. See *Insanity*.

Magic. Any form of magic in a dream predicts unexpected changes. To dream of being mystified and/or amused by a magician indicates a reunion with a long-lost friend or the rekindling of a past love affair.

Magnet. The attraction of a magnet featured in your dream predicts sexual vigor and pleasing popularity with the opposite sex.

Magnifying Glass. A dream of using a magnifying glass forecasts an increase in material wealth or a sudden stroke of money luck.

Magpie. You are flogging a dead horse in regard to a matter of unrequited love or personal friendship, and these birds in your dream are telling you that now is the hour to give up the enervating exercise. New interests will soon console you.

Mahogany. To admire or polish mahogany in your dream predicts an improvement in your living conditions, possibly due to an inheritance.

Maid. The meaning of this dream depends on your circumstances. To dream of your own maid is a good omen if you actually have one; if not, it is a dream of contrary signifying financial reverses or loss of status. For a woman to dream of being a maid is a sign that she can expect to regain lost social status.

Mail. See *Letter* and *Package*.

Makeup. See *Cosmetics*.

Malaria. See *Fever, Illness,* or *Disease*.

Malice. Whether shown by yourself or someone else, a display of malice in your dream is an omen of contrary and predicts help through influential, well-disposed friends.

Man. A dream featuring mankind as a whole is a warning of nervous depression due to overwork; either slow down or take a vacation. To dream of a strange man augurs well for family affairs, but the meaning is modified to some extent by the details of his appearance (if you were aware of them) and his actions (if any), so these factors should be considered. See also *Hair, Height, Eyes, Colors,* etc.

Manacles. See *Handcuffs*.

Mandolin. See *Music* and *Musical Instruments*.

Mangle. See *Ironing*.

Maniac. See *Insanity*.

Manicure. If you are in the habit of being manicured, the dream has no significance, unless there was something unusual about it, in which case the unusual aspect must be analyzed to determine the meaning. If you are not in the habit of getting manicures, then the dream is warning you to conserve your resources, as you are likely to have to meet some exceptional expense shortly.

Manna. A straightforward omen of "pennies from heaven." Unexpected money should soon come your way; and following a dream of this kind should be a propitious time to take a chance, if you have been considering one.

Manners. To dream of bad manners, whether your own or those of others, suggests that you are

245

standing in the way of your own progress due to an inferiority complex which you should try to overcome; but a dream featuring overprecise manners indicates that you are contemplating some social climbing which will not work out well—give it up.

Mansions. A dream of contrary. If the mansion was luxuriously furnished, be prepared to accept some changes that will not be to your liking; however, if it was empty or in bad condition, you can expect the change to be for the better, although it may not at first appear that way.

Manufacturing. See *Factory* and *Machinery*.

Manure. As with feces, manure in a dream is a symbol of money luck, wealth, profits, and/or general prosperity.

Manuscript. A dream in which a manuscript is featured portends a disappointment concerning some current plan or project, unless your work normally involves manuscripts, in which case the dream has no significance except in the event of some unexpected factor.

Map. Maps, as one would expect, signify journeys and changes. The larger the map was in your dream, the more distant will be the travel and/or the greater the change. The more brightly colored the map, the happier the forecast. If, in your dream, you were drawing a map, the travel or change will have a lucky aspect providing you used a pencil; if you used a pen, it signifies complications.

Maple. This beautiful tree, or anything made of its wood, is a symbol of family unity and/or a happy homelife. To dream of maple sugar, maple syrup, or anything flavored with maple signifies a happy love life and extraordinary sexual vigor.

Marble. Whether the marble was in a quarry, in a building, or in some other form, it predicts love troubles or personal disappointment; but to dream of the marbles used by children, or to play a game of marbles in your dream forecasts the surprise resurgence of a past love affair or the renewal of a valued friendship. See also *Colors*.

March. To dream of March when it isn't predicts disappointment concerning an expected change. A dream of marching signifies sad news if the marching was slow, but good progress if it was brisk.

Marigold. See *Flowers* and *Colors*.

Marijuana. If you actually use this drug, then the dream has no special significance; otherwise, a dream concerning its use would suggest that you are contemplating something that would not be to your credit—think it over carefully and then don't do it. It's usually better to be a happy chicken than a sick tiger.

Mark. A dream featuring a birthmark, identification marks, silver marks, or any distinguishing-type mark, predicts interesting new friends who will turn out to be useful as well as enjoyable.

Market. The interpretation of this dream depends on its details. If the market was well-stocked and neat and you were shopping or there was business going on, the augury is of abundance and prosperity; but if the food (or merchandise) was in bad condition or of poor quality or if the

place was empty or unattended, the portent is of hard times ahead due to overlooked opportunities.

Marmalade. See *Jam* and *Fruit*.

Marriage. For single people to dream they are married indicates that they are involved in an affair of diminishing returns and would do well to seek a new alliance. Otherwise, see *Wedding*.

Marrow. A dream concerning bone marrow (which is very rare) is likely to be of physical origin and suggests that a medical checkup would be beneficial. For a dream about vegetable marrow (zucchini or green squash), see *Vegetable(s)*.

Mars. Any dream featuring either the Roman god or the planet of this name is, as might be expected, a straightforward omen of approaching clashes, stupid arguments, petty quarrels, and general conflict. Try to maintain some sort of equilibrium till the dust settles.

Marsh. You must make a sharp effort to avoid getting dragged into the unsatisfactory affairs of friends or relations if your dream featured a marsh. Give advice if you can but don't take responsibility.

Marshmallow. Toasted or plain, these mushy morsels signify an unusual new friend of the opposite sex. See also *Candy*.

Martyr. To dream of being a martyr is a warning that your greed could alienate those you care about; any other dream concerning martyrdom is a forerunner to recognition for work well done, either your own or that of someone close to you.

Mascot. If your dream featured a mascot of any kind, you can expect a sudden change of events which will make a beneficial alteration in your future prospects.

Mask. Deceit from an unsuspected quarter is indicated in a dream of a person (or people) disguised by a mask. If your dream concerned wearing one yourself, it predicts that you will end up with a profit from a scheme intended to cheat you.

Mason. Bright prospects are forecast in a dream featuring anything concerned with Freemasonry. Otherwise, see *Bricks* and *Stone(s)*.

Masquerade. To dream of a gay masquerade party or ball predicts a surprise opportunity which could secure your future if you can summon up the courage required to latch on to it.

Mass. An outdoor Mass is an omen of good tidings, but inside a church it is a sign of coming difficulties.

Massage. A dream of having a massage (facial or body) signifies that your unfounded doubts of a friend's sincerity are, in fact, groundless. To dream of giving a massage indicates approaching good news.

Mat. Mats, anywhere except in front of a door, are held to signify obstacles of a size in ratio to the size of the mat; in front of a door, they forecast unwelcome visitors.

Match. To strike a match in your dream is a sign of unexpected gain or increased income. To match things up (shoes, gloves, or whatever) in your dream signifies a sudden increase

Mattress. The meaning of this dream is in line with the condition and/or comfort of the mattress; if the mattress suited you, then the augury is good; if not, it is a warning to start saving for the rainy days ahead.

Matzoth. If you dreamed of eating or serving this unleavened bread, you can expect that some past kindness will be returned to you in a surprising form.

May. Temporary financial setbacks are forecast in a dream of it's being May when it isn't.

Maze. See *Labyrinth*.

Meadow. See *Field*.

Meat. To dream of meat, as such, is a fortunate omen for business affairs; a dream of buying meat suggests an auspicious time for a risk or even a gamble; cutting meat in a dream indicates a coming increase in material wealth, possibly a legacy or inheritance. Cooking meat predicts a change of circumstances; throwing meat away is a warning against extrava-

gance, unless it was spoiled, in which case it indicates a lucky escape from a potential danger or obstacle. See also under *Beef, Veal, Pork, Bacon, Sausage(s), Lamb, Barbecue*, etc.

Medal. Wearing medals predicts recognition for work well done; observing medals on others or in a display is a warning to control your vanity and/or your jealousy.

Medicine. A dream of contrary if you took it yourself; your troubles will prove to be trivial indeed; however, if you gave it to someone else in your dream, you can expect to have to put in some painful effort before you enjoy the pleasure of success.

Medium. See *Occult*.

Melody. See *Music*.

Melon. Melons in your dream are an omen of hope and/or a surprising turn of events in connection with whatever concerns you most at the time. See also *Cantaloupe*.

Menace. See *Threat*.

Mend. To dream of mending clothes predicts an unexpected new source of in-

249

come; a dream of mending anything else portends an approaching need to retrench—but only for a short time.

Menu. A dream which featured a menu promises a long period of comfortable, if not luxurious, living.

Mercury. If your dream concerned the Roman messenger of the gods, it predicts good news; if it pertained to quicksilver, it is warning you against indiscriminate or casual sex relations; if it featured the planet, it augurs a sudden rise in status.

Mermaid. A mermaid in your dream is a symbol of your current love or personal affairs, and its meaning depends on the nature of the action and the general atmosphere of the dream. If those elements were pleasant, you can expect things to go well; but if they were unpleasant or generated a feeling of confusion or dissatisfaction, the dream portends a disappointment.

Merry-go-Round. To dream of riding on, or observing, a carousel with happy children aboard signifies a coming improvement in your life conditions; but to be on it alone or to

see a deserted or derelict one predicts a period of discouragement, but don't despair—new doors will eventually open.

Mess. A dream of contrary. Whatever may be worrying or confusing you will soon come to an orderly conclusion.

Messenger. If you dreamed of acting as a messenger, it signifies an offer of a lucrative, albeit somewhat questionable, deal. Otherwise, see under *Letter*.

Metal. A dream concerning metal takes its meaning from the action as well as the type. To dream of molten metal indicates formidable, if not insurmountable, obstacles in your path and suggests consideration of a change of goal or direction. Buying metal signifies money luck, and selling metal augurs progress after hardships. See also *Gold*, *Silver*, *Iron*, *Copper*, *Platinum*, etc.

Meteor. To see, in your dream, a meteor streaming across the sky, is a sign of a sudden flash of success that will be very exciting but very short-lived. Be prepared to enjoy it while it lasts—then forget it.

Microscope. Using a microscope in your dream predicts the sudden discovery of a new talent or skill; to dream of breaking a microscope, or of a broken one, indicates that your integrity may be challenged from an unexpected quarter.

Midgets. One (or more) of these little people in your dream signifies a new acquaintance (probably male) who will develop into a valuable friend.

Mildew. Disappointment in love or in a previously trusted friend is the forecast in a dream of finding mildew on clothing, furniture, paper, or books, but mildew on food signifies a lucky escape from danger.

Milk. Cow's milk featured in a dream predicts vigorous good health; goat's milk signifies business advancement; mother's milk is one of the luckiest of omens and augurs enduring happiness through intelligent application of ability and adjustment to the realities of life. Sour milk portends setbacks or difficulties created by your own foolish actions, and spilled milk indicates that your grasp is greater than your reach.

A dream of milking a cow or a goat promises prosperity through hard work. To skim the cream off the milk forecasts social popularity, but spilled cream is a caution against new ventures—stick to known paths for the next few months. See also *Buttermilk,* *Cow,* and *Goat.*

Mill. An average-sized picturesque water mill in your dream augurs a peaceful, happy homelife, but a very large (commercial type) mill signifies wealth acquired through the efforts (or ideas) of others. A sawmill portends upsetting news, and a windmill is a warning against being too quick to trust strangers. To dream of a miller at work is a sign of a coming improvement in your circumstances.

Millionaire. This is NOT a dream of contrary, but its meaning is modified by its details. If you dreamed of being a millionaire, you are likely to profit indirectly from a past favor freely given. If, in your dream, you used your money to help your family, friends, or worthy causes, you can count on a stroke of good luck being just around the corner. A dream of meeting a millionaire is a caution to listen to wiser heads before making a new commitment.

Mimic. If you dreamed of mimicking someone, the dream is warning you against that person, and if you couldn't identify the one you mimicked, you are being cautioned to beware of deceit in an important matter. If your dream concerned watching a mimic, you are likely to encounter opposition from an unknown source.

Mine. To dream of working in any kind of a mine predicts eventual wealth through your own efforts. For up or down, see under chapter on general guides for interpretation. See also *Gold, Silver, Metal,* etc. For an explosive-type mine, see *Bombs.*

Minister. A political or diplomatic minister in your dream is a sign of increasing status and/or improving conditions, but a minister of religion is a symbol of a need for solace and is likely to be a forerunner to a disappointment.

Mink. Not an auspicious omen. The fur is a warning against a tendency to selfishness and greed; the

animal predicts hard work and not much play.

Minnows. Pleasing recognition from your colleagues is forecast in a dream of using minnows for bait, but success with the opposite sex is predicted if you caught them in your hands.

Mint. A dream of this fragrant and palatable herb signifies happiness to the healthy and improvement to the ailing. A money mint in your dream forecasts an expected rise in status but after unexpected delay.

Miracle. You can contemplate the future with great confidence if you dreamed of seeing, or hearing about, a miracle.

Mirror. Although ancient sources disagree widely on the forecast in most mirror dreams, they practically all agree that a broken mirror signifies sad news and/or a troubled period ahead. To see yourself in a mirror is a warning of deceit among your friends, and to see others reflected in a mirror portends dishonesty in your associates.

Miser. Any dream concerning a miser or miserly ways is an unfortunate omen for either love or business

affairs. You would probably profit from an all-around change of atmosphere.

Missionary. To dream of being a missionary portends failure of a long-term plan —you'll have to reorganize your thinking. To dream of being converted by a missionary indicates success in your current undertakings.

Mistake. If, in your dream, you admitted the mistake and/or took responsibility for it, it's an omen of contrary and you can expect your interests to flourish; but if you tried to hide the error or shift the blame, it portends lack of progress due to overconfidence or poor planning; listen to competent advice.

Mistletoe. Business or professional people who dream of this Christmas symbol will have to have more patience than anticipated before attaining their current aims; but if your main concern at the moment is love, or personal affairs, you can expect things to run smoothly. See also *Plant(s)*, *Foliage*, etc.

Moan. See *Groan*.

Mob. An angry mob in your dream is a warning that some activity in which you are being urged to join could prove dangerous. Be firmly cautious. See also *Crowd*.

Molasses. This sticky substance featured in your dream is a sharp warning against gossip. Guard your tongue; any kind of loose talk will tend to backfire at this time.

Mold. Whether for food, metal, plastic, clay, or what have you, a shaped mold in your dream signifies improving financial conditions. Otherwise, see *Mildew*.

Mole. A dream featuring this underground burrower is a straightforward sign that you are in danger of being undermined by someone you trust; you needn't be generally suspicious but do be generally discreet. However, if you caught or killed the animal, you can expect a rise in status. Body moles are a very complex subject and to determine their meaning in a dream you must correlate their size, shape, color, and location, so only a general guide can be given here. A large mole intensifies the omen as does a very dark color, and a small mole minimizes it, as does a very light color. A round shape signifies good luck; an oblong one indicates modest good fortune; and an angular shape foretells a mixture of ups and downs. A hairy mole portends difficulties, as does a left-sided position; but a mole with one hair (or only a few) modifies the forecast for the better, as does a right-sided location. See also *Blemish, Skin,* etc.

Money. The meaning of money in a dream is as variable as its meaning in conscious life, and although there is some disagreement among authorities, the great majority concur that to pay, give, or lend money augurs well for all that concerns you. Receiving money is also a good omen, providing it was honestly come by; it signifies security through development of your own resources. To dream of finding money is a sign of mixed blessings; your financial success will be accompanied by disappointment in its effect. Losing money in a dream is an omen of contrary; you are likely to have a windfall. To change money (as paper for coins or large denominations for small, etc.) indicates problems created by your own carelessness

in the handling of your affairs; a dream of exchanging money (as for foreign currency) means an increase in material wealth; to borrow money signifies a need to retrench and a warning against extravagance. To spend money prophesies an unexpected profit, and to steal it predicts an unexpected stroke of luck. To dream of counting or saving money promises personal happiness providing it was NOT done in a miserly way. See also under *Miser* and *Coins.*

Monkey. See *Ape* or *Animals.*

Monocle. This pretentious type of eyeglass featured in a dream is a caution against pretending to be other than you are. Being yourself is always the easiest position to maintain or sustain.

Moon. The meaning of a moon depends on the details, but is, in the main, favorable. As with the superstition, to dream of seeing a new moon over your left shoulder predicts a lucky month ahead. A bright, waxing moon in a clear sky forecasts a new and exciting project (or change); but if it was covered or dimmed by drifting clouds, you will have to overcome some obstacles before reaping a well-earned reward. A full moon means unusual success in love matters, and a harvest moon signifies unusually good returns on your investments of either energy or money. Very bright moonlight is a prophecy of family unity and/or domestic happiness. All moon omens are intensified if they were seen reflected in water. To dream of moon travel or of the man or lady in the moon is a warning that you could lose the happiness close at hand by being too preoccupied with distant mirages.

Moose. If you dreamed of a moose in its natural habitat, you can expect a beneficial change of circumstances, unless you shot it, in which case you can expect some family trouble which has been brewing to boil over. A baby moose in your dream means a lucky break—probably in connection with a journey. See also *Animals*.

Mop. A new or clean mop suggests that a pleasant hobby or community activity could develop into a profitable venture; but an old or dirty mop is telling you that you could soon be seriously embarrassed by neglected duties if you don't make more effort.

Morgue. Difficult and/or disagreeable duties are forecast in a dream of a morgue. If your dream featured being aware of your own corpse in a morgue, it is warning you to take better care of your health; a medical checkup would probably prove beneficial.

Morphine. If you dreamed of taking this drug (or others using it), you are being warned that you must quickly get off the fence in regard to an important decision; further delay could have undesirable consequences. Of course if you actually use morphine in any form, the dream has no prophetic significance.

Mortgage. A dream of odd contrast, for if you dreamed of paying off a mortgage, you are likely to be faced with an unexpected drain on your resources; but if you dreamed of a mortgage foreclosure, it signifies a lucky financial break. To apply for or get a mortgage of any kind forecasts a welcome release from worry.

Mosquito. This buzzing pest is a warning against damage to your reputation through unsavory companions. Be firm about shaking off undesirable associations.

Moss. If the moss in your dream was dry and/or discolored, it portends disenchantment; but if it was soft and green, it predicts romantic bliss.

Moth. Moth holes in clothing or blankets portend family sadness or disappointment; a dream of trying to catch moths is a sign of trouble from hidden hostility or jealousy, but if you succeeded in catching and destroying them, you will outwit your enemies.

Mother. See *Parents*.

Mother-in-Law. See *Parents*.

Motor. Any smoothly running motor in a dream is an omen of solid progress, but if it gave any trouble or wouldn't start, it suggests that a reassessment of your aims with an eye to a change of direction might prove advantageous.

Motorcycle. A dream featuring a motorcycle takes its meaning from the function of the motor, as above, and if a passenger was involved, the forecast refers to affairs with the opposite sex.

Mountain. Another classic obstacle dream. The forecast depends on the outcome of the dream action and other elements which must be correlated, but the interpretation is substantially the same as climb. See also *Trees, Cedar, Colors,* etc.

Mourning. See *Grief* and *Sorrow*.

Mouse (Mice). Discord among friends and/or family is the main keynote in most dreams concerning mice, but this is altered in some circumstances by the action. If you scared the mice away in your dream, the indication is that you will overcome your difficulties and/or outwit your enemies; if, in your dream, you felt a mouse in your clothes, it is a warning that someone you trust is maligning you. To be frightened by a mouse portends a social embarrassment; to kill one signifies financial gain; and to catch one in a trap indicates unwelcome news (or visitors) from a distance. If your dream concerned a mouse (or mice) being chased or killed by a cat, it is a warning not to allow others to meddle in your affairs; listen to advice but act only according to your own judgment.

Mouth. To dream of an open mouth is a straightforward warning that you tend to use yours too much; try to listen more. An open mouth with teeth showing indicates a false friend—be on guard. A small but shapely mouth predicts approaching money, and a large but shapely one forecasts a valuable new friend. Otherwise, see *Lips*.

Movies. The omen here depends on whether or not you enjoyed what you saw; if you did, the augury is one of pleasant social times ahead; but if you were depressed, displeased, or disgusted, you are being warned against being deluded by a dishonest avowal of love or cheated by an insincere declaration of friendship.

Moving. Another obstacle dream. If the move in your dream proceeded smoothly, so will your progress over the difficulties in your path; but if the move was troublesome, unsatisfactory, or uncompleted in your dream, you are likely to be faced with a choice between a retrenchment or a new start.

Mowing. See *Lawn*.

Mucus. Believe it or not, this disgusting body secretion featured in a dream is an omen of contrary signifying good health, and if it was running profusely from your own nose, it predicts a substantial increase in material wealth.

Mud. As in the amusing song lyric, "Mud, mud, glorious mud," a dream of it predicts glorious good luck.

Mule. See *Donkey*.

Murder. See *Killing*.

Muscle. Not a very auspicious omen. A dream of sore or painful muscles signifies emotional upsets, and a dream of displaying muscles, whether your own or someone else's, indicates frustration in regard to social ambitions.

Museum. Unanticipated good luck through a social contact is likely to follow soon after a dream of seeing, or going through, a museum of any kind.

Mush. Whether you ate it, cooked it, or served it, this cereal in your dream means good times ahead.

Mushrooms. A dream of mushrooms growing forecasts the accumulation of wealth through intelligent speculation; to dream of picking the mushrooms predicts prosperity and protection; to eat them signifies an improvement in status due to influential social contacts.

Music. Beautiful, harmonious music, heard in a dream, augurs great good fortune in all that deeply concerns you, but unpleasant, cacophonic, or out-of-tune music signifies discord in personal relations and/or business difficulties.

Musical Instruments. To dream of playing a musical instrument (other than one you can or do play) forecasts a sudden and surprising change in your lifestyle. A broken musical instrument is a warning to guard your health; to break a string on an instrument while playing predicts a broken love affair. A dream of putting new strings on an instrument indicates good news in the offing. Carrying a musical instrument is a sign of success with the opposite sex.

Musk. The smell of musk in your dream is the forerunner of a passionate new love affair; if not your own, it will be close enough for you to share the excitement.

Mussels. To eat them is a sign of increasing social popularity; to gather them forecasts contentment.

Mustache. A dream featuring a mustache is a warning not to let irritations grow into large heartaches; to dream of shaving off a mustache predicts an unhappy sexual experience, but don't get discouraged—a new love will soon console you.

Mustard. The Bible says, "if ye have faith as a grain of mustard seed . . . nothing shall be impossible unto you," and so it is more or less with a dream concerning mustard; whatever its form was it signifies good news and fruitful efforts.

Myrtle. Popularity and sexual vigor are the messages contained in a dream featuring this lovely fragrant tree. See also *Trees, Flowers,* and *Color.*

Mystery. Any dream in which you were aware of a mystery is telling you that your worries are self-induced, and if you can relax they will, in fact, evaporate.

Mystic. See *Occult*.

Myth. A dream concerning any of the great mythical characters or any of the ancient myths is telling you that flattery can get you everywhere, so put your tongue in your cheek and start spreading the oil.

Nagging. If you were doing the nagging, you were using the dream as a subconscious safety valve which indicates that you are swallowing a big dose of resentment; better let off the steam to the person involved, or better yet, talk it over with a trusted friend first. If you dreamed of being nagged, it's a warning to be very cautious in whom (and also about what) you confide.

Nail(s). A dream of hammering nails predicts that you will, in fact, by dint of hard, slogging effort, be able to achieve something you thought beyond your reach. To see shiny and/or new nails in your dream forecasts unexpected news, but bent or rusty nails signify either minor reverses or slow progress. See also *Fingernails.*

Naked. In one aspect this is a dream of contrary, and that is if the nakedness was your own, you can expect a stroke of money luck or an improvement in circumstances; but dreaming of others being naked suggests that you will inadvertently uncover a deception within your close circle.

Name. The meaning depends on the circumstances. If you dreamed that you couldn't remember your own name, or that of someone you know well, the dream is warning you against an illicit affair or a questionable deal that you would find difficult to justify. To be called by a wrong name in a dream portends grave difficulties on the personal side of life, but they will ultimately lead to better understanding. See also *Call.*

Nap. To dream of taking a nap during the daytime is a sign of emotional as well as financial security.

Napkin. If you dreamed of using a napkin, it indicates that you will find the energy to complete a task which you thought beyond your powers. To fold a napkin in your dream predicts a much desired social invitation.

Narcissus. Growing in a garden these lovely flowers are a happy omen for the future, but indoors or in pots they are a warning against vanity and overconfidence.

Narrow. To be aware of something excessively narrow for its purpose is a form of obstacle dream, and its meaning depends on the outcome of its action. However, it seems likely you are worried by the suspicion that you have bitten off more than you can chew, in which case some outside advice might be helpful.

Nasturtium. A dream of eating the seeds or stem of nasturtiums predicts an unusual sexual experience. Otherwise, see *Flowers.*

Nausea. Being nauseous in a dream portends a challenge to your honesty or integrity; be on guard against "help" from untrustworthy friends or associates. See also *Vomit.*

Navel. If your dream concerned your own navel, it is more than likely you will soon be considering a new venture which could produce long-term benefits. To dream of someone else's navel indicates a new love affair in the offing. A dream of Buddha contemplating his navel augurs a period of good fortune.

Navigation. To dream of studying navigation signifies extended travel, but a dream of being a navigator portends complex problems in your life which will require powerful concentration to solve.

Neck. Practically all the oracle sources agree that ANY dream featuring the neck is a sign of approaching money, unless the dream concerned a broken neck, in which case it is a warning against mismanagement of your affairs; pay more attention to your own and less to those of others.

Necklace. A necklace is said to be a fortunate dream

symbol pertaining to love affairs, unless it broke or fell off, in which case it signifies domestic quarrels or romantic disappointment. However, all the elements, such as design, jewels (if any), metal, color, etc. should be correlated with the action, i.e., giving, receiving, finding, or whatever, in order to determine its meaning.

Necktie. To dream of having difficulty with a necktie is a sign that you are chafing under an emotional hold that you would be wise to break.

Nectarines. See *Fruit*.

Needles. Threading a needle in your dream is a lucky omen for your current interests providing you did it with average ease; however, if you had difficulty and/or became irritated, you can expect a period of frustration. To prick yourself with a needle portends problems due to the bad luck of a relative or close associate; to find a needle suggests unnecessary worry; and to lose one is a warning of danger through your own careless conduct. See also *Sewing*.

Needlework. See *Embroidery*.

Neighbor. To dream of helping a neighbor predicts an unexpected gift or minor legacy, but to dream of quarreling with neighbors is a warning of possible troubles through being quick-tempered.

Nephew. See *Relatives*.

Nervous. Whether you dreamed of being nervous yourself or of noticing the symptoms in others, the dream is warning you to control your tendency to be overgenerous with your resources.

Nest. See under *Birds, Chickens, Eggs,* etc.

Nettles. Nettles are a dream of contrary and signify success due to effort coupled with courage, unless they stung you, in which case they portend a need to protect yourself from a deceitful friend or lover.

Neuralgia. If you dreamed of a painful attack of neuralgia, you can expect some sort of emotional upheaval, but though the shock may be sharp, it will also be short.

News. This is a classic example of contrary omen; the worse the news in your dream the better will be the news you get, and vice versa.

Newspaper. To read a newspaper in a dream signifies that events at a distance are conspiring in your favor; to buy a newspaper predicts a quick rise in status; to use a newspaper for wrapping or in any other way indicates a happy reunion with absent friends or relations or the reestablishment of a past happy association.

New Year. A dream featuring the new year (at any other time) is an augury of satisfaction due to hopeful developments in your affairs.

Nickel. See *Coins, Metal,* and *Silver.*

Nickname. Calling anyone by a nickname—or vice versa—in a dream is a caution to stick to well-established paths for yet a while; the old and new will blend better at a later time.

Niece. See *Relations.*

Night. Obstacles and delays are the keynote of this dream, but the interpretation should be modified by the prevailing conditions. The clearness of the night, any moonlight, stars or sign of dawn reduces the adverse aspect. See also *Darkness.*

Nightcap. See *Hat* or *Drink.*

Nightingale. The song or sight of this lovely bird in a dream is a happy augury for love affairs if you are single, and if you're married, it forecasts a pleasing advance in your social status.

Nightmare. To dream of having a nightmare is an extremely rare phenomenon and suggests you are probably repressing a rather deep-seated emotional problem; if you know what it is, talk it over with someone you trust; otherwise get help from a professional psychologist.

Nightshade. This poisonous member of the potato family is an omen of contrary and signifies a good time for taking a chance on new ventures or untried activities.

Nipple. A dream of an adult taking nourishment through a nipple is telling you that your personal debts are on the verge of getting out of hand, but to dream of a baby or a child using one signifies a happy release

263

from worry. If your dream was of the erotic type the meaning depends on the details. A dream of firm, pleasantly colored nipples is a favorable omen for either sex and if they seemed to be very large they predict an increase in material wealth. Painful or ulcerated nipples are warning you that you could do with a medical check-up. To dream of having more than the normal complement of a pair signifies that your only sex problems will be discretion in your choice of partner(s). You'll have no lack of opportunity. A dream of being touched on the body by someone else's nipples indicates happy tidings.

Nobel Prize. If you dreamed of winning this prestigious distinction, you are being cautioned against arrogance and reminded of what goes before a fall, but a dream of rejoicing in this achievement by a friend or relation is a forerunner to happy family news. Of course if you happen to have actually collected one of these coveted awards, the dream has no significance.

Noise. Loud and/or peculiar noises heard in a dream portend domestic dissension, unless the noise actually woke you up, in which case you can expect a change for the better.

Nomination. You are likely to have a period of commiserating with the disappointment of others if you dreamed of being nominated for any sort of official duty.

Noodles. Progress with a cherished plan is forecast in a dream of cooking, serving, or eating noodles.

Noon. See *Hour*.

Noose. See *Rope* or *Hanging*.

North. A dream in which a northerly direction is featured is a forecast that you will eventually find the right direction in life. See also *Compass*.

Nose. To dream of seeing your own nose is a sign that you have more friends than you think; blowing one's nose predicts a welcome decrease in obligations; a dream of tweaking someone's nose or having your own tweaked signifies popularity with the opposite sex; to dream of a swollen nose augurs abundance and porsperity, but a nosebleed is a warning of possible financial stress and a caution to avoid lending money for the next few months. A cold nose is a warning against indiscriminate sex relations, and a snub nose is a warning against indiscreet gossip. A clogged nose signifies hidden opposition, and a cut or injured nose portends family troubles but not close enough to disturb you seriously. See also *Mucus*.

Notary. Any dream featuring a notary predicts a sudden and unexpected demand on your resources, so you'd better go easy on any unnecessary spending for the time being.

Novel. To dream of writing a novel portends trouble and vexation, but to dream of reading one augurs happy social activity ahead.

November. A dream of it's being November when it isn't predicts contentment in the late years of life.

Novocaine. The use of this pain-killer in a dream predicts the sudden solution to a long-standing problem.

Nugget. If you found (or received) a nugget of any precious metal in your dream, you can expect an opportunity which would lead to a spectacular change of circumstances and/or surroundings in the near future.

Numb. A feeling of numbness in a dream generally arises from an external physical condition such as too tight bedclothes or lying in an awkward position; however, it could have an organic origin and a medical checkup would be a good idea.

Numbers. Only a general guide can be given here, as the meaning of numbers in a dream varies according to the context and other details which should be correlated, but if you had the rare experience of being aware of the number of people (or things) in your dream, it signifies an increase in personal power and/or prestige. To dream of numbers which you cannot recall on awakening predicts a period of confusion and surprises regarding the affairs of others; to remember the numbers in your dream forecasts good luck ahead possibly connected with the dreamed number or some derivative or multiple of it.

Nun. See *Convent*.

Nurse. A dream featuring a professional nurse signifies marriage for the single and family unity for the married, unless you are a trained nurse or in daily contact with them, in which case the dream has no prophetic significance.

Nursery. See under *Baby* or *Children*.

Nursing. General good luck is the message contained in a dream of a child being breast-fed, or in a dream of tending the sick.

Nut(s). Nutmeats, as such, are considered a generally fortunate omen, unless they were wormy or stale, in which case they forewarn of problems arising from deceit and/or hostile competition. Cracking nuts prophesies success in your current endeavors, and eating nuts signifies improving health for the ailing and contentment for the healthy.

Nutcracker. A dream featuring a nutcracker (but not being used) is telling you that, whatever your hang-ups may be, they can be overcome by intelligent application of the means you have at hand.

Nutmeg. Grating it in your dream is a sign of increased entertaining, but tasting or smelling it is a warning that you need to look more carefully into the motives of those around you if you want to avoid being used to your own disadvantage.

Nutshells. Empty nutshells in a dream portend futile efforts, unless you cracked them by stamping on them, in which case the omen is reversed.

Nut Trees. Slow but steady accumulation of wealth through sensible planning and intelligent use of energy is forecast in a dream featuring nut trees.

Nylon. This synthetic fiber in a dream is a reminder that things are not always what they seem and you would benefit from being less preoccupied with appearances and more with basic qualities.

Nymph. A dream of a nymph predicts an interesting romantic experience.

Oak. If your dream featured oak in the form of furniture, woodwork, beams, paneling, doors, etc., it is a symbol of strength in all areas of life, signifying emotional security for the single, solidarity for the married, steady progress for the career oriented, and a comfortable healthy long life. See also *Trees* and *Acorn.*

Oar. This is another example of a bad news–good news dream. The bad news is that if you lost or broke the oar, you are in for trouble; and the good news is that it will be the kind of trouble you can quickly overcome by using your head. See also *Row.*

Oasis. Success of an important magnitude in an exciting new endeavor is forecast in a dream featuring an oasis.

Oath. A rise in social and/or business status can be anticipated if your dream concerned hearing or taking a legal oath.

Oatmeal. Cooking oatmeal predicts a period of ups and downs, but serving or eating it prophesies a season of steady progress.

Oats. Whether growing in the field or harvested, a crop of oats in your dream is a forerunner to financial gain; however, if the oats were still green, you can expect a sticky period to precede the progress, but don't get discouraged—the frustration won't last long.

Obituary. An omen of contrary; good news is on the way.

Observatory. A dream featuring an observatory is telling you to guard against impulsive relationships that you may later regret.

Occult. If your dream concerned mystic or occult matters, it predicts that you will come into possession of some confidential information which will be of great advantage to you.

Ocean. The meaning of this dream varies according to its details and action. The ocean, as such, is a good omen if calm, a sign of mixed fortune if choppy; but if very rough or stormy, it is a warning that real courage will be needed to overcome your obstacles, and the following interpretations must also be modified by the foregoing weather conditions. An ocean voyage predicts a lucky escape from an irritating problem; to swim in the ocean signifies that you will soon be enlarging your sphere of influence and/or activity.

October. To dream of October when it isn't is a sign that you will have to use all the self-restraint you can muster to resist some strong persuasion to make a hurried change which would be to your eventual disadvantage. Be firm; your momentary discouragement will soon pass.

Oculist. Any dream featuring an oculist contains the obvious warning from your subconscious that you are not seeing an important matter in its true perspective. Consider the possibility that you are deceiving yourself and then act accordingly.

Odor. Unidentifiable odors in a dream have a straightforward meaning in relation to your personal reaction to them; pleasant ones are a good omen, unpleasant ones predict anxieties which could be major or minor depending on the degree of unpleasantness. If the odor in your dream was identifiable, then check under separate listings, i.e. *Roses, Beef, Meat, Lotus, Lily,* etc.

Offense. A dream of strange contrast in meaning. If you dreamed of being offended, you are likely to convert a former enemy into a friend; but if, in your dream, you were guilty of giving the offense, it is a warning that you are, in fact, in danger of turning a friend into an enemy by careless speech or ill-considered actions.

Offer. To dream of making or receiving a good offer is a straightforward omen of advancement, and even if the dreamed offer was not particularly attractive, you can still expect an improvement, but it is likely to be subject to delays and/or greater effort.

Office. Oddly enough, a dream concerning an office pertains to emotional affairs rather than business matters. To dream of being in your own office predicts a probable change in your love life; to be worried by office matters indicates domestic strife; a new or strange office is a sign of an important new friendship. Obviously, if you dreamed of an office in which you actually work, the interpretation must be made by reference to the action only (not the place).

Officer. If your dream featured a police officer, it forecasts an embarrassment due to the financial carelessness of a friend or relation; however, a dream featuring an officer of any of the armed services signifies security and protection.

Ogre. You are either con-

templating, or indulging in, a dangerous vice or passion if you conjured up imaginary monsters in your dream. In either case you'll be doing yourself a real favor if you find a new interest.

Oil. To dream of an oil field or of striking oil forecasts the pleasant jingle of approaching money, which is also the case if you dreamed of having it on your person or clothing. Oiling machinery is a sign of recognition in your field of endeavor or in community affairs. Buying oil predicts a happy improvement in love (or domestic) affairs but selling it suggests an inclination to cooperate in a questionable proposition—resist it! Cooking (or cooking with) oil suggests that a person of whom you are doubtful is in fact trustworthy; to drink oil is a sign of improving health for yourself or someone close to you. Spilling oil indicates that you will soon have to "pour oil on troubled waters." Anointing yourself with cosmetic oil or the use of medicated oil predicts that you will solve your current problems without outside assistance.

Oilcloth. A dream of strange contrast in meaning. If the oilcloth featured in your dream was shiny and/or new, it is a caution to stick to your own ideals and avoid anything even vaguely illicit. To be thought square in the evening is better than hating yourself in the morning. However, if the oilcloth in your dream was shabby or cracked, it signifies that you might benefit from a bit of a fling with the opposite sex.

Oil Painting. If you were impressed by the painting in your dream, it is a reminder that social snobbery (or pretensions) frequently result in lost opportunities.

Ointment. The use of ointment in your dream, on yourself or others, portends that you are in danger of losing the stars within your grasp by reaching for the moon.

Old. See *Age* or *Antiques*.

Old Maid. See *Spinster*.

Oleander. These beautiful blossoms are a sign of sexual and/or marital satisfaction. See also *Trees*.

Olives. Whether they were ripe or green, to see, eat, or pick olives in a dream predicts happy contentment, but stuffed or pitted olives are a warning that your disregard for the feelings of others could leave you out on a shaky limb—try to consider the viewpoint of others at least part of the time.

Omelet. A successful light omelet predicts a passing but passionate new love affair; a heavy flat omelet portends onerous new duties which will, nevertheless, prove ultimately beneficial.

Onions. Although there is a good deal of difference of opinion concerning the meaning of onions in a dream, a consensus of authoritative sources leads to the conclusion that to see onions forecasts a season of ups and downs; to eat them augurs an unexpected increase in material wealth, possibly through a legacy or a lucky gamble; to peel them prophesies family trouble (especially if your eyes watered); to cook them portends the estrangement of an important friend, and to serve them warns against too much emphasis on trivial pleasures.

270

Onyx. To dream of breaking this rather brittle stone is an omen of contrary and signifies upcoming luck; otherwise, this type of quartz featured in your dream forecasts indecision concerning an important change. Get competent advice, as delay will not be to your advantage.

Opal. Contrary to the widespread superstition that opals are unlucky unless they happen to be your birthstone, to dream of them signifies a season of unexpected good luck, and the omen is intensified if they were fire opals.

Opera. A dream of enjoying an opera, either at a live performance or on records, suggests that you are practicing a measure of deception which could prove embarrassing if discovered; and if your dream involved the use of opera glasses, you are likely to have to defend your reputation.

Operation. An important change in your fundamental life-style is forecast in a dream of undergoing surgery; to dream of observing an operation predicts unexpected news. However, neither of these dreams has any signifi-cance if you practice (or are connected with) any form of medicine.

Opium. Any dream featuring this addictive fruit of the poppy is a warning against even a casual association with people of unsavory habits. Although judging a person by the company he keeps may be considered square, it is nevertheless widely practiced.

Opponent. See *Adversary.*

Opossum. This amusing animal in a dream is reminding you that ignoring your problems is a surefire method of building a time bomb under yourself; vigorous positive action is the only safe road to relief.

Optician. A dream of going to an optician is telling you that more energetic effort will be required to avoid a loss of status; stop moping and get cracking!

Oracle. See *Occult.*

Orange. To see them growing or boxed for shipment is a forecast of a slow but steady improvement in your circumstances; to eat them or drink the juice predicts a short but unforgettable love affair; and orange blossoms, as expected, signify news of a wedding. See also *Fruit*, *Trees*, and *Colors*.

Oration. To deliver an oration in your dream indicates embarrassment due to a long neglected duty or obligation; to listen to one predicts the need to sever a debilitating relationship.

Orchard. General good luck will surely follow a dream of an orchard in bloom; an orchard of ripe fruit signifies attainment of your deepest wish; an orchard of green fruit predicts slow progress but eventual success; a stripped orchard portends modest achievement due to modest effort.

Orchestra. See *Music*, *Concert*, *Conductor*, *Hall*, and *Musical Instruments*.

Orchids. These exotic blooms are a warning to curb either your extravagance or your exotic habits, whichever applies.

Orders. To obey orders is a sign that better times lie ahead; to give orders portends domestic discord.

Organ. Pleasant organ music heard in a dream is an omen of satisfying sexual prowess. See also *Music*,

Musical Instruments, or *Sexual Organs*.

Orgy. This dream is a warning that your excesses or your repressions (whichever applies) could get you into trouble; moderation is the key to contentment.

Orient. See *Foreign*.

Oriole. You'll soon be singing for joy if you dreamed of this attractive warbler. See also *Birds* and *Colors*.

Ornament. Profit from the sale of property or some other asset is forecast in a dream of personal ornaments; but futile efforts are predicted if your dream featured a collection of household ornaments, unless you broke one (or more), in which case it signifies good luck. See also *Decorate*.

Orphan. You are being warned that your self-centered attitude could lose you a valuable friendship if your dream featured an orphanage, but any other dream concerning orphans predicts a sudden gain in material wealth from a previously unknown source or an unexpected legacy.

Osteopath. To dream of an

osteopath or of osteopathic treatment is a warning that you are in an accident-prone phase and should be extra cautious for the next few weeks.

Ostrich. This strange bird in a dream is a good omen and especially so if it kicked you; cash will be more plentiful than usual and gay social activity will follow.

Otter. Whether in or out of the water, this animal in your dream is telling you to conserve your resources now because you've got some rainy days ahead.

Ottoman. A dream of contrary. You will have to wait yet awhile before you can put your feet up.

Oven. A warm or hot oven signifies fruitful efforts, but a cold oven indicates regret over a lost friend or missed opportunity; one should learn from what's past, not yearn for it—look ahead! See also *Bake* and *Roast*.

Owl. This hooting night bird in your dream is an omen of reverses and/or disappointments, unless you drove it away, in which case you can expect an improvement in your circumstances. An owl in the house forecasts family discord.

Oxen. A herd of oxen in your dream is an omen of great prosperity; particularly if they were grazing, they signify the accumulation of wealth through lucky speculation and success in all your current undertakings. See also *Animals*.

Oxygen. Whatever the action, if oxygen was the main feature of your dream, it predicts that you will overcome the main obstacle presently in your path.

Oyster. Opening oysters in your dream is a warning that you have misplaced your confidence and are in danger of being cheated by someone you trust; reconsider any dealings you might be contemplating with friends. Eating oysters is a sign of good luck in love affairs, but if your main concern is business, this dream suggests that you will have to be more energetic and/or aggressive in asserting yourself if you want to succeed.

Pace. A dream of striding back and forth is telling you that your impatience could be your undoing. Restrain your attempts to force the pace and you'll get there quicker.

Pack. Any form of packing is an omen of contrary; you can expect a period of plodding along a familiar rut.

Package. To dream of carrying a package suggests that you are shouldering a responsibility which you feel should be undertaken (or shared) by someone else; don't swallow your resentment, speak up. See also *Wrap, String, Box,* etc.

Pad. See *Paper, Pack, Footsteps, Bandage,* etc.

Paddle. See *Canoe, Oar, Water, River, Stream,* etc.

Paddock. See *Horse.*

Padlock. See *Lock, Key(s),* etc.

Page. Turning book or magazine pages in your dream predicts good luck with small investments.

Pageant. If your dream featured a colorful pageant, it signifies the renewal of a lost friendship or the discovery of a previously unknown relative.

Pagoda. Unexpected travel is forecast in a dream featuring a pagoda.

Pail. The meaning of this dream depends on the circumstances and other elements, such as whether the pail(s) were shiny or dull, metal or plastic, etc., but as a general guide: to carry a pail signifies improving conditions; empty pails indicate delayed satisfaction, whereas full ones forecast minor achievement. To knock one over or spill the contents is a warning to be more careful with money or in money matters.

Pain. A dream of being in pain most frequently arises from a physical source and has no prophetic significance, but if you are sure this was not the case, then the meaning depends on the location as follows: general (all over) pain predicts success; in a limb, signifies embarrassment due to impulsive actions; in the heart, portends marital or romantic problems; in the teeth, a period of minor difficulties; in the head, an unpleasant surprise; in the throat, a warning against gossip; in the chest, financial gain. See also under *Back, Neck, Abdomen,* etc.

Paint. To dream of a house being painted indicates that information which has been kept from you will soon be forthcoming; if you dreamed of painting anything (like furniture, woodwork, etc.), it suggests that you are contemplating some activity which you would prefer to keep secret—think it over well before you commit

yourself. A dream of artist's paint signifies important changes if it was watercolors. To dream of lacquer, gilt, or shellac predicts a passionate new love affair. See also *Decorate.*

Painter. Other than under *Paint,* see *Artist.*

Paintings. See *Oil Painting* and *Pictures.*

Pair(s). Pairs of things featured in a dream predict an unusual event on your horizon. See also under *Match.*

Pal. This alter-ego-type friend in your dream forecasts a season of general good luck.

Palace. If you dreamed of seeing a palace from the outside, you can expect an improvement in your affairs; but if your dream concerned the inside, you are being warned that your vanity could generate some harmful hostility. Listen more and toot your own horn less.

Palisades. An obstacle dream with a meaning similar to cliff or cave, depending on whether you were in or out.

Pallbearer. A rise in status is forecast by a dream of being a pallbearer.

Pallor. To be aware, in your dream, of your own pallor predicts an unexpected gain. To notice anyone else looking pale forecasts an illness or a shock for that person. If the pale person was unknown to you, the dream is warning you to look for a hidden danger to your business or your investments, whichever applies.

Palm(s). A legacy or an unexpected valuable gift is likely to follow a dream featuring the palms of your own hands or those of others.

Palmist. See *Occult*.

Palm Tree. This tree in your dream is a symbol of disappointment in one whom you believed to be a loyal friend.

Pan. You will soon be able to laugh your troubles away if your dream featured the Greek god with the pipes. If your dream concerned a cooking pan, prosperity is just around the corner.

Pancakes. Making and/or serving pancakes in a dream forecasts an exciting and gratifying increase in social activity; eating them signifies success in your current undertakings; and if they were made of buckwheat, the augury is of a calm life with slow but steady progress.

Panda. This lovable Chinese bear in your dream is telling you that, if you'll just stop feeding your worries, they'll go away.

Pansies. Oddly enough, these pleasant flowers featured in a dream forecast an unpleasant experience or misunderstanding with someone of your own sex; but don't let it depress you—remember that into each life some rain must fall. See also *Flowers*.

Panther. See under *Animals*.

Pantomime. See *Charades*.

Pantry. A well-stocked pantry predicts prosperous times ahead; a partly filled pantry signifies comfort but no luxury; a bare pantry is a warning to curb extravagance.

Paper. Clean or new paper in a dream is a symbol of efforts, and its meaning must be interpreted according to its color. Waste-paper predicts a fine new opportunity which you should not waste time about accepting. See also *Wallpaper* and *Parchment*.

Paprika. This lovely red Hungarian spice is a warning to control your excesses, unless you believe the corny old joke about overindulgence being a pleasant way to die.

Parachute. If the use of the parachute was trouble free, you can expect a happy love life; but if there was any difficulty involved, you are likely to be let down by someone on whom you relied.

Parade. To dream of leading a parade means recognition in community affairs; to march in a parade forecasts annoyance due to unexpected visitors; to watch a parade from the sidelines is a sign of an increase in income.

Paradise. See *Heaven*.

Paralysis. Generally, this disability in a dream, whether your own or someone else's, suggests an emotional conflict or sexual inhibition. If the paralysis was total, it is likely that you are fighting your conscience over something you

want to do and feel you shouldn't; if the paralysis was only partial, it indicates a fear of frigidity, impotence, or latent homosexuality. Alternatively this dream could arise from a repressed desire for freedom from responsibility or from an organic malfunction. In any case, medical or psychological advice would be beneficial.

Parapet. Minor obstacles which can be overcome by patient determination is the message in a dream concerning a wall of this kind.

Parasol. A lucky omen for love affairs if carried outdoors; to open one indoors predicts an unexpected gift, probably money.

Parcel. To receive or mail a parcel signifies a change of circumstances in the near future. See also *Package*.

Parched. See *Drought*.

Parchment. Any form of parchment in a dream augurs a release from current worry, or alternatively a successful outcome of pending legal matters if you have any.

Parents. As a rule, fathers represent authority and

mothers symbolize love, and you will have to figure out the meaning of your dream by correlating the action with your parental attitude and other elements of the dream, but as a general guide: if the parent you dreamed of is dead and he or she spoke to you, you can expect to hear important news; otherwise, a dream of your mother signifies happiness in love or personal affairs, and a dream of your father forecasts progress in business, professional, or career matters. To dream of being a parent (if you aren't) augurs a surprising turn of events concerning a cause you believed to be lost; and a dream featuring a parent- (or parents-) in-law portends an awkward situation which will require all your diplomatic skill to surmount. To dream of the parents of others indicates that you can count on the help of friends when you need it.

Paris. This beautiful city is a symbol of gaiety and predicts a season of carefree social activity—but be careful not to get drawn into doing things you cannot easily afford. See also *Foreign.*

Park. A public park predicts exciting love affairs, unless it was untidy or in poor condition, in which case it portends a lonely period of readjustment.

Parking. Parking or trying to park a car in a dream suggests that it would be a significant time to start tapering off a relationship which no longer interests you.

Parliament. See *Congress, Government,* or *Politics.*

Parrot. As you would expect, talking or noisy parrots in a dream forecast irresponsible gossip from which you will have to protect yourself; be energetic about it. See also *Birds.*

Parsley. Success is the message in a dream featuring parsley. If you saw it growing, your accomplishment will be due to steady hard work, but if you served or ate it, you will achieve your goal through a combination of intelligent effort and unusually lucky breaks.

Parsnip. This pedestrian vegetable in a dream is a caution against hitching your wagon to a plow horse when there is a star available.

278

Parson. See *Clergy*.

Partner. Personal and/or financial success is the augury if you dreamed of having a satisfactory partner; however, if there was any hint of dissatisfaction or suspicion between you, it portends a season of shifting tides.

Partridge. You will need fortitude and oxlike patience to sit out the troubles on your horizon if you dreamed of these game birds; however, don't despair, the troubles will be annoying rather than serious.

Party. Another example of a sort of good news—bad news symbol of mixed fortunes and contrary omens. Pertaining to social matters, it is considered more fortunate to dream of going to a party than to dream of giving one, and the less pretentious the function the better the augury. In either event, the dream takes its meaning from the general atmosphere of the function and the degree of pleasure (or displeasure) experienced by the dreamer.

Passage. An obstacle dream similar in meaning to Hall.

Passenger. Easy success is the forecast in a dream of being a passenger in a wheeled vehicle, and the message contained in a dream of being a passenger on ship, plane, boat, rocket, balloon, or what have you is escape from worry and/or responsibility.

Passion. See under *Sex* or *Rage*.

Passport. To dream of getting a passport indicates an approaching opportunity for profitable travel; to dream of losing a passport suggests a depressing lack of progress due to unappreciative or hostile influences around you. Try to find a new channel or a new environment for your activities.

Paste. See *Glue*.

Pastor. See *Clergy*.

Pastry. Pastry, as such, signifies an important decision or discussion in the offing. Otherwise, see *Bake, Eating, Dough, Kneading, Fruit*, etc.

Pasture. See *Field*.

Patch. A dream of having necessary (mending variety) patches on your clothing is an omen of contrary and signifies prosperity or wealth by inheritance; decorative patches or items made of colorful patchwork suggest that this is a likely time for speculation or for a bit of a flutter at gambling. An eyepatch in a dream predicts an unusual sex experience.

Patent. Following a dream of getting (or applying for) a patent on an invention is a favorable time for risky ventures or games of chance.

Path. A broad path in your dream predicts a happy life and good friends, but a narrow one portends struggle and deceit; however, you can overcome it by being cautious in your close associations.

Patience. To dream of the exercise of this compassionate quality, by yourself or anyone else, is a lovely omen of contrary, indicating that you won't need much patience to see the last of current worries.

Patio. If the main feature of your dream was a pretty patio, it predicts exciting new social contacts.

Patterns. Sewing, embroidery, or construction patterns in a dream are a suggestion from your subconscious mind to refrain from straying into unknown paths. For a dream featuring changing patterns see, *Kaleidoscope, Colors,* and *Decorate.*

Pauper. See *Beggar.*

Pavement. If the pavement in your dream was in good condition, or if you saw new pavement being laid, you can expect your current interests to proceed smoothly; but bumpy or damaged pavement in your dream is warning you that you are in danger of losing both face and influence unless you learn to control (or conceal) your feelings of envy.

Paw(s). Animal paws in a dream signify a possible loss of status due to careless manners and/or questionable companions; you've been warned!

Pawn. Any dream concerning a pawnbroker or pawnshop is an omen of good luck and predicts that whatever your troubles may be you will find a way to rise above them.

Pay. See *Bills* or *Money.*

Peace. Contentment through

spiritual inspiration is forecast in a dream of world peace.

Peach. Trivial but uplifting personal pleasures are predicted in a dream of eating or having a peach. See also *Fruit, Trees* and *Colors.*

Peacock. A dream of these strutting birds is an omen of contrary containing a warning of possible loss of status or failure due to vanity and/or overconfidence; it sometimes works wonders.

Peanuts. Whether salted or in their shells, peanuts are a sign of increasing personal popularity. Peanut butter indicates remorse over a past injustice; either confess it or forget it—regret is an enervating exercise in futility.

Pearls. A dramatic increase in wealth and social position are forecast in a dream featuring pearls, unless the string broke or you lost them, in which case you may expect some reverses before the advances; however, if you managed to gather them up or restring them, the reverses will be minor and the delay inconsequential.

Pears. Canned pears signify an unexpected profit, fresh pears predict that you will hear some scandalous gossip which will prove to be useful to you, and fruit-laden pear trees forecast expanding opportunities. See also *Fruit* and *Leaf.*

Peas. To open a can of peas predicts a variety of small complications of your own making; to see peas growing indicates vexation due to the troubles of a close friend or relative; for a man to dream of shelling peas means that an influential (or wealthy) woman will be responsible for his success; and for a woman to dream of shelling peas forecasts that her mate will talk a better game of love than he can play.

Pebbles. Picking up pebbles predicts a period of lonely depression due to a lost friend or broken relationship, but try not to mope, the forging of new links will soon fill the void. Tossing pebbles in a dream is a warning that indiscriminate gossip could make wider waves than you suspect, so restrain your chin-wagging or be prepared to sidestep the boomerang. Sitting or walking on pebbles signifies that you will have an unexpected chance to repay (in kind) someone who took unfair advantage of you; before you react, remember that while revenge may give you a sweet moment of satisfaction, forbearance carries the seeds of lasting self-respect.

Pecans. You can expect an advantageous social invitation if you dreamed of eating pecans. See also *Nut(s)* and *Trees*.

Peel. If you dreamed of peeling fruit, you will discover a secret which will prove useful to you; to dream of peeling vegetables forecasts sad or disappointing news of a distant friend. See also under *Skin*.

Pelican. Pelicans in a dream are a symbol of prosperity through sensible frugality. See also *Birds*.

Pen. As one would expect, pens in a dream signify news from a distance; if you broke or damaged the point or the pen went dry, you are being warned that you are endangering your reputation by associating with people of questionable character.

Pencil. Good health, good luck, and the time to enjoy them is the message in a dream featuring pencils, and this applies even if your dream involved having to sell them.

Pendulum. A sudden change of plans will upset your regular routine if you dreamed of a pendulum; however, if you can manage to accept the change without a display of undue anxiety, it will prove to be ultimately beneficial.

Penguin. This funny earth-bound bird in your dream is telling you that your problems are not as serious as you believe, and if you keep your cool, they will melt away.

Penny. A new or shiny penny portends deceit in someone you trust; giving pennies away predicts money luck, but receiving a penny (or pennies) indicates a financial loss. See also *Coins*.

Pension. The main message in a dream featuring a pension is security, and if you want to ensure yours, you must pay closer attention to your own plans and interests and make your own decisions in that context.

Penthouse. A dream of contrary. This elegant and expensive type of cliff dwelling in your dream is a warning against living beyond your means, unless you actually live in a penthouse, in which case the location has no significance and the other main elements of the dream should be analyzed.

Peony. Peonies are one of the few flowers of unhappy omen, as they signify anxiety. However, the meaning is somewhat modified by their color. See also *Colors* and *Flowers*.

Pepper. To dream of using this hot spice is a warning to cool your temper; restraint is a happier companion than regret.

Peppermint. If you dreamed of eating or serving peppermint, you are likely to have a legacy from, or an unexpected benefit through, a very distant relation. See also *Candy*.

Perch. As one would expect, it is a straightforward prediction of increased status if you dreamed of climbing onto any kind of perch.

Percolator. A new percolator (or coffee maker) in your dream predicts a change of residence for the better;

an old one signifies that you will make pleasant improvements in your present living quarters. See also *Coffee*.

Perfume. For a woman to dream of using perfume on herself predicts an unusual new heart interest; for a man this dream signifies misunderstandings in both personal and business affairs. To smell pungent or heady perfume in a dream is a forecast of a passionate and exciting new love partner; delicate scent that gently stirs the emotions suggests a pleasant, but not exciting, romantic experience.

Periscope. Surprising news from a distance is forecast in a dream of looking through, or seeing, a periscope.

Perjury. You are being warned to forget about some shady deal or questionable method of making money which you have been contemplating if you dreamed of committing perjury; as a matter of fact, after such a dream don't even consider a slight jiggle with your taxes, never mind a fiddle! If your dream concerned someone else perjuring themselves, it is a sort of omen of contrary and indicates that you are likely to benefit now from an injustice done to you in the dim and distant past.

Permanent Wave. See *Hair* and *Curls*.

Peroxide. See *Disinfect* or *Hair*.

Persimmon. Eating a persimmon in a dream forecasts a surprise meeting with a past friend or former associate, but if the fruit was puckery, the meeting will not be pleasant.

Perspiration. This dream is reminding you that the formula for success is inspiration plus perspiration, so don't rest on your oars; if you want to enjoy the rewards, you'll have to endure the efforts.

Petal. If you dreamed of pulling the petals from a flower, or of seeing them fall, it signifies sadness due to a lost friend or broken relationship; try to bear in mind that every experience, even a sad one, adds to your fund of understanding and is likely to be of benefit in your next encounter.

Petticoat. Petticoats in a dream pertain to marital or romantic affairs, and their meaning depends on the action and other aspects of the dream which must be correlated, but as a general guide: petticoats which the dreamer considered as pleasing or pretty (rather than strictly utilitarian) are a warning against vanity and conceit; buying petticoats is a caution against extravagance; changing a petticoat predicts that the dreamer will soon be "off with the old, on with the new"; losing a petticoat is a sign of unexpected rivalry for the affection of someone the dreamer takes for granted; a torn petticoat indicates disenchantment; a mended petticoat (or to mend one) is a warning against foolish pride; it is frequently better in the long run to sit on your pride than to stand on your dignity. See also *Clothes* and *Colors*.

Petunia. Growing out of doors these flowers signify pleasant friendly social affairs, but otherwise they predict a period of boredom; a vacation or a new hobby is likely to prove helpful.

Pewter. Pewter in your dream is a sign of a useful new social contact on the horizon. See also *Metal*.

Phantom. See *Ghost*.

Pharmacist. You will make a successful investment, but it will involve you in a bit of gossip. See also *Drugstore*.

Pheasant. This bird in your dream is a warning to be prudent with your credit for the time being, as you are likely to have an unexpected call on your resources soon; however, if in your dream you cooked or ate the pheasant, the omen is reversed and augurs a new source of income. See also *Birds* and *Fowl*.

Photography. To dream of looking at photographs forecasts the pleasing renewal of an old friendship. See also *Camera*.

Piano. A dream of playing the piano yourself predicts success in all your plans and hopes, unless the instrument was damaged or out of tune, in which case you can expect some difficulties and delays along the way. To dream of shifting or moving a piano signifies solid achievement; tuning a piano (or hearing a piano tuner at work) forecasts good news; if you dreamed of hearing piano music beautifully played by someone else, it is a promise of better financial times ahead. See also *Music* and *Musical Instruments*.

Pick. This sharp-pointed tool is a straightforward symbol of hard work, but a dream of it holds a promise of satisfying rewards if you persevere. See also under *Flowers*, *Teeth*, *Fruit*, etc.

Picket. If your dream featured a picket fence, it indicates minor troubles which you can easily overcome by positive action; a dream concerning picketing for a cause predicts recognition for a job well done. See also *Hedge*.

Pickle. Overall satisfaction with the general state of your life, love, and pursuit of happiness is forecast in a dream featuring pickles.

Picnic. The meaning of a picnic dream depends entirely on the general atmosphere (pleasant or awkward) prevailing and on the details of the other elements involved which must be correlated. See *Sky*, *Field*, *Flowers*, *Food*, *Landscape*, *Eating*, etc.

Pictures. Watercolors, drawings, or modern pictures predict minor changes;

otherwise, see *Oil Painting, Photography, Portrait, Artist, Camera, Museum, Landscape, Colors*, etc.

Pie. The meaning contained in a dream of eating or serving pie depends entirely on the contents of the pie. See *Fruit, Meat, Chickens, Nut(s), Chocolate*, etc.; also *Bake*.

Pier. See *Quay*.

Pig(s). Another example of the good news had news, contrast-in-meaning-type of dream omen signifying vexation in family affairs but satisfaction in business or professional matters. However, the omen is modified by the condition of the animals, intensified if the pigs were fat and diminished if they were lean. See also *Animals*.

Pigeon(s). A dream of pigeons flying is a prophecy of important changes ahead brought about by news from a distance. Pigeons on the ground signify minor family troubles, but sitting on ledges or windowsills they are fortunate for love affairs. If you dreamed of feeding pigeons or watching them eat, you can expect to be preoccupied shortly with some un-anticipated but temporary financial problem.

Pile(s). If you dreamed of putting things in piles or of seeing piles of things, you are being cautioned about a forgotten (or neglected) obligation which could suddenly embarrass you; don't compromise your integrity for the sake of passing pleasures. For the physical condition, see *Hemorrhoids*.

Pilgrims. An omen of contrary, you can expect the general quality and enjoyment of your life to improve following a dream featuring these hardworking, courageous pioneers.

Pill(s). To dream of taking or giving pills signifies new responsibilities which will, nevertheless, be rewarding. Buying pills forecasts a change of residence. Of course, if the pills in your dream were those you habitually use, the dream has no significance.

Pillow. You can expect troubles due to your own imprudent behavior if the pillow was soiled or rumpled; otherwise the meaning of this dream symbol is the same as *Mattress*. See also under *Bedclothes* and *Colors*.

Pimple(s). See *Skin*.

Pin(s). Pins, as such, in a dream signify petty annoyances such as family squabbles, hurt pride, or minor disappointments; to dream of actually hearing the proverbial pin drop is a prophecy of contentment; sitting on a pin predicts a happy surprise; pinning up an article of clothing (i.e., ladies' dresses or mens' slacks) forecasts a coming social embarrassment; to dream of swallowing a pin suggests that careless planning will lead you into an unpleasant situation, but a lucky circumstance will get you out; pricking yourself or being pricked by a pin (unless you sat on it) signifies that you will have to help cope with someone else's problems; finding a pin is a sign of general good luck in all your current interests. See also under *Jewelry*.

Pincushion. A full pincushion is a sign of solid achievement, and the more pins there were in it, the greater will be your accomplishment; but an empty pincushion is a symbol of wasted effort and suggests you would be wise to consider rechanneling your energy.

Pine. Same as *Cedar*.

Pineapple. Eating or serving it predicts social success; drinking the juice signifies business success; and to dream of seeing this cactus fruit harvested or growing promises a passionate new love affair. See also *Fruit* and *Colors*.

Pine Cones. Whether seen in a decorative arrangement, gathered in the forest, or used as kindling for a fire, pine cones in your dream forecast unexpected news, probably of a birth.

Ping-Pong. A game of Ping-Pong in a dream, if reasonably evenly matched, is a sign of fairly easy attainment of your current aims, but if the contest was definitely one-sided, you will have to contend with some strong rivalry before you get what you want; and this applies whether you participated in the game or only watched it.

Pink(s). These pungent small blooms predict happy social times with enjoyable companions. Otherwise, see *Colors*.

Pinking. You will discover an interesting and rewarding new talent if you dreamed of the use of pinking shears.

Pipe(s). The ability to meet your obligations and solve your own problems is promised in a dream of smoking a pipe, and this augury applies to any dream featuring a tobacco pipe, unless it was broken, in which case it signifies a parting from a valued friend. Plumbing pipes, gas pipes, or chemical pipes indicate that your pessimistic outlook tends to make you a victim of circumstances; try trading your worm's-eye view for a bird's-eye view.

Pirate. Storybook-type pirates in your dream suggest a strong inclination to enter into an exciting new venture, but be cautious about your associates and investigate before you invest.

Pistol. See *Guns* and *Shoot*.

Pit. An obstacle dream similar in meaning to *Cavern* or *Abyss*.

Pitch. See *Tar*, *Sports*, or *Ball*.

Pitcher. To dream of pouring from a pitcher is a sign of abundance; a cracked or broken pitcher in your dream is a warn-ing that you are jeopardizing a valuable friendship by extreme self-indulgence.

Pitchfork. This implement in a dream portends financial headaches due to overindulgence; try underindulgence as a cure.

Pity. A dream of contrary. Having pity on another person in your dream portends a season of petty vexations and/or family discord; but if someone pitied you, it is an augury of good fortune in all your affairs.

Placard. You will discover some startling news and/or make a surprise change for the better if your dream featured a placard of any kind.

Plague. See *Epidemic*.

Plaid. See *Colors* or *Kilt*.

Plan(s). To dream of looking at architects' plans is a forecast of a new and important friendship; if you dreamed of drawing plans, it is a warning of possible trickery regarding an offer or a deal you are currently contemplating. It is likely to cost more than you've been told, so think it over carefully.

Plane. See *Carpenter* or *Airplane*.

Planet(s). If your dream featured other planets, it suggests a strong desire for adventure and/or change from your present routine which you feel would be unwise; try to resolve the conflict by finding a new extracurricular interest as an outlet for your unsatisfied drive.

Plank. A dream of planks, as such, is a warning to guard against a loss, possibly by robbery; extra precautions would be advisable. If you dreamed of walking on a plank, it signifies a period of indecision which in turn indicates a choice to be made concerning a new offer or opportunity; try to resist being pushed into hasty action.

Plant(s). Healthy plants, growing indoors or out, are an omen of general good luck in your current undertakings, and the omen is intensified if the plants were in bloom; however, if they were wilted or in poor condition, they signify a warning of possible difficulties due to careless planning. A dream of repotting, watering, feeding, or setting out plants is a promise of a contented homelife in comfortable circumstances. See also *Foliage, Flowers, Garden,* and *Colors*.

Plaster. Mixing plaster in a dream forecasts a period of money luck; putting plaster on a wall is an omen of increasing prosperity; however, cracked or falling plaster portends family troubles. If you dreamed of wearing a medical plaster or a plaster cast, you are likely to have to defend your reputation as a result of your own careless behavior, but if the plaster was on someone else, you are likely to be called on to help a friend or relative who is in trouble.

Plastic. The meaning depends on what the article was and whether or not the plastic factor created an element of disappointment in your dream. Plastic, as such, predicts a friendship which will, surprisingly, turn out to be useful as well as enjoyable.

Platform. You can expect a really significant rise in status if you dreamed of being on a platform, but if the structure was shaky or in poor condition, it is a sign that you will need to impress a powerful person before you get what you want. A combined display of strength and tact should turn the trick.

Platinum. Whether your dream featured this precious stuff as jewelry or in some other form, it predicts the attainment of something (an ambition, friendship, or possession) which you believed to be beyond your reach.

Play. To see children at play is an omen of success in love or personal relationships; watching the performance of a play in your dream is a symbol of good times ahead if you enjoyed it, but if you found it sad or unpleasant in any way, the dream is warning you of brewing financial embarrassment—guard your credit.

Pledge. See *Oath*.

Pliers. Whatever your problems are you will find a way to get around them if your dream featured the use of pliers.

Plot. Be prepared for a season of ups and downs with emphasis on the downs if you dreamed of being party to a plot against someone else; but if your dream concerned a plot against yourself, you can expect a pleasant improvement in your financial affairs.

Plow. If you dreamed of a horse-drawn plow, it signifies slow but steady progress in all that concerns you; a motor-drawn plow is a forecast of achievement with a strong assist from lady luck.

Plug. To dream of plugging up anything, or of plugs, indicates abundance due to prudence.

Plum(s). Eating fresh plums in a dream or drinking plum juice signifies recognition for work well done, but canned or sour plums portend disappointment due to slipshod planning. Damson plums indicate important beneficial news on your horizon. To dream of picking plums predicts an approaching change of circumstances. See also *Fruit, Colors,* and *Leaf (or Leaves)*.

Plumbing. Elegant, bright, shiny, or new plumbing featured in your dream forecasts an unexpected opportunity, plus the necessary, to realize a long-standing travel ambition; old, dull, or leaky plumbing portends vexation over an annoying misunderstanding with a friend or colleague.

Pneumonia. A health warning is contained in a dream of pneumonia; better have a medical checkup.

Pocket(s). If your dream featured pockets but you weren't aware of whether or not they contained anything, you will be surprised and annoyed (if not inconvenienced and embarrassed) by the unexpected stinginess of a friend or associate. To dream of having (or finding) something in your own pocket signifies that you will have an easier time than you anticipate, with a person in authority, concerning a pending matter of importance to you. A dream of having a hole in your pocket suggests chagrin due to off-the-cuff judgment or hasty action. Guard against impulsive reactions.

Pocketbook. See *Handbag*.

Poet. A poet in your dream is a symbol of an impecunious friend who is likely to ask you for a loan. Don't make it more than you can afford to give away

because it will turn out to be a donation.

Poetry. To dream of writing poetry predicts that you will make an unusually interesting new friend; reading or listening to poetry forecasts a gratifying increase in popularity with the opposite sex.

Poison. A dream of taking poison portends a period of tension due to your unwillingness to compromise your principles. Stand pat; your refusal to conform will pay dividends later. If your dream concerned giving poison, it portends a broken friendship or love affair. To dream of others taking poison signifies success in spite of unfair competition and/or opposition. Poisoned animals in a dream indicate domestic troubles. Throwing poison away suggests the lucky discovery of a deceitful friend who could have caused you a severe financial loss.

Poison Ivy. This noxious creeper in a dream, or suffering the results of contact with it, portends a painful misunderstanding with a very special friend of the opposite sex.

Poker. Whether you participated or just kibitzed, a game of poker played in your dream forecasts happy social events shared with good companions. Using a fire poker signifies wasted effort in trying to rekindle a dying flame. Don't fret; a new fire can be built even before the ashes are cold.

Polar Bear. Due to its color, a polar bear in a dream is a good omen signifying an improvement in your circumstances. See also *Animals*.

Police. Police in your dream are a symbol of security in your life, and even if your dream involved trouble with them, it is an omen of contrary and signifies that you will get unexpected help with a current problem. See also *Arrest, Handcuffs, Jail, Black Maria*, etc.

Politeness. See *Manners*.

Politics. Discussing politics in your dream is considered a sign of success, providing the conversation was with someone of your own sex and the discussion wasn't heated; however, to talk politics with someone of the opposite sex suggests you are currently engaged in a futile effort. To

dream of being involved in a political campaign predicts added responsibilities with inadequate compensation.

Polo. A dream of playing or watching polo predicts an approaching increase in material wealth, probably through a legacy. See also *Horse*.

Pomegranate. See *Fruit, Colors,* and *Leaf (or Leaves)*.

Poncho. Help in time of trouble and/or protection when needed is the keynote in a dream of featuring a poncho.

Pond. Prosperity through industry is the message contained in a dream of a clear millpond, but if your dream featured any other kind of a pond, its meaning depends on the condition of the water and other elements. See also *Water, Landscape, Colors, Fish*, etc.

Pool. A swimming pool is a symbol of social gaiety, unless it was empty, dirty, or in poor condition, in which case it is a warning against gambling or speculation. A garden pool is a happy omen for love affairs. To dream of playing pool suggests that you would benefit from cultivating new interests and new companions.

Popcorn. If the popcorn in your dream was fresh, crisp, and tasty, it predicts love, vigorous health, and the means to enjoy them, but if it was stale, limp, or not fully popped, you are likely to hear some disappointing news.

Poplar. Poplars in a dream are a warning against reckless companions who will try to tempt you into foolishly dangerous adventures; be sensible—it's better to be square than squalid.

Poppy. Yellow poppies predict sensual delight, but red ones are a warning to control your passion and/or your temper. See also *Flowers*.

Porcelain. Whether new or old, fine china seen or used in a dream forecasts a gratifying improvement in your life-style.

Porch. To dream of sitting on a porch forecasts personal contentment, but a dream of sleeping on one portends social embarrassment.

Porcupine. This prickly creature is another good news-

bad news omen. You will have an increase in prestige but it will be accompanied by an increase in business worries. See also *Animals*.

Pork. Any form of pork in a dream predicts continued prosperity—if you're well fixed—or if you're not, you soon will be; and this applies whether you ate the pork, cooked it, served it, or bought it. See also *Meat*.

Porridge. See *Mush* and *Oatmeal*.

Port. Port wine in a dream is a sign of social popularity. Otherwise, see *Harbor*.

Porter. See under *Baggage* and *Travel*.

Portfolio. See *Briefcase*.

Porthole. If you dreamed of looking through a porthole, the meaning depends on what you saw, unless you saw another ship, in which case you are likely to have a surprise encounter with a forgotten friend or acquaintance from your past. See also *Ocean*, *Water*, *Sky*, *Landscape*, etc.

Portrait. To give or receive a portrait in your dream

is a warning of deceptive flattery around you; if your dream concerned having your portrait painted, or made by photography, it portends disenchantment in love; a dream of seeing someone else sitting for a portrait signifies a rise in status. See also *Artist, Oil Painting, Ancestors, Pictures, Colors,* etc.

Portugal. See *Foreign.*

Postcard(s). This friendly form of communication is, oddly enough, an omen of contrary, for if you sent, wrote, or bought one in your dream, you can expect to have some awkward moments over a past indiscretion, and if you received one, the awkward moments will concern a recent financial indiscretion.

Postman. This fellow in your dream is a straightforward symbol of news on the way.

Post Office. See *Letter, Package, Document,* etc.

Postponement. See *Delay.*

Pot(s). Flowerpots in your dream are a mixed omen; you may not have much money, but you'll have lots of joy and laughter. Cook-

ing pots are another reminder of the "trust everyone but cut the cards" rule. Broken pots portend a short season of sadness. See also *Pan* and *Jars.*

Potato. Serenity and security is the happy message contained in a dream of eating potatoes in any form; and a stroke of business luck is forecast if you dreamed of digging, cooking, planting, buying, or serving them. See also *Peel.*

Pouch. You will discover some useful information if you dreamed of a pouch, unless it was empty, in which case it is a warning against extravagance.

Powder. If you dreamed of spilling powder, it suggests that you are in a state of mental turmoil due to conflicting advice concerning a pending decision; get away by yourself and give your instincts a chance to work it out. Gunpowder in a dream predicts a lucky escape from danger. See also *Cosmetics.*

Power. This is a straightforward symbol of success in whatever concerns you most, and the greater the power was in your dream —regardless of its form—

the greater will be your achievement.

Prank. See *Joke*.

Prayer. Peace of mind and contentment with your lot in life are promised in a dream of offering up prayers; to dream of hearing others pray is a sign of loyal and lasting friendship.

Prediction. See *Occult*.

Pregnancy. For a woman, this dream forecasts a happy increase in material wealth, but for a man, it is a warning against indiscriminate sex relations.

Premonition. A (very rare) dream of having a premonition is telling you to avoid all possible risks for at least a month.

Prescription. A dream of contrary if the medicine was for yourself; if it was for someone else, you are likely to be disappointed in a friend or lover.

Present. See *Gift*.

President. See *Power, Politics, or Election*.

Prick. See under *Needles, Pin(s), Tack(s), or Nail(s)*.

Pride. An omen of contrary. If the pride in your dream was your own, you are likely to have to combat a challenge to your integrity, but if the pride was displayed by others, you will soon take a giant step upward.

Primrose. A dream featuring this charming plant forecasts a passionate but stormy love affair—for yourself or someone close to you. Fortunately it will soon blow over.

Prince (or Princess). A good news–bad news type of prediction is contained in a dream of meeting or seeing this rank of royalty. You can expect ever-increasing prestige, but you will have to guard against opportunist friends who will try to take advantage of it.

Print. If you dreamed of being a printer or of the printing business, it is a prediction that you will always have sufficient for your needs. To read something in print indicates the satisfactory solution to a current problem. A dream of seeing a printer at work or of watching printing presses in operation is telling you that you can attain your goal but it won't fall in your lap—you'll have to reach for it.

Prison. See *Jail.*

Privy. See *Toilet.*

Prize. To dream of receiving a prize suggests that you will be successful in your current endeavors; a dream of giving a prize indicates an increase in material wealth, possibly through an inheritance. See also *Nobel Prize.*

Prizefight. See *Boxing.*

Profanity. The meaning depends on the sex of the user. If it was a man who used the profane language in your dream, you can expect a temporary decrease in your income; but if the profanity was used by a woman, you are being warned about a casual love affair which could develop into a serious embarrassment unless you are extremely tactful. Try to remember that, when you are through with (or tired of) someone, it is a safer policy to lay him or her aside than to throw him or her away.

Professor. A dream of being a professor forecasts an improvement in your circumstances; to dream of being instructed by, or listening to, a professor, suggests that you will discover a new talent or find a rewarding new hobby.

Profit. If you dreamed of making a profit, you are being cautioned to keep your private affairs to yourself for the next few weeks and to avoid being drawn into the personal affairs of others.

Promise. This dream pertains to friends, and its meaning depends on whether you gave or received the promise. If you gave it, you are likely to forgive an enemy and gain a friend; if you received it, an unexpected happening will reveal a friendly enemy.

Propaganda. To dream of trying to influence the opinions of others portends that you will have to try to hold your own against an underhanded attack on your reputation; don't be a proud fool—fight back.

Propeller. If the propeller in your dream was in sound condition and/or working properly, it predicts swift progress; but if it was broken or you lost it, you are being warned that your carelessness or apathy will be someone else's gain.

Property. See *Land*.

Proposal. Whether the dreamed proposal was made or received, for a woman it predicts great popularity with the opposite sex; for a man it is a warning not to let his financial success go to his head—one cannot live by bread alone.

Prostitute. You are probably suffering from a fear of sexual failure or inadequacy if a prostitute featured in your dream; however, other aspects and elements in the dream must be correlated to determine its meaning, but as a general guide: If the prostitute involved in your dream seemed to be a sympathetic type, you are likely to be successful in some volunteer or non-commercial project. If she (or he) was a brazen, hard-boiled harlot type, you are being warned that unscrupulous behavior may cause you to be scorned by someone whose opinion you value. To dream of being solicited by one is a reminder that while flattery may get you everywhere, getting everywhere leads to arriving nowhere —so be selective with your favors. To dream of being a prostitute signifies good news from an unexpected source, unless you are one, in which case the dream obviously has no significance.

Prude. A dream of contrary. Prudishness in yourself or others is a warning to control your tendency to be too outspoken or you could lose a friend you'd like to keep.

Prunes. These dehydrated plums in a dream predict a change of residence, unless they were stewed, in which case they signify improving health. See also *Fruit*.

Ptomaine. To dream of suffering from food poisoning is a straightforward warning to watch your diet.

Publicity. A dream of reading something in print signifies a satisfactory solution to a current problem; however, if the publicity was about yourself or someone you know, the dream is reminding you that how you get on depends on how you handle other people—diplomacy is the watchword.

Publish. If you dreamed of having something published, you can expect an improvement in your circumstances; but if your dream involved being (or meeting) a publisher, it is a warning that you should guard against financial loss by relying on competent advice rather than entirely on your own judgment.

Pudding. Pudding featured in your dream predicts a satisfactory but unexciting life, unless it was a plum pudding, in which case you can expect your fortunes to vary from feathers to chicken.

Puddle. A disagreeable (or embarrassing) social experience is forecast in a dream of being splashed by a puddle, but if you escaped, or stepped around it, you can expect to be helped out of an awkward situation.

Pulpit. Be prepared for a period of lack of progress if you dreamed of a pulpit, unless you stood in it or spoke from it, in which case it signifies recognition in community affairs.

Pulse. An exciting new interest in life is forecast if your dream concerned your own pulse; but if your dream featured any other pulse, it is cautioning you against getting too confidential too soon with recent acquaintances.

Pump. The meaning of this dream varies according to the action and other elements, and in some aspects it can be considered an obstacle dream; but as a general guide: clear water flowing freely from an efficient pump is a symbol of gratifying rewards for your efforts, but if the water was cloudy or unclean, it portends a partial disappointment with some current plan. To push a pump handle without getting results is a caution that some help which you expect will not be forthcoming. A frozen pump signifies hard work for modest rewards, but if you successfully primed a pump, you are likely to have a pleasing albeit temporary stroke of luck. An oil pump forecasts eventual great wealth; an air or bicycle pump is a sign that the solution to any problems or difficulties you may have lies within your own power.

Pumpkin. Any form of pumpkin featured in your dream predicts a happy, comfortable homelife.

Puncture. A puncture in your dream is telling you

to stop being a victim of your own inflexibility. Try giving a chance to someone else's ideas occasionally; you might discover new horizons. See also *Tire*.

Punishment. See *Chastise*.

Puppet(s). These dolls featured in your dream are a sign that you are worried about being controlled by outside influences—or repressed fears—which are preventing your progress and/or enjoyment in life. Professional counseling would be likely to help you resolve your conflict.

Puppy. See *Dog*.

Purge. To dream of a political purge suggests you may be called on to arbitrate in a dispute between friends or colleagues. Try to avoid the Solomon bit or you are likely to end up backbitten.

Purple. See under *Colors*.

Purse. You are likely to be pleasantly surprised by a long overdue payment or repayment if you dreamed of finding a purse, but if you lost one, it signifies disillusionment with a friend or lover. See also *Handbag*.

Pus. The meaning of this dream depends upon the area where the wound or infection was seen. See under parts of body, also *Infection*.

Push. A happy omen of contrary. To dream of pushing anything predicts that whatever your troubles may be, you will rise above them or overcome them by your own efforts.

Push Button(s). A super surprise is signified in a dream featuring push buttons of any kind.

Putty. This material in your dream is a warning against wasting time and money on trivial passing pleasures.

Puzzle. An obstacle dream, and its meaning will relate to whether (or how easily) you solved it.

Pygmy. Whether they were hostile or friendly, these small people in your dream forecast emotional distress due to an unfortunate misunderstanding. Have patience and try not to grieve; the situation will eventually clear up.

Pyramid. You can expect a pleasant change of pace (possibly foreign travel) if you dreamed of a pyramid, unless it was lying on its side, inverted, or damaged, in which case it suggests approaching family or financial worries.

Python. This big snake signifies that someone is trying to snow you by intimidation. No matter how strong the pressure, stand your ground and victory will be yours.

Quack. If a medical-type quack was featured in your dream, you are being cautioned against accepting new acquaintances at face value. Otherwise, see under *Ducks*, *Geese*, or *Fowl*.

Quadrangle. You are approaching a satisfactory solution to your current problems if you dreamed of this kind of geometrical figure or courtyard.

Quadruplets. Double trouble is forecast in a dream featuring quads, but it will be minor and temporary.

Quail. A dream of eating it predicts an improvement in your living conditions; to dream of hunting it indicates an agreeable surprise. See also *Fowl*.

Quaker(s). Members of this sect are a generally favorable dream omen signifying a peaceful life through family unity and helpful friends.

Quality. To be concerned, in your dream, about the quality of anything suggests you are procrastinating regarding an important decision. Get off the fence; further delay may result in a loss by default.

Quantity. A very large quantity of anything suggests you are in danger of being overwhelmed by your responsibilities; keep calm and you'll find you can manage.

Quarantine. If a quarantine was the main feature of your dream, you can confidently expect that a current threat to your security will turn out to be a tempest in a teapot.

Quarrel. This is mainly a

301

dream of contrary signifying love and full accord, unless you dreamed of quarreling with a stranger, in which case it predicts a change of residence. See also *Argue*.

Quarry. Don't expect to rest on your oars if you dreamed of a quarry; you'll have to work hard for everything you get. See also *Stone(s)*.

Quarter. Be prepared for some delays or alterations in your current plans if your dream featured a fourth of anything. Otherwise, see *Coins*.

Quartet. To dream of playing or singing in a quartet signifies a decrease in status.

Quartz. A lovely piece of quartz in a dream is, oddly enough, a warning that you are in danger of being cheated by someone you trust. Be extra cautious concerning any business with friends.

Quay. Ships alongside a quay are a straightforward omen of travel, but a quay without ships is a warning of possible disappointment due to idleness or neglect of duty. See also *Dock, Harbor, Water,* etc.

Queen. See *King*.

Questionnaire. Irritating delays in the progress of plans already under way are forecast in a dream of filling out a questionnaire.

Questions. To ask questions in a dream is an omen of general good luck; but to be questioned is an obstacle dream the meaning of which relates to whether or not you could give satisfactory answers.

Queue. A benefit from family advice or generosity is forecast in a dream of waiting in a queue or observing one; to dream of seeing a Chinaman wearing an old-fashioned queue is a sign of approaching good luck.

Quick(s). You will be obliged to defend your honesty and/or integrity if you dreamed of cutting (or tearing) a nail down to the quick.

Quicksand. Pulling someone (or something) out of quicksand in your dream predicts a steadily increasing income; a dream of sinking in quicksand is a strong warning against mixing or prying into the personal affairs of others.

Quicksilver. See under *Mercury*.

Quiet. A dream of absolute silence or unusual quiet suggests a state of repressed nervous shock—see a doctor.

Quill. Plucking or using a quill in your dream predicts the receipt of important information which will be lucky for you.

Quilt. To dream of a luxurious down quilt is an omen of increasing prosperity; a patchwork quilt signifies domestic happiness. See also *Bedclothes*.

Quince. Cooked quince—as in jelly—indicates an annoying mystery regarding the behavior of a friend. Don't jump to conclusions; time will eventually disclose the truth. If you dreamed of eating fresh quinces, it is a reminder that your tendency to be too casual about your debts and/or responsibilities could suddenly embarrass you. See also *Fruit*, *Trees*, *Leaf*, and *Colors*.

Quinine. Whether you took it or gave it, this bitter dose in a dream is telling you that you are in bondage to old habits or associations that are holding you back. Freedom may be hard to achieve but the effort will be rewarding.

Quintuplets. No matter how immovable the obstacles in your path may seem at the moment, you will either overcome them or find a way around them if your dream featured quintuplets.

Quip. You can expect a pleasing invitation if you heard someone make a clever quip in your dream; if you made the amusing remark, you will soon be among new faces in new places.

Quirt. You are being warned against an unreliable friend if your dream concerned carrying or using a riding crop.

Quiver. A dream in which you were aware of the quivering of a person or an animal suggests that you are subconsciously worried by some form of obsessive overindulgence (such as sex, liquor, or gambling). If you can't kick the habit on your own, get professional help. To dream of a quiver full of arrows is an indication that closer attention to the target is needed if you are to attain your aim.

Quiz. See *Questions*.

Quoits. Quoits in a dream pertain to love affairs and your success in romantic matters will depend on how pleasant (or frustrating) you found the game. If you got a "ringer," it predicts that you will find an exciting partner who will bring out the best in you.

Quotations. Gratifying social success in intellectual circles is forecast in a dream featuring quotations from well-known sources, but obscure quotations are a warning to guard against a pretentious acquaintance who may try to exploit you.

Rabbi. Whatever your faith, a rabbi in your dream is a symbol of favorable influences around you. If you are Jewish, this dream signifies prosperity through fruitful efforts; if you are not Jewish, it indicates friends who will demonstrate their regard by helping you to achieve your ambitions.

Rabbit. Many rabbits in your dream signify an increase in responsibilities which will be pleasant rather than onerous; rabbit fur or anything made of it is a sign that you will eventually be able to afford sable. Otherwise, see *Hare*.

Rabies. This dire disease featured in your dream is a sharp warning that you have an unsuspected active enemy; take off your rose-tinted glasses and have a good look around your close circle.

Raccoon. Raccoon fur or articles made from it predict that you will find a new talent or hobby which will prove profitable as well as enjoyable. Otherwise, see *Animals*.

Race. To watch any kind of race being run is a form of obstacle dream in that it predicts success in whatever concerns you most, providing that in your dream you bet on (or rooted for) the winner. If you dreamed of running in a race yourself, you can expect an exciting new offer whether you won or lost. A dream featuring race relations signifies progress if the climate was pleasant, but disappointment if it was not.

Racket. A tennis or sports

racket in your dream is a caution to control your tendency to be too outspoken. Otherwise, see *Noise*.

Radiator. Remorse over an alienated friend is signified in a dream of a cold radiator; regret is a futile waste of energy but try to profit from the experience by thinking before you speak in future. A hissing radiator in your dream is a sharp warning to stop considering a shady deal or furtive affair; if you give in to the temptation, you might mortgage your whole future. If your dream concerned an overheated car radiator your love life needs unsnarling.

Radio. If the volume and/or program was pleasant, it signifies a happy domestic life; but if it gave trouble or was irritatingly loud, it predicts arguments or serious differences that need to be reconciled.

Radishes. These crisp roots in your dream signify swift success, unless you ate them, in which case you should be prepared to suffer some stiff competition or opposition before you get what you want.

Radium. Almost unlimited wealth but very little personal satisfaction is forecast in a dream featuring radium. If your dream concerned a radium burn, it is a warning to avoid all personal risks for the following month or so.

Raffle. Winning a raffle in your dream is a straightforward omen of an upcoming lucky phase. If you're inclined to take an occasional gamble, following this dream would be a propitious time to do it.

Raft. The meaning of this dream depends on various elements, such as the condition and kind of water, etc., which must be correlated to the action, but as a general guide: to dream of floating on a raft suggests that your indolence will lead to someone else's gain; a dream of building or repairing a raft is a forecast of achievement through your own efforts.

Rag(s). Clean rags predict a period of prosperity, but dirty or soiled ones suggest that you need to reassess your behavior and/or your current companions from a moral standpoint. If your dream concerned ragged clothing or other articles, see under separate listings.

Rage. If you dreamed of flying into a rage, you are being warned that you could lose the support of an influential person through lack of self-control; try to keep your cool in company and let off your steam on a punching bag or pillow. A dream of trying to calm someone else's rage suggests you are on a sticky wicket in regard to your current activities and a change of pace or location would probably be beneficial.

Raid. To dream of being in a raid is a caution to guard against loss of personal property; but if you dreamed of participating in a raid, you are likely to make a small profit in some unusual manner.

Railroad. Whether they were old-fashioned or streamlined type, railroad tracks in your dream signify good fortune in the offing; if you were walking the ties, you will achieve your aims through prudent hard work, but if you were walking the rails, you will be helped by influential friends. See also *Locomotive, Train,* etc.

Rain. This is a dream of strange variation in meaning depending on your circumstances and on the character of the rain. A soft spring rain is a lucky omen promising many good things to come, including possible benefits from work done in the forgotten past. If you are struggling or only modestly well off, a heavy downpour predicts a substantial improvement in your circumstances; but if you are one of the affluent society, it signifies a period of reverses. A fine drizzle portends petty difficulties which will soon pass; to be out in an average kind of rainfall indicates the happy demise of an ailing affair, but to be drenched in a blowing rainstorm is an augury of unexpected wealth, likely to be through a legacy.

Rainbow. Whatever the action may have been, if the main feature of your dream was a rainbow, it predicts the end of all your troubles followed by great happiness.

Raisin. If you ate the raisins in your dream, you can expect a season of cash going out faster than it comes in, so keep a tight grip on your spending as of now. Other than eating them, raisins in a dream signify pleasant social times ahead. See also *Fruit*.

Rake. To dream of using a rake is an omen of a happy family celebration; to step on a rake predicts a surprise which will be especially exciting if the handle hit you. See also *Hay* and *Leaf (or Leaves)*.

Ram(s). A dream featuring these aggressive creatures is telling you that it's high time to stop allowing yourself to be dominated by others; be independent even if it means making mistakes; at least they'll be your own.

Ranch. The meaning of this dream depends on the action and the type of ranch featured. If it was a dude ranch, you are being warned against repeating unfounded rumors; to dream of owning a ranch predicts prosperity after a period of hard struggle; a dream of working on a ranch indicates a coming season of sadness; selling a ranch suggests you will soon change old friends for new.

Rancid. Rancid food in a dream is a warning to guard your health by avoiding excesses in food,

drink, or whatever you're inclined to do to excess.

Ranger(s). Travel is forecast in a dream featuring these guardians of nature.

Ransom. Regardless of the action, if the main feature of your dream was ransom, you are likely to come by an unexpected and fairly impressive sum of money through a strange combination of circumstances. See also *Kidnap*.

Rape. Whatever form it took in your dream, this act is a warning to avoid loose companions or careless behavior that could seriously damage your reputation by giving a false impression to those whose opinions are important to your welfare.

Rash. See *Blemish, Skin*, etc.

Rasp. See *File*.

Raspberries. On the bush, in season, raspberries signify business and/or family unity; harvested or eaten from a bowl they predict passing pleasures.

Rat(s). These nasty rodents in your dream portend trouble through active but hidden jealousy; however, if they were white, you will be protected by benign forces. If you heard them gnawing but didn't actually see them, the dream is a warning that you are wasting your life in meaningless pursuits.

Rattle. A baby's rattle in a dream is an omen of contrary; you will find the satisfactions of maturity outweigh the responsibilities. However, an annoying and/or unidentifiable rattle in a motor or anything else portends a number of small worries.

Rattlesnake. As one would expect this dangerous snake in a dream is a symbol of unsuspected treachery from someone you trust, but if you heard its warning rattle and/or avoided its strike, you are likely to forestall the hostile maneuvers. If it bit you, you must be prepared for a fight.

Rattrap. To dream of catching a rat in a trap is a sign of improving circumstances; a dream of setting a trap augurs a sudden release from worry.

Raven. See *Crow*.

Ravine. See *Abyss*.

Ravioli. See *Spaghetti*.

Ray. A dream featuring destructive rays or radiation is a warning to guard your health. See also *X Rays*.

Razor. The meaning of this dream depends a great deal on the action and the condition as well as the kind of razor. If it was the old-fashioned barber's type and the blade was dull, it is a warning to control your temper and/or your passion or be prepared for serious consequences; if the blade was bright and sharp (or you honed it), the dream predicts that your ability to cut through irrelevant issues will bring you gratifying recognition. If you dreamed of cutting yourself on a razor (or razor blade), you will have to overcome some hostile opposition before you get what you want; fighting or slashing with a razor portends reverses due to impulsive, badly timed actions. However, a safety razor in your dream predicts achievement through clever application of your ability to organize. See also *Shaving*.

Read. Reading in a dream is a generally favorable omen signifying progress. If you were reading aloud, it predicts help from outside sources; to hear someone else read foretells future comfort and peace of mind. See also under *Book, Newspaper, Print,* and *Letter.*

Real Estate. A real-estate transaction in your dream, whether purchase, sale or transfer, predicts an increase in material wealth probably through inheritance. See also *Land.*

Reaper. See *Harvest.*

Rebellion. See *Revolution.*

Receipt. Whether you gave it, got it, signed it, or whatever, a receipt featured in your dream is a promise of better times ahead.

Reception. If you attended a reception in your dream, it signifies gratifying recognition for community or philanthropic work; if you gave a reception in keeping with your actual means, it predicts a rise in social status; but if you gave one that was ostentatious or pretentious, you are being cautioned against abusing your credit. See also *Party.*

Recipe. A recipe featured in your dream is telling you that all work and no play is a good formula for a

nervous breakdown, and all play and no work is a likely road to ruin; try to get your proportions in balance. See also *Cooking.*

Record. To dream of a record player or tape recorder (as equipment) is a sign of a deteriorating love affair; otherwise, the meaning of the dream must be determined by reference to what was being recorded or played.

Red. See *Colors.*

Reduce. An exciting new love affair is forecast in a dream of successfully slimming your figure. See also *Weighing.*

Reeds. Garden reeds are a symbol of unstable friendship and another reminder to trust everyone but cut the cards! For musical reeds, see *Musical Instruments.*

Reel(s). The meaning of the dream depends on what kind of reels were involved, but as a general guide reels are a symbol of success through perseverance. See also *Films, Thread,* etc.

Refrigerator. Putting food in predicts continued (or increasing) prosperity; taking food out is a forecast of unexpected guests.

Refugee. If refugees were featured in your dream, it means that you will have to defer your own needs to those of others for the time being. If you dreamed of being a refugee yourself, you are likely to reap an unexpected benefit from a favor done for love.

Regret. A dream of contrary; you will soon have reason to rejoice.

Reindeer. These dignified animals in your dream forecast a surprise gain. You are likely to recover something you thought lost (possibly a forgotten loan) or to discover that something you thought worthless is, in fact, quite valuable.

Relatives. Freedom from worry is forecast in a dream concerning cousins; aunts and uncles signify money matters; and other relatives (apart from immediate family) are an omen of help when needed. Of course the dream action must be correlated to get an accurate interpretation. See also *Parents, Sister,* and *Brother.*

Relief. A classic example of

contrary omen. If you dreamed of being on relief, you can be sure that better times are just around the corner.

Religion. Small troubles are portended if your dream featured the interior of a church, but to experience a spiritual feeling of religion in your dream augurs contentment and peace of mind. See also *Church, Cathedral, Prayer, Clergy, Rabbi,* etc.

Removal. See *Moving.*

Rent. If you dreamed of collecting it, you can expect a period of financial strain; if you paid it, you are in for a season of discontent; but if you dreamed that you were unable to pay rent when it was due, a pleasant surprise and/or unexpected gain is sure to follow.

Repair(s). A dream concerning household repairs predicts a sudden series of difficulties regarding your residence or living arrangements. A change might be beneficial.

Reptile. See under separate listings, as *Alligator, Python, Snake(s),* etc.

Rescue. Avoid all unnecessary

risks as you are likely to be in an accident-prone phase for a few weeks following a dream of being rescued; but if your dream involved rescuing someone else, or others being rescued, it signifies sudden success in overcoming a previously sticky obstacle.

Reservoir. The message contained in this dream relates to the amount of water contained in the reservoir. If it was full up, it predicts full prosperity; if it was empty, it portends difficulties though not of your own making. Partially full suggests sufficient resources for your requirements, and if the reservoir was in the process of filling, the wind of change will soon be blowing some new opportunities your way.

Resign. To dream of resigning from a position is an omen of contrary and signifies steady progress; and if you have any legal matters pending, they are likely to be resolved in your favor fairly soon.

Resolutions. See *New Year*.

Resort. Summer or winter resorts featured in your dream indicate a new romantic interest which should be kept within the bounds of lighthearted flirtation.

Rest. A real contrary one. You can expect some extra hard work to follow a dream of taking a rest, but the results will be rewarding.

Restaurant. This is a dream of contrast in meaning which relates to your personal circumstances. If the restaurant was, by your standards, very posh and/or ostentatious, it is a warning that temporary reverses or a sudden extra demand on your resources will entail a need to economize; if the restaurant was of the type you would normally patronize, it signifies pleasant social activities connected with business; but if the restaurant was in the cheap, greasy-spoon category or a counter café kind, you can expect an increase in your income soon.

Retirement. Yet another omen of contrary, for if you dreamed of retiring you are likely to be engaged soon in a new (or extra activity.

Reunion. Any kind of reunion featured in your

dream indicates that you will have outside help in furthering your ambitions.

Revenge. Chagrin and personal problems arising from your lack of sympathy with any viewpoint except your own are indicated in a dream of revenge. Remember that you must give consideration if you expect to get it.

Reverses. A peculiar form of contrary omen, for if you dreamed of having reverses, you can expect to have some, but they will be the kind from which you will quickly recover and eventually benefit. To dream of someone else suffering reverses predicts a sadness or illness for that person.

Revolution. If your dream concerned a bloody, shooting-war-style revolution, you are likely to have a complete change of circumstances; but if it was a bloodless political-coup type, it indicates a change of status.

Revolver. See *Guns*.

Revolving Door. A dream featuring a swinging door is telling you that the rut in which you are traveling is leading you nowhere;

marshal your assets and consider a new start, or if that isn't practicable try to rechannel your efforts within your present situation.

Reward. To receive a reward in your dream predicts an unusual stroke of luck; to offer one is a caution against complacency.

Rheumatism. See *Arthritis*.

Rhinoceros. Seen in his native surroundings this fellow is a warning against carelessness in meeting your obligations; but if he was in captivity or in a zoo, the dream suggests that you will have a social benefit due to your sexual prowess.

Rhubarb. Eaten, cooked, or growing, this vegetable in your dream is a symbol of satisfactory progress in your current undertakings.

Rhyme. See *Poetry*.

Rib(s). Any pain in, or injury to, your ribs in a dream is a warning that you are in danger of being cheated by being unwilling to recognize the trickster; brush the scales from your eyes before it's too late.

Ribbon. The meaning of ribbons in your dream depends a great deal on their color and use which should be correlated to the action; however they pertain mainly to your love life and are a warning against casual sex affairs. See also *Colors*.

Rice. An exceptionally happy domestic (or romantic) phase is the augury in a dream of eating rice; to see, serve, or cook it is a sign that you will be able to fulfill some obligations which have been worrying you; if you picked it yourself, or saw it being harvested, you can expect the development of a profitable business trend; to dream of throwing rice at a bridal pair predicts good news, probably concerning a trip.

Rich. If your dream concerned being more affluent than you actually are, it is, unfortunately, an omen of contrary and portends a protracted period of patience before your circumstances will improve. See also under *Money, Cake, Food*, etc.

Riddle. See under *Puzzle* and *Questions*.

Ride. See under *Horse, Automobile, Passenger, Carriage*, etc.

Rifle. See *Guns*.

Right. A dream in which the right side of anything or a right turn or direction is featured suggests that you are caught in a conflict between your desires and your principles. Usually the best solution to this type of problem is to let your conscience be your guide. To dream of being right-handed if you are not predicts success in pending legal matters (if any) and/or a pleasant rise in status.

Ring. To dream of losing or breaking your ring is a fortunate omen for business or financial affairs; if you found a ring or received one as a gift, it predicts a new love interest or an important new friendship. See also *Jewelry, Colors, Gold, Silver, Platinum*, etc., or under *Circle*.

Rink. An ice rink is a symbol of pleasant social activity, but a roller rink portends minor disappointment in a fickle friend.

Rinse. See under *Wash* or *Hair*.

Riot. A riot featured in your dream is a sharp warning to curb your extravagance

314

and/or sensual overindulgence.

Rise. To rise from the ground signifies victory over opposition; from a chair portends a temporary upset; from a couch or bench indicates an unexpected obstacle to be overcome. See also *Arise*.

Rival. An obstacle dream of contrasting symbolism. If your dream concerned a business rival, it pertains to personal affairs, and if a personal rival was featured, it pertains to business affairs. The meaning depends on how you coped with the dream situation. See also *Adversary*.

River. As with all water dreams the meaning is modified by the condition and appearance of the water. If you fell in the river, it indicates approaching domestic difficulties, but if you jumped in, you are being warned against hasty actions. To dream of sitting on, or walking along, the bank of a river is a sign that if you continue along your present lines success will follow. See also *Water, Sky, Landscape*, etc.

Rivet. For a woman, a dream featuring rivets suggests that she is involved in a relationship which has become either too possessive or overrestrictive, and an effort should be made to adjust the situation before it becomes a health hazard. For a man, this dream symbolizes a sex problem for which psychological counseling is likely to be beneficial.

Road. A straight broad road in good condition signifies steady smooth and satisfying progress; but unpaved, bumpy, narrow, or twisting roads represent difficulties to be overcome, and the meaning of the dream will depend on the outcome of your dream action in relation to the road. Road signs featured in a dream point to minor but pleasant changes in your living conditions.

Roar. The roar of rushing water in your dream is telling you that you are likely to defeat your own purpose by overaggressiveness; try a little gentle persuasion. If your dream featured the roar of machinery, it is a warning of unsuspected rivalry. Otherwise, see under *Lion*, etc., or *Animals*.

Roast. Although the oracles vary considerably in their

interpretation of this dream, the majority appear to agree that eating roasted food is an omen of general good luck; to carve, serve, or buy a very large roast is a forerunner to a family celebration, and a roast fish is a sign of a happy conciliation or reconciliation. See also *Lamb, Beef, Pork, Chickens,* etc.

Robber. Oddly enough, this dream pertains to affairs of the heart and suggests that you are in danger of losing your head over an unworthy (albeit fascinating) person; try to look behind the dazzling facade. See also *Robbery*.

Robbery. To dream of losing your valuables in a robbery is an omen of contrary and signifies unexpected gain, unless the robbery involved a loss of money, in which case it is a warning to be careful how you handle your cash.

Robin. One of the most fortunate omens you could dream up; great happiness is sure to follow.

Rock(s). An obstacle dream. Persistent difficulties which you will have to circumnavigate patiently are portended if you couldn't move the rock in your dream; if you were able to move it, or get around or over it, you can expect a general improvement in conditions. A rock fall is a sign of change.

Rocker. If the rocking chair was occupied, it forecasts contentment and relief from worry; if it was empty, it portends a period of loneliness and frustration, but don't despair— like the seasons it will soon pass.

Rocket(s). Easy come, easy go is the message contained in a dream featuring rockets.

Rocking Horse. Whether you rode it yourself or saw someone else sitting on it, a rocking horse in your dream is a fortunate omen for your personal interests.

Rod(s). A dream featuring rods suggests that you will eventually achieve your ambition by virtue of strong-willed determination. However, the interpretation of this dream will be modified by the material of the rod. See *Iron, Steel, Silver,* etc.

Rolling Pin. Use of a rolling

pin in your dream for its proper purpose indicates a happy family reunion, but if used in any other manner, it is a warning against hasty actions inspired by temper.

Rolls. See *Bread*.

Rolls-Royce. This international status symbol featured in your dream suggests that a new offer or opportunity (either now under consideration or soon to come) will actually be better than it appears and you would be wise to accept it.

Romance. See *Love*.

Roof. The action and other elements must be correlated to get an accurate interpretation of this dream, but as a general guide: a tiled roof signifies swift success; a thatched roof is a warning of danger through repeating idle gossip; to climb or stand on a roof predicts an impressive improvement in your circumstances; to see a roof on fire suggests that the things you worry about most will never happen; a dream of repairing a roof prophesies new sources of income; a shingled roof is a sign of emotional security; and a leaky roof indicates emotional and/or sexual problems. To dream of falling off or climbing down from a roof signifies a flash in the pan temporary success, which will be pleasant while it lasts but you should try for something less spectacular next time.

Rook. See *Crow* or *Chess*.

Room. If a strange room was the main feature of your dream, the meaning depends on the action and other elements which should be correlated, but as a general guide: to enter a strange room is a warning that a casual affair could turn out to be an incubus if you aren't careful; to find yourself in a strange room signifies sudden success if it was reasonably well-furnished, legal troubles if it was empty or only partly furnished. If the room was a very small one, it indicates a lucky last-minute escape from a regrettable mistake. See also *Furniture, Colors*, etc.

Rooster. See under *Cock*.

Root(s). Whether the roots involved were those of plants, trees, or flowers, the dream is telling you that you must assert yourself more actively if you want to prevent an aggressive rival from getting the benefit of your efforts. See also *Teeth*.

Rope. To dream of seeing or handling a coil of rope signifies the successful completion of a difficult task or assignment; to uncoil rope predicts the beginning of a new chapter in your life; if your dream featured the making of rope, you will soon learn the reason behind a longstanding mystery or puzzling situation; a rope noose indicates an unfortunate personal entanglement which will entail some unpleasant moments to loosen. To dream of walking a rope signifies a propitious period for speculation; to see someone else walking a rope is a sign of gain through influential friends. See also *Knot, Hanging, Cord, Skip, Ladder*.

Rosary. Telling (or counting) the beads of a rosary in your dream is a sign of greater contentment than you have previously known. See also *Prayer*.

Rosemary. See *Herbs*.

Roses. Gathering fresh roses of any kind in your dream predicts great joy; to give roses signifies that you will be well and truly loved; to receive roses promises extraordinary social success. Artificial roses, however, portend deceit or jealousy on the part of a trusted friend. See also *Garden, Flowers*, and *Colors*.

Rotten. See under *Fruit, Meat, Food, Eggs*, etc.

Rotunda. See *Dome*.

Rouge. See *Cosmetics*.

Roulette. See *Gambling*.

Row. If you dreamed of rowing a boat, or of being rowed in one, you can expect to make steady progress along your chosen path. See also *Oar* and *Race*.

Royalty. See *King*, etc.

Rub. Business or material success is the message in a dream of rubbing any inanimate object. Otherwise, see *Massage*, or *Animals*.

Rubber. Any form of rubber featured in a dream forecasts freedom from worry.

Rubbish. See under *Mess* or *Garbage*.

Ruby. Rubies are considered

to be a symbol of passionate love. See also under *Jewelry* and *Colors*.

Rudder. If the rudder was damaged or broken, the dream is warning you to avoid travel for the following two or three weeks; featured in any other way it indicates that your present course will lead to happiness. Persevere.

Rug. See *Carpet*.

Ruin(s). Ancient ruins featured in your dream are a lucky omen of improving conditions, but a contemporary ruin is a forecast of unhappy news concerning a close friend or relative.

Ruler. Measuring with a ruler in your dream suggests that you can achieve your aims through careful planning and cautious organization of your assets.

Rum. See *Alcohol* or *Drink*.

Rumble. News from a distance which may entail a hurried trip is forecast in a dream of strange rumbling noises; but digestive rumbles in a dream are a

straightforward caution to watch your diet.

Rummage. Small profits are predicted in a dream featuring rummage.

Run. A dream of running suggests that you are involved in a situation (or obligation) from which you would like to escape; talk it over with a competent adviser or friend before the resentment has serious repercussions. To dream of being unable to run indicates a lack of self-confidence. Try asserting yourself now and then; you might be surprised at the results. See also *Race*.

Rupture. If you dreamed of having a rupture, it is a straightforward warning against overexertion; slow down!

Rust. An omen of contrary; you will make an unexpected profit through your careful attention to detail.

Rye. To see it growing or harvested predicts prosperity; a dream of fresh rye bread forecasts an interesting new friendship. See also *Alcohol, Bar*, etc.

S

Sabbath. See *Sunday*.

Sable. This is a dream of contrast and contradictory symbolism, so its details must be carefully correlated to determine its meaning. If the main feature of your dream was the brown color of the fur, it predicts a stroke of money luck; if the luxurious fur itself was the important factor, the dream is telling you to curb your extravagance; if you saw the animal alive, it indicates the advent of a new and unusual friend into your life.

Sabot. See *Clogs*.

Sabotage. Observing or being involved in any type of sabotage in your dream portends arguments and/or disagreements with family or business associates which could have serious consequences, unless you exercise great tact. Be persuasive rather than aggressive.

Sack. Good luck in your current affairs is forecast if the sack was full; if it was empty, it signifies obstacles to be overcome.

Sacrifice. A dream of contrary; you will soon have reason to rejoice.

Sacrilege. If you dreamed of committing a sacrilege yourself, you are being warned against the influence of unsavory companions; but if your dream featured sacrilege on the part of others, it indicates a lucky escape from a dangerous situation. See also *Blasphemy, Profanity, Curse*, etc.

Saddle. To dream of any difficulty with a saddle suggests that you would be wise to give more careful attention to your personal affairs. Some revision in your current plans might prove beneficial. See also under *Horse, Leather,* etc.

Sadness. A dream of contrary. Whatever your worries or troubles may be, they will soon be over.

Safe. This dream is one of peculiar contrast in meaning, as a full safe (or strongbox) portends a series of unexpected worries; however, regardless of any present obstacles, an empty safe featured in your dream predicts ultimate great success.

Safety Pin(s). An excellent omen indicating that success is likely to follow if you continue along your present lines.

Saffron. This yellow spice in your dream is a warning that your tendency toward envy could alienate a valuable friend. If you can't control your jealousy, at least try to conceal it.

Sage. You'll be lucky if the sage you dreamed of was a wise man; if it was the spice, you can expect some changes for the better.

Sail(ing). If you dreamed of handling or observing the sails on a boat, it predicts approaching happiness; to dream that you were sailing under pleasant conditions and with favorable winds predicts prosperity, but uncomfortably choppy seas or dead calm portends disappointment. If you dreamed of sailing into harbor in a small boat, the forecast is of sudden success or unexpected good fortune.

Sailor(s). To dream of being a sailor suggests that you are dissatisfied with your present life conditions and you need a refresher. Consider making a change or taking a vacation. A dream featuring sailors onshore (or being in their company) indicates a probable new and exciting romantic interest; sailors on board a ship predict news from a distance which is likely to settle some uncertainty concerning business (or financial) matters.

Saint. A dream of seeing a saint is telling you not to lose heart; you can overcome your present difficulties if you persevere; however, if your dream concerned talking with a saint, you should consider making amends for some past indiscretion or injustice.

Salad. The meaning of this dream varies according to the action as well as the sex of the dreamer. If the main feature of the dream concerned the preparation of the salad, for a man it is a warning that his affections are not well-placed, and for a woman it is a caution against idle flirtation. However, if the dream concerned eating or serving a salad, it predicts approaching luck in financial matters for a man and a pleasing increase in social status for a woman.

Salary. Money from an unexpected source is predicted in a dream of being refused an increase in salary; however, if the requested raise was granted, it is a warning that you could suffer a loss of status (or a demotion) unless you pay more attention to your work. If you dreamed of spending money on the basis of a raise, it is a warning to economize, as you are likely to have to cope with either a temporarily reduced income due to business reverses or an unanticipated drain on your resources. To dream of paying a salary is a forecast of financial gain. See also *Money.*

Sale. An increase in material possessions through a legacy or valuable gift is forecast in a dream of going to a sale; to dream of the sale of personal belongings predicts an approaching increase in income.

Saliva. If your dream featured the saliva of a dog, it indicates that you are needlessly concerned regarding the loyalty of a friend or colleague; you can stop worrying. A dream of the saliva of a horse is a forecast of prosperity, and the saliva of other animals suggests that you will shortly find a way to overcome your present obstacles and/or outwit your opposition. Otherwise, see *Drool* or *Spit.*

Salmon. Canned salmon featured in a dream predicts an unconventional adventure; eating fresh salmon portends trivial lovers' quarrels or family disagreements, but the differences can be reconciled if you really care. See also under *Fish.*

Salt. In all respects an excellent omen, for even if you spilled the salt in your dream, the predicted difficulty will be of short duration.

Salvation Army. You will soon find yourself in a more contented frame of mind if your dream concerned this band of sincere do-gooders.

Sanitarium. A dream of being a patient in a sanitarium is telling you to take better care of your health, but a dream of visiting someone else there suggests you are worrying needlessly. In either case a medical checkup is likely to prove beneficial.

Sand. Whether the sand you dreamed of was on a beach, in your food, or in your shoes, it is warning you to be wary of a new acquaintance who will try to exploit you. See also *Desert*.

Sandals. To dream of wearing comfortable sandals predicts a new romance, but if they hurt your feet or were featured on someone else, they portend vexation concerning small money matters.

Sandpaper. Petty irritations involving relatives or close friends are forecast in a dream featuring sandpaper.

Sandstorm. See under *Desert*.

Sandwich. An interesting dream of varied omen depending on details. If you ate (or prepared) a sandwich at home, you will soon have an opportunity to improve your situation; if you ate the sandwich in a restaurant or at a lunch counter, it is a warning against confiding in casual acquaintances. Toasted sandwiches or sandwiches eaten outdoors on a picnic suggest that you are contemplating (or involved in) a love affair which could cause you serious embarrassment; in either case, think again.

Sapphires. Seen on others or in a display these lovely blue gems forecast an improved social status through influential friends; however, if you dreamed of wearing them yourself, the dream is warning you to restrain impulsive behavior. See also *Jewelry* and *Colors*.

Sardines. A dream of eating them is a warning to be on your guard against some hidden but active jealousy around you, but a dream of opening a can of sardines suggests that you are repressing a hostility or resentment which should be aired before it causes you acute mental distress; talk it over with a trustworthy friend or a professional adviser.

Sash. Happy domestic or love affairs are forecast in a dream featuring a sash. See also *Colors* and *Ribbon*.

Sash Cord. A dream concerning the sash cord on a window is a warning to take more careful precautions against possible intruders.

Satan. See *Devil*.

Satin. See *Silk*.

Satellite. This celestial hanger-on in your dream is telling you that you can achieve better relationships by asserting more independence of thought. You can listen to others, but don't be completely influenced by outside opinions.

Sauerkraut. Good health and happy social occasions are forecast in a dream of eating sauerkraut, cooking it, or drinking its juice.

Sausage(s). You are likely to be happily surprised by a sudden turn of luck concerning business or financial matters if your dream featured a variety of sau-

sages such as are displayed in a delicatessen or market; but a dream of eating sausages suggests you could be the cause of a broken marriage or love affair. Don't be mischievous in the matter or it might backfire.

Savage. If your dream featured being frightened or captured by one (or a few), it suggests that you have (or will have) an opportunity to retaliate for worry and/or embarrassment caused you by petty dishonesty in a friend or colleague; however, if your dream concerned many (or a tribe) of savages, it signifies that you need help to extricate yourself from difficulties arising through your own indiscreet behavior. Confide in a trusted friend.

Savings. See *Money*.

Saw. The interpretation here must be correlated with the action and type of tool. If you dreamed of a band saw, the dream is telling you to persevere and you will win the approval you seek; a jigsaw portends the breakup of a romantic attachment; a buzz saw is a warning that you are endangering your reputation and/or credit through association with undesirable companions; a hacksaw predicts an increase in responsibility but with unexpected compensations; an ordinary handsaw indicates difficulties and obstacles to be overcome during a change which will ultimately be an advance.

Saxophone. See *Musical Instruments* and *Music*.

Scab. Whether on yourself, others, or animals, scabs in your dream are an omen of contrary and predict an increase in material wealth.

Scaffold. Seen in your dream, a hangman's scaffold is a warning of serious danger to your future through your own indiscretions; you can avoid the impending disaster if you heed the warning and stop tempting fate! Scaffolding on buildings or houses is a sign of improving status and/or new opportunities. See also under *Rope* and *Hanging*.

Scald. Small difficulties followed closely by a stroke of good luck is the augury in a dream featuring a scald or scalding.

Scale. Scales, as such, in your dream are a symbol of important decisions to be made; to scale a fish is a sign that you will uncover a false friend. Otherwise, see *Weighing*.

Scallops. Raw scallops predict an unexpected but pleasant trip; eating or cooking them forecasts an improvement in living conditions.

Scandal. To dream of being involved in a scandal suggests that you would be well advised to clear your conscience regarding something you regret, but if the dreamed scandal concerned only others, you can expect to have to cope with a challenge to your integrity.

Scar(s). You are in for a short period of ups and downs if your dream featured scars on others; but if you dreamed of scars on yourself, it's your conscience nudging you to stop doing (or contemplating) something of which you are ashamed.

Scarf. A bright scarf in your dream forecasts a happy love affair.

Scarlet. See *Colors*.

Scenery. See *Landscape*.

Scent. See *Perfume* or *Odor*.

School. A dream of being in school suggests that your reluctance to break old associations is retarding your progress; to dream of leaving school or of seeing a school from the outside predicts a sudden stroke of money luck, but don't go wild; it will be transitory.

Scientist. To dream of this experimental-type fellow is a forerunner to an improvement in status.

Scissors. Scissors, as such, featured in a dream are thought to portend a broken relationship; but to use scissors signifies that you can outwit a jealous competitor by prompt action.

Scold. You are being warned against overconfidence if you dreamed of being scolded; but if you did the scolding, you can expect to find yourself in the midst of a family quarrel. Try to be diplomatic if you want to avoid a serious rift.

Score. A dream featuring anything to do with keeping a score is a warning to guard against activating the latent jealousy around you.

Scorpion. This poisonous spider in your dream is a warning of danger from treacherous friends or associates, especially if you killed it; however, you will overcome the hostile influences if it bit you.

Scrapbook. General good luck is forecast in a dream featuring a scrapbook.

Scrape. If the scraping in your dream featured metal, it portends a broken friendship, if it involved stone, it is a sign that you will shortly have reason to be grateful to the good influences which surround you; scraping by sand or sandpaper augurs some pleasant romantic news—possibly a wedding.

Scratch. Bleeding scratches are a warning against hidden hostility; nonbleeding scratches indicate that you have protective influences around you; to scratch yourself (especially your own back) in a dream forecasts an unexpected windfall of money.

Screams. A sort of dream of contrary in that to hear the scream of others signifies that you are likely to hear distressing news; however, to dream of screaming yourself is considered a fortunate omen for all that concerns you closely.

Screen. Any type of screen featured in your dream is a straightforward symbol of a desire to cover or hide a mistake. Either confess or forget it; worrying is a nonconstructive exercise.

Sculpture. If your dream featured sculptures, as such, it is a warning to pay more attention to your own personal affairs and less to those of others; to dream of being a sculptor or seeing one at work predicts an opportunity to make an exciting and interesting change.

Scythe. To observe a scythe in your dream suggests that unforeseen circumstances will cause a disagreeable encounter during which you must guard against hasty speech and/or actions; but to dream of a scythe in use forecasts an increase in material wealth.

Sea. See *Ocean*.

Seahorse. This tiny creature in a dream augurs pleasant adventures and/or travels in the offing.

Seal(s). Prosperity is predicted by a dream featuring seals (or their fur), unless you killed them, in which case you can expect a season of hard going as far as business is concerned. If the seal was the monogram or crest variety, as in a ring or fob, it signifies passing legal worries. A wax seal forecasts early success.

Seam(s). A suggestion to moderate your spending is contained in a dream featuring seams; you are likely to be in for a season of unanticipated demands on your resources.

Seance. To dream of a seance is a warning not to let foolish pride stand in the way of accepting needed help. See also *Occult*.

Search. The meaning of a search dream must be determined by reference to the purpose and object of the action; however, to dream of searching for an unknown purpose or thing is your subconscious reminding your conscience that you are wasting your time in meaningless activity and/or relationships.

Searchlight. Observing, or being in, the beam of a powerful searchlight is a sign that you can get what you want but you will have to concentrate on it to the exclusion of all else; to see many searchlights crisscrossing the sky indicates coming danger from hostile competition. Forewarned should be forearmed!

Seat. To dream of falling from your seat is a straightforward warning of possible loss of status through your own careless behavior. Pay some attention to the opinion of others.

Seaweed. Tangled seaweed in a dream is a suggestion to resist being influenced to behave contrary to your own principles. A firm stand will pay long-term dividends.

Secret. Intrigue among those you have trusted is forecast in a dream of hearing a secret. To repeat a secret is a sign that you will have to defend yourself against malicious gossip.

Secretary. If you dreamed of being a sceretary, it is an indication that you are in bondage to habits which are holding you back; a dream of engaging a secretary is a sign of improving status.

Seduction. See *Rape*.

Seeds. New experiences through new opportunities is the message in a dream of seeds. The winds of change are blowing your way; don't be deterred by misplaced loyalty.

Seesaw. A short-lived but exciting love affair is forecast in a dream of a seesaw; enjoy it while it lasts.

Senator. Whether the dream involved being one or seeing one, for a man, it predicts that he will be called on to do a favor for a friend; for a woman, it forecasts an improvement in social status.

Separation. A dream of contrary. You can expect to reach a better understanding with the object of your affection.

September. Changes for the better are predicted in a dream of September during other months.

Serenade. A dream of being serenaded signifies a happy outcome to your current problems. See also *Music* and *Singing*.

Sermon. To hear a sermon inside a church is a warning to expect a delay in some cherished plan; to deliver a sermon suggests that your doubts concerning a trusted friend are groundless.

Serpent. See *Snake(s)*.

Servant(s). A dream of contrary. To dream of being a servant signifies long-awaited happiness; but to dream of having servants portends financial reverses.

Sewing. In some respects an obstacle dream, but the interpretation varies according to the action. To see someone else sewing is a sign that you would be wise to be more diligent in providing for your future; but if you dreamed of doing the sewing, an exciting new opportunity for advancement will soon come your way. Hand sewing suggests hard work ahead; machine sewing indicates a need to be more cautious about giving confidences. To finish the sewing forecasts success in your current undertakings, but to leave it unfinished is a sign of troubles to overcome.

Sex. For a woman, a dream of changing her sex predicts an unexpected honor or success in the family; but for a man to dream of having a sex change portends a necessity to make an embarrassing ex-

planation regarding his sexual inadequacy. Sexual teasing in a dream indicates the realization of an unworthy ambition. Otherwise, see *Intercourse, Orgy, Impotence, Incest,* or *Sexual Organs*.

Sexual Organs. In some aspects a dream of contrary. A dream of having diseased sex organs is telling you to practice a bit of under-indulgence for a time; to dream of having deformed organs is a warning against casual sex relations; if your dream concerned unusual organs, it augurs an increase in social popularity; to dream of having no sexual organs suggests you could benefit from some competent advice regarding your sex life; and if you dreamed of exposing your sex organs, you are being warned that your reputation is in danger through your own indiscretions.

Shabby. A dream of contrary. See under *Clothes, Dress, Coat,* etc.

Shade. Lowering a shade is a sign that your grasp is greater than your reach; back up and reassess your position. To dream of raising a shade predicts success in the enterprise that interests you most; a shade snapping suddenly to the top of the roller indicates sudden surprising news.

Shadow. Most authorities seem to agree that to be aware of your own shadow in a dream is a sign of a beneficial legal matter, likely to be an inheritance or legacy. However, if the shadows were not your own, their meaning must be gleaned by correlating the other details of your dream. To dream of the shadow of a dead person is an indication of a temporary obstacle; the shadow of a living person is believed to be a warning against travel or unnecessary risks for a few weeks' time.

Shake. See under *Hand.*

Shampoo. See *Hair.*

Shamrock. See *Clover.*

Shark. This disagreeable swimmer is an omen of danger from dishonest friends or associates; be extra cautious in all financial matters for the time being.

Shaving. As a general guide, to dream that you are shaving or being shaved is a warning of financial pitfalls ahead. Don't borrow, lend, or invest for a period of three months and be very careful in whom you confide. See also *Hair, Beard,* and *Razor.*

Shawl. If you dreamed of wearing a shawl on your head, you can expect your love affairs to be satisfactory; to dream of wearing a shawl on your shoulders, or of carrying one, is an omen of a temporary financial difficulty followed by an unexpected gain. A shawl on its own symbolizes money and/or security and should be correlated to the dream action as such. See also *Colors, Lace,* etc.

Sheep. If there was a black or gray one among them, the dream is warning you to watch your step as regards your personal behavior; otherwise, sheep are an excellent omen for all that concerns you deeply. See also *Lamb.*

Sheet(s). See *Bedclothes.*

Shelf. Be prepared for unexpected delays and hitches in your current plans.

Shell(s). Seashells are an omen of unusual experiences and/or events; nutshells are a symbol of success if they were full, disappointment, if empty. Strange news from a distant place is the forecast if you dreamed of listening to the roar in a conch shell.

Sheriff. Family quarrels are the forecast in a dream featuring a sheriff; stay out of it if you can, and if you can't, try to pour oil on the waters.

Sherry. See *Wine.*

Shin. See *Leg* or *Bone.*

Shine. See *Light, Metal, Shoes,* and in the interpretation chapter.

Shingle(s). Shingles in your dream represent success through hard and painstaking effort. To dream of buying them in large quantity predicts a money windfall.

Ship. Whether powered by sail, steam, or motor, ships in your dream are an augury of profitable ventures. To be in a shipwreck portends a situation in which you will have to defend your reputation. To see or build a model of a ship promises a mad new love affair within the year. A single battleship seen in your dream indicates an improvement in your living conditions; a fleet of ships is a sign of business success. In any dream of ships, the condition of the water and weather must be taken into consideration.

Shirt. A clean shirt in a dream is an omen of good luck, but a soiled or messy one portends a period of gloom. See also *Clothes.*

Shock. An omen of contrary. Whatever your difficulties may be, you'll find a way to overcome them.

Shoes. Shabby or worn shoes are an omen of success; new shoes are a warning against overconfidence; to dream of losing your shoes indicates that you are wasting your efforts in unproductive activity; to shine your shoes predicts an unexpectedly fortunate venture. To see a shoemaker at work is a sign of an unanticipated new business offer.

Shoot. See *Guns.*

Shop. Buying in one predicts petty financial problems which can be overcome by the use of a little self-restraint; working in one forecasts a stroke of money luck.

Shore. See *Beach, Sand, Tide(s), Ship, Boat, Port,* etc.

Shorthand. See *Secretary*.

Shovel. If a shovel was the main feature of your dream, you can expect an increase in your responsibilities in the near future.

Shower. To dream of taking a shower is an omen of coming prosperity. Otherwise, see *Rain*.

Shrimp. Cooking, eating, or serving shrimp in your dream is a promise of pleasant social times to come.

Shroud. A dream of contrary signifying an unusual celebration ahead, likely to be connected with a legacy.

Shrubs. Peace of mind and prosperity is the message contained in a dream of healthy shrubs, but if they were withered or dead, it is a warning of difficulties in your personal relations due to inconsiderate behavior.

Shuffle. Whether the shuffling was done by yourself or someone else, it predicts an approaching crisis in your love affairs and/or domestic life.

Shy. If your dream featured your own shyness, it is a forecast of success in your current undertakings; but if you dreamed of the shyness of others, you are likely to be thwarted in an immediate plan by the sudden backing out of someone you rely on.

Siam. See *Foreign*.

Sick. See *Illness*.

Sieve. Any dream in which a sieve is the main feature is a warning to curb your extravagance if you want to avoid a serious embarrassment.

Sigh. A dream of contrary, and the deeper the sighing, the happier will be the coming events.

Sign. To dream of a road sign predicts an approaching opportunity to make an important change. Get competent advice b e f o r e making the decision.

Signal. The meaning of this dream varies considerably according to the details of its action, but as a general guide, signals represent the realization of long-delayed wishes or ambitions.

Signature. Putting your signature to anything in a

dream is an indication that, though you may enjoy only limited prosperity, you will have unlimited security. Signatures other than your own signify long-term loyalty from friends and/or associates.

Signpost. See *Sign*.

Silence. See *Quiet*.

Silhouette(s). However featured, silhouettes in a dream augur contentment and happiness in life.

Silk. A dream of wearing silk is a fortunate omen which promises all the necessities of life and some of the luxuries as well. If your dream featured spun silk or bolts of silk, it is a warning to guard against joining the "flattery will get you everywhere" brigade.

Silo. To dream of taking anything out of a silo is a warning against too much high living in low places; a dream of putting anything into a silo is a caution to guard your credit.

Silver. Silver money featured in a dream is an omen of plenty but coupled with heavy responsibility; however, to dream of silverware suggests that you may be ignoring the spiritual side of life in favor of the materialistic.

Singing. This dream must be interpreted according to its details, much the same as a music dream and its meaning depends, to a great extent, on whether or not the sound was pleasing, but as a general guide: to sing in your dream signifies passing troubles; to dream you hear others singing foretells happy news; if you were aware of a bass voice, it is a warning that there may be some irregularities in your business or financial affairs, or if your main preoccupation is with love affairs, you can expect some sudden quarrels or a possible estrangement. To dream of a soprano singing solo predicts a gradual introduction into a new and exciting social environment. To hear or join in the singing of hymns indicates recognition in community affairs.

Single. For a married man or woman to dream of being single again is a warning against getting involved with companions whose fast reputation could rub off to your detriment.

Sink. Unhappy news concerning a friend is the portent

in a dream featuring the sinking of anything.

Siphon. New and exciting events are forecast in a dream featuring a siphon.

Sister. The meaning varies according to context and sex of the dreamer. For a man, it signifies emotional security, but for a woman, it portends domestic disagreements. An objective dream of sibling unity between sisters is an indication of emotional stability.

Sister-in-Law. Same as *Sister*.

Sit. This dream follows, to some extent, the general rule of up and down. If you dreamed of sitting on a high seat or place, you can expect an improvement in status; if your dream featured sitting on a low seat, it is telling you that you could benefit by asserting yourself more.

Skate. Good times are predicted by a dream of either ice or roller skating; however, if you fell or went through the ice, it is a warning against trying to advance at the expense of others.

Skein. Romantic disappointment if the threads were tangled, but happiness in love if they were smooth.

Skeleton. A skeleton featured in your dream predicts news of a legacy, unless it was seen as part of a medical display or in a museum, in which case it augurs new and interesting friends and events.

Skid. A dream of skidding suggests that you are heavily involved in a problem (or problems) concerning which you are reluctant to make a decision. You can't evade the issue so get advice—if you need it—then take the bull by the horns. If you recovered from a skid in your dream, you can expect a favorable turn of events in financial matters.

Skin. The meaning varies according to the details of the action, but as a general guide: smooth attractive skin signifies happiness in sexual and/or domestic affairs; blotchy skin suggests emotional difficulties and a need to unsnarl your love life; peeling skin predicts a period of unhappiness but followed by a rewarding new relationship.

Skip. If your dream featured skipping, it predicts that you will get help when and where you least expect it.

To skip rope in your dream signifies that your self-doubts are unfounded; you are generally well-liked and your friends are loyal.

Skirt(s). This dream omen follows the same pattern as do the fashions in relation to the economic cycles; if your dream featured short and/or tight skirts, it is telling you to be prepared for a season of financial strain; long and/or full skirts prophesy an increase in material wealth. Otherwise, see *Clothes* and *Colors*.

Skull. See *Skeleton* or *Death's Head*.

Skunk. To see or smell a skunk in your dream predicts a social disappointment. Don't brood; you can't win them all, and new doors will eventually open.

Sky. The omen here depends on the weather details. A clear sky, whether light or dark, signifies happy times ahead; a few clouds, dispersing, are a sign of minor difficulties easily overcome; a few clouds, gathering, indicate obstacles which will require more effort; and a stormy sky portends a period of stress that will require courage and determination. A gray sky is a sign of reliable friends who will stand by you in all kinds of weather.

Slap. A dream of contrary: If you got slapped, you will win some well-deserved but unexpected social kudos; if you observed, or did the slapping you are likely to suffer a social embarrassment.

Slate. Coming prosperity is indicated in a dream featuring a slate roof. See also *Roof* or *Blackboard*.

Slaughter. Whether your dream involved animals or people, in a slaughterhouse or elsewhere, it suggests that you are sacrificing personal happiness on the altar of material success. If you want to avoid unpleasant repercussions, try to achieve some kind of balance.

Sled. An exhilarating ride on a sled in your dream predicts a hectic love affair; if you fell off into the snow, the affair will be a very brief encounter.

Sleep. Many of the more modern psychologists believe that this rare dream demonstrates a wish to escape reality and is a possible sign of approaching illness; however, reference to the older oracles suggests that the omen in the dream depends on whether its main feature was who (or what) the dreamer slept with or alternatively WHAT the dreamer slept on, as follows:

WITH	OMEN
A stranger	Embarrassment
A spouse	Happiness
A lover	Uncertainties
A child	Family joy
A friend	Security
Animals	Warning against accidents

ON	OMEN
Wool	Fulfillment
Water	Danger
Street	Sadness
Straw	Rejuvenation
Hay	Material wealth
Sand	Disappointment

Sleet. See *Snow*.

Sleeve(s). One sleeve predicts unexpected travel; short sleeves mean a slight disappointment; long sleeves indicate community recognition; tight sleeves forecast sexual pleasures; full sleeves are a warning to control your temper. See also *Coat, Dress, Clothes, Colors, Repair(s), Mend*, etc.

Slide. See under *Skid, Sled,* and *Ice*.

Slip. To dream of losing your footing on something slippery is a warning to be more selective about where you place your confidence. Otherwise, see *Petticoat, Ice,* or *Skid*.

Slipper. Comfortable slippers signify contentment, uncomfortable ones indicate domestic problems; otherwise, see *Shoes*.

Slot Machine(s). Whether you played them, observed others playing, won, lost, or broke even, these one-armed bandits featured in your dream are telling you to conserve your resources because you are likely to have some unanticipated demands on them in the near future.

Smallpox. Strangely enough, a dream of having, or being exposed to, this serious disease is an omen of unexpected profits through new and influential friends.

Smile. A straightforward happy omen whether you did the smiling or observed others smiling. You are likely to have an unanticipated reward for a long-forgotten favor.

Smoke. If your dream featured smoke from a known source (i.e., a fire or chimney), it signifies improving financial conditions; however, if you saw or smelled the smoke but couldn't identify its source, you are likely to be in for a period of annoying worries or petty disappointments. Keep your chin up; you'll soon find comfort in new experiences. See also *Cigar (or Cigarette)*, *Pipe(s)*, *Coal*, etc.

Smuggle. Be prepared for a sudden exposition of your family skeleton (if any), or something you've kept carefully hidden, if your dream featured smuggling or smugglers; however, the embarrassment will soon pass, leaving you in a better frame of mind than ever before.

Snail(s). There is a wide variation as to the meaning of snails in a dream, but the consensus seems to be that they represent personal and/or love affairs. As a general guide: to see them crawling signifies a long-awaited social achievement; to see one with long horns indicates an unfaithful lover; and to step on one warns of a false friend in your close circle. If you cooked or ate them in your dream, you can expect a long period of domestic contentment.

Snake(s). In its psychological interpretation a snake in your dream is a phallic symbol, and to dream of one, especially if it was coiled around you, or otherwise on your body, is a warning that you may be a slave to either your sexual passions or repressions. However, according to the oracles, snakes in a dream are warnings of various troubles, obstacles, or treachery. Of course the colors and other details must be carefully considered, but as a general rule: to dream that you were bitten by one portends a period of struggle against unfortunate circumstances, and if it was a cobra, it carries a special warning to guard against accidents in the following few weeks. If your dream featured a snake wound around you which you could not throw off, you are being warned to expect treachery where you least suspect it. To dream of being surrounded and unable to kill more than one or two indicates that you are in danger of being seriously cheated by someone you trust, but if you managed to kill (or get rid of) them all, it is a sign that you will succeed in spite of any hostile opposition; to walk over snakes without trying to kill them suggests that you will, in the end, actually turn the tables on those who are trying to block your way. To dream of playfully handling snakes suggests that you are in danger of being led astray by unprincipled friends or associates; and if your dream featured a professional snake charmer at work, it indicates that you will have to defend your reputation against malicious gossip.

Snare. See *Trap(s)*.

Snatch. If you did the snatching, the dream is telling you to leave important issues for the time being or you may thwart your ambitions and/or hopes; however, if the snatching was done by others, the omen is of success, but only after a series of delays.

Sneeze. If you dreamed of sneezing, it means that nothing is likely to upset your applecart for some time to come; but if your dream concerned others sneezing, the indication is that you may have to do a bit of scheming and/or fighting to get what you want. Persevere.

Snow. This is a generally good omen, unless you ate the snow, in which case it portends a coming season of sadness. To dream of deep snow or of a snowstorm signifies hard work but with an unexpected big success at the end; wet snow on trees, etc., is an omen of profitable investments; snow in the autumn indicates unusual happiness; in the spring it predicts an unanticipated material gain; in the summer it means a good business season ahead; in the winter it predicts success after minor difficulties; on the mountains it forecasts important good news; to wash in it is a sign that you will soon see the end of any troubles you may now have; to shovel it augurs h e l p from influential friends. A dream featuring snowshoes predicts a surprise reward for a past kind deed.

Snuff. Happy social times ahead are promised in a dream featuring snuff.

Soap. Scented soap featured in a dream predicts satisfaction in love affairs; soap flakes or laundry soap suggest that you will have to cope with strong competition to achieve your aims; medicated or antiseptic soap is an omen of revealed mysteries.

Sob. An omen of contrary, Good news will shortly follow.

Socks. See *Stockings*.

Soda. Soda water in your dream predicts contentment and comfort through your own hard efforts; ice-cream soda forecasts an exciting new friendship.

Sofa. See *Furniture* or *Couch*.

Soil. See *Earth* or *Dirt*.

Soldiers. For a woman to dream of soldiers is a warning against casual love affairs; but for a man, it predicts surprising business (or professional) changes.

Soles. See under *Fish, Shoes,* or *Feet*.

Solitaire. Playing solitaire in your dream predicts an unexpected increase in responsibilities, unless you won, in which case it predicts an unexpected windfall of money.

Sorcery. See *Magic*.

Sore(s). If you dreamed of sores on yourself, you can expect an improvement in general personal conditions; but if the sores in your dream were on others, or on animals, you'd better be prepared for a period of self-sacrifice in the interest of others. See also *Scab*.

Sorrow. A dream of contrary. You will be comforted.

Soup. Hot soup in a dream indicates a struggle from which you will emerge better than you hoped; cold soup portends an unsatisfactory love affair or unsympathetic companion; don't flog a dead horse and feel sorry for yourself if it fails to respond—try for a new relationship, or if that's not practical, try for a new hobby. To dream of being annoyed by a noisy soup slurper indicates an exciting invitation.

Sour. A dream of eating something excessively sour suggests that you may be in danger of sacrificing personal happiness for material success; reassess your values.

South. To dream of being in southern places or of moving or traveling southwards is a sign of coming security.

South America. See *Foreign*.

Sow. See *Plant(s)* and *Seeds*.

Spade. See under *Ace, Cards*, etc., or *Shovel*.

Spaghetti. Gay social times are forecast in a dream featuring spaghetti, and if you dripped the sauce on yourself, you can expect a real celebration soon.

Spain. If you dreamed of Spain or of anything Spanish, see *Foreign*.

Spaniel. Any type of spaniel in a dream is an augury of a pleasing improvement in home conditions. See also *Dog* and *Colors*.

Sparrow. These busy birds featured in your dream are harbingers of lean times ahead, unless you chased them away, in which case it signifies good business news. See also *Birds*.

Spear. An exciting love life is usually the message in a dream of using a spear, especially if it was used to catch fish; however, if you're not eligible or susceptible, the dream suggests a clearing of obstacles in your path.

Spectacles. See *Eyeglasses*.

Specter. See *Apparition, Ghost*, or *Occult*.

Speech. Improved status in social position and/or business is forecast in a dream of making a speech. See also *Oration*.

Speedboat. Achievement of an important objective is predicted in a dream of riding in or driving a speedboat.

Spell. If you dreamed of spelling words correctly, it signifies success in your current affairs, but if you misspelled any, it is a warning to be on guard against hidden hostility.

Spend(ing). A contrary omen warning you to economize for the time being. See also *Money* and *Extravagance*.

Sphinx. An omen of contrary. You will soon have the answers to some things which have puzzled you in the past.

Spice(s). Pungent spices featured in a dream are a warning that you are in danger of being exploited by an unscrupulous member of the opposite sex. See also under individual listings as *Cloves, Ginger*, etc.

Spider(s). Spiders with one exception (see *Tarantula*) in a dream are a sign of general good luck; to kill one signifies good news; if it was spinning it augurs approaching money; climbing a wall it's a harbinger of success in all that concerns you most deeply.

Spin. Industrious perseverance will generate the power to carry you to your goal if your dream featured spinning. See also *Cotton, Silk,* and *Colors.*

Spinach. The omen varies according to the details. A healthy happy life is forecast by a dream of eating spinach, unless you found it gritty or bitter, in which case it portends quarrels with friends or family. See also *Vegetable(s).*

Spine. See *Bone, Back,* and *Skeleton.*

Spinster. The meaning of the dream depends on its details in relation to your sex and status, but as a general guide: a group of unmarried ladies in a dream forecasts happy social events; an old maid type featured in your dream is a warning against impulsive behavior. For a married woman to dream of being a spinster predicts an unexpected change of circumstance and/or status. For a single woman it indicates a serious new attachment on the horizon.

Spire. True love and friendship are the omens in a dream of a spire outlined against the sky. However, if the spire was twisted or leaning, it is a sign that you will have some difficulties to overcome before you achieve your goal.

Spirit. A dream of seeing or speaking with a spirit is a warning of deception where you least suspect it. See also *Occult, Seance,* and *Ghost.*

Spit. A rift with a friend is likely to follow a dream of seeing someone spit; try to be more diplomatic in putting forward your opinions.

Spite. A dream featuring spite suggests a physical malfunction; have a medical checkup.

Splinter. If you dreamed of having a splinter in any part of your body, it is a warning to control your temper; if your dream featured a splinter in someone else, it is a warning to pay closer attention to your personal affairs if you want to avoid a loss.

Sponge. The meaning of this dream varies according to

the action, but its omen is generally good. If you washed with the sponge, it forecasts satisfying recognition for work well done; if you squeezed water out of it, you can expect an increase in your income; but if you tried to squeeze it and found it dry, you are being warned against indulging in any form of gambling at the present time.

Spool. Here again the omen depends on the action and the details. A full spool indicates pleasantly busy times ahead; an empty spool suggests a possible loss of status through improvidence; winding onto a spool is a sign that you may be retarding your own progress by being overcautious; unwinding from a spool predicts a new and profitable venture. If your dream featured slipping or falling on a spool, it is warning you against indiscriminate sex relations.

Spoon(s). Spoons in a dream are a symbol of domestic happiness, unless you lost them or snitched them, in which case you are being warned against a loss due to an unwise deal; before you invest—investigate.

Sports. Any display of sports-manship in a dream is a generally favorable omen and indicates advancement in your chosen endeavor through the help of influential friends. More specifically; Badminton suggests important decisions in the offing; Baseball promises a happy homelife; Basketball predicts competitive but satisfactory sex affairs; and Cricket forecasts boring but useful social affairs. It is especially lucky to dream of winning in any athletic or sports endeavor. To injure (or strain) yourself in a game or contest augurs business and/or social advancement.

Spot(s). As a general guide spots are an omen of new opportunities, but other elements of the dream must be coordinated, such as what the spots were on, their size, nature, etc. See under *Skin, Stain(s), Cloth, Clothes, Colors,* etc.

Spotlight. See *Searchlight* and *Light*.

Sprain. If you dreamed of spraining any part of your body, you are likely to receive an unexpected honor, and the more painful the sprain the greater the recognition.

Spring(s). To dream that spring has sprung before it has is a favorable omen for new enterprises; otherwise, a dream of spring out of season suggests a renewal of sexual vigor and/or happiness in affairs of the heart. Bedsprings featured in a dream pertain to changes in living conditions, and mechanical springs are a warning of disloyalty in personal relationships or infidelity in love. Otherwise, see *Water* or *Well.*

Spruce. See *Trees.*

Spur(s). If the spurs in your dream were bright silver, they predict wealth; otherwise, they suggest that you should try to adjust, or cut off, a relationship under which you are chafing.

Spy. If you dreamed of being spied on, you are being warned against impulsive behavior; but if your dream concerned being a spy or spying on others, you can expect some exciting new offer or adventure to come your way fairly soon.

Squall. See *Storm(s)* or *Ocean.*

Square(s). Eventual success and security will be yours if your dream featured anything in this form.

Squash. A profitable opportunity which you should make the most of will come your way if your dream concerned cooking or eating squash. See also *Vegetable(s).*

Squint. For a woman, this dream pertains to love affairs and is a good omen; for men, it relates to business or professional affairs and predicts improving conditions.

Squirrel(s). The omen in a dream featuring squirrels varies according to the action. If you fed them or observed them eating or carrying nuts away, it signifies comfort through prudence and diligence; to see them running or chasing each other aimlessly suggests you are heavily involved in a profitless love or business affair which you would be wise to forget about; to see squirrels running up—or sitting in— a tree is a warning of possible financial embarrassment; pull in your belt before you stretch your credit to the breaking point.

Stable. A dream of contrary. A full stable is a warning

against greed, but an empty stable predicts health and prosperity. See also *Horse, Colors, Manure,* etc.

Stadium. See *Sports.*

Stag. An antlered stag featured in your dream is a symbol of sexual vigor and/or personal power, unless it was brought to bay, in which case it is a warning that you are in danger of losing status due to overaggressiveness; cool it!

Stage. See *Acting.*

Stagecoach. See *Carriage.*

Stagger. To dream of staggering is a caution against the flattery of those who wish to exploit you; if your dream concerned others staggering, you can expect to be asked to help a friend who is in trouble.

Stain(s). As a general guide stains symbolize worries, and in order to interpret your dream, you must correlate them to what kind they were, i.e., blood, fruit, rust, etc., and what they were on, i.e., clothes, carpets, walls, etc. See also *Colors.*

Stairs. This dream follows the general "up" is good, "down" not so good, rule (see the chapter on inter-

pretation); however, as an additional guide: to fall upstairs augurs well for love affairs, and to fall—as opposed to stumble—downstairs is a warning to be less controversial in your expressed views; if you dreamed of sweeping or scrubbing the stairs, you are likely to have an unexpected improvement in your life-style.

Stall. See *Stable, Horse, Car,* or *Motor.*

Stamp(s). If your dream featured rare stamps of any kind, it predicts a good financial year ahead; stamping letters is an omen of improving status; to buy stamps indicates an increase in material wealth; collecting foreign stamps is a prophecy of advancement through influential friends.

Star(s). To dream of a particular bright and/or twinkling star predicts that your destiny will be fulfilled through the help of a powerful friend of the opposite sex. Many bright stars are a promise of success, but pale stars portend a period of poverty. A dream of a shooting or falling star indicates assured success but not as soon as you had hoped. See also *Sky* and *Comet.*

Stare. You are likely to suffer a social embarrassment if you dreamed of being stared at; if you did the staring, you must correlate the action to the cause.

Starfish. This is a dream symbol for an influential person, so you must interpret according to the action; i.e., if you found one in your dream, it suggests you will make an important new friendship, etc.

Starvation. This dream—as opposed to one of ordinary hunger—is a strong warning against extravagance; you are in for a season of financial stress, so start to retrench now.

Static. You will have to account for some erratic behavior if your dream featured static of any kind.

Stationery. Increasing prosperity is the omen in a dream featuring stationery or office supplies. See also *Paper.*

Statue(s). If you dreamed of seeing one come to life, it indicates the reforging of a broken friendship and/or the sudden realization of an abandoned hope. Otherwise, see *Sculpture.*

Steak. To dream of cooking or serving it indicates an increase in social activity; to dream of eating it predicts an increase in income.

Steal. A dream of stealing is a warning to be extra cautious in money or investment matters for the next few months, unless you were caught, which is a dream of contrary and signifies good luck. See also *Spoons.*

Steam. The omen varies according to the action. If you were burned by the steam, the dream is telling you to look out for deception within your close circle; to hear the sound of escaping steam portends quarrels and/or disagreement; a dream of turning off the steam is a sign that you will get a wish—or overcome an obstacle—which you thought was impossible. Operating a steamroller forecasts success in all your undertakings; but if you dreamed of being run over or hit by one, you are being warned of hidden, but nevertheless active, hostility.

Steel. Used constructively, steel seen in a dream is a symbol of enduring love and/or friendship, and if you handled it, you can anticipate a resounding success; however, if it was featured in any destructive form as blades, weapons, etc., it is a warning to be on your guard against jealousy.

Steeple. See *Spire*.

Step(s). See *Stairs* or *Ladder*.

Stereo. Travel at home and abroad is the omen in a dream featuring stereoscopic sights or sounds.

Stethoscope. An unusual accomplishment of your own, or shared with someone in your immediate circle, is forecast in a dream concerning a stethoscope.

Stew. Cooking or serving stew in your dream signifies news of a birth; eating it predicts a surprise reunion with an old friend. See also *Beef*, *Lamb*, etc.

Stiletto. See *Knife*, *Steel*, *Cut*, etc.

Stilts. A caution against arrogance is the message in a dream of using stilts, unless you fell, in which case it signifies good news on the way.

Stink. See *Odor*.

Stockings. The omen here varies according to the ac-

tion and details as follows:

Putting them on—profit and security.
Taking them off—changing conditions
Torn (or runners)—minor financial difficulties.
Mended or darned—domestic contentment
Holes in them—new adventures
Silk or nylon—money luck
Woolen—security
Cotton—friendly pleasure

See also *Colors*.

Stock Market. A dream of contrary. If your dream featured gains, it is a warning against speculation, but if it involved losses, you are likely to have a stroke of money luck.

Stole. See *Shawl*.

Stomach. See *Abdomen* or *Indigestion*.

Stone(s). Stepping-stones signify slow but steady advancement; Bloodstones portend unhappy love affairs; Cobblestones are a warning against gambling, and a dream of throwing stones is a sign of regret over a missed opportunity; let it be a lesson to you, but don't waste energy in vain postmortems. To dream of being a stonemason or seeing one at work predicts a season of hard work followed by a small advance.

Stoop. You are likely to discover a new talent or hobby if you dreamed of stooping.

Store. See *Shop.*

Stork. Woe is you if you dreamed of this long-legged bird, but your troubles will be small and soon forgotten.

Storm(s). Storms are obstacle dreams and portend a season of discontent from which you will only recover when you realize that you are the master of your own fate. See also *Rain, Snow,* and *Hail.*

Story. To dream of writing a story portends a season of sadness, but to dream of reading or listening to one is a sign of happy times to come.

Stove. A cold stove pertains to problems in sexual or personal relations for which you should seek professional advice or friendly counsel; a hot stove indicates a need to control your temper and/or excessive passions. See also *Cooking.*

Straitjacket. An obstacle dream pertaining to financial stress. Its meaning depends on the outcome of the dreamed action. If you succeeded in releasing yourself or were released by someone else, you are likely to get unexpected help out of your difficulties; otherwise, you must be prepared for a period of sharp economy.

Strangers. A dream of contrary. Strangers in your dream forecast happy reunions with valued friends.

Strangle. This could be classified as a form of contrary obstacle dream, for if you dreamed of strangling yourself or being strangled, it suggests that you are standing in the way of your own desires due to overcautiousness created by repressed fear; you would be wise to get psychological help. To dream of strangling someone else is a warning to listen to your intuition regarding someone you feel for but don't quite trust.

Straw. If your dream featured heaps of straw, it signifies security through increased savings; stacks of straw predict an increase in material wealth; burning straw is a warning against loss of money due to care-lessness; wet straw suggests loss of freedom due to foolish behavior; and a straw bed forecasts an improved income, unless you slept on it, in which case it means you are in for a lover's quarrel.

Strawberries. Happiness is the message contained in a strawberry dream. If you picked them, you are likely to have an unexpected and delightful vacation; otherwise, whether you ate them, served them, bought them, or cooked them, they signify happy domestic and/or love affairs.

Stream. This dream is thought to symbolize the general flow of life forces, so if in your dream the stream was clear and flowed smoothly, you can expect your life pattern to do likewise; but otherwise, you are likely to encounter obstacles in ratio to the turgidity or roughness of the water.

Street(s). Strange streets signify profitable new ventures or associations. Curving or crooked streets indicate travel and surprises. A very long street suggests that you will need much patience before you get what you want.

Strength. A sort of omen of contrary in that to dream you have great strength suggests that your ambition outstrips your ability and you would be well advised to readjust your sights; to dream of a show of strength by another predicts a sudden passionate but unfriendly love affair. Give it up, it's basically destructive.

Stretch. An obstacle dream. If the stretch was satisfactory, all will go well for you; otherwise, expect delays.

Strike. Whether you participated or just observed, progress toward your aims is the message in a dream featuring a strike or protest demonstration.

String. A dream of bits of string or of struggling to save used string suggests you may be suffering some form of sexual repression or repressed fear; a short session with a psychotherapist might be beneficial. See also under *Cord, Rope, Knot,* etc.

String Bean(s). Eating them predicts gay social times ahead; cooking or serving them forecasts a change in living conditions. See also *Vegetable(s).*

Strip. If your dream featured a striptease act of any kind, it suggests that you are contemplating some sort of indiscreet behavior; the price will be higher than you think possible, so avoid it. See also under *Naked.*

Stroke. To dream of having a stroke indicates a probable organic malfunction, and a medical checkup would seem advisable; a dream of someone else suffering a stroke indicates news of an illness. See also under *Paralysis.*

Struggle. An obstacle dream, but its meaning depends on what was involved in the struggle, therefore the details must be correlated; however, it is generally considered to be an omen of contrary relating to health.

Subway. To dream of being on or in the subway portends a series of minor setbacks and/or petty disappointments. Don't get discouraged; they will soon be a faded memory.

Success. Success in your dream is a straightforward omen of satisfactory achievement in your current aims.

Suffocation. A warning to see your doctor is contained in a dream featuring suffocation.

Sugar. However featured in your dream, sugar is an omen of happy success.

Suicide. This dream is a signal that you need a change of scene or more mental relaxation. Try sharing your troubles with a trusted friend or adviser, but in any event stop brooding.

Summer. You are likely to hear some surprising news if you dreamed of summer in any other season.

Sun. The meaning of the dream depends on the details and conditions featured. Bright clear sunlight forecasts success in all that concerns you, but a dim circle around the sun or an overcast sun is a warning of domestic trouble; a red sun predicts a struggle from which you will emerge victorious; to see the sun rise indicates the opening of new doors; to see it set, especially if it shows lovely colors, is a promise of exciting change for the better.

Sundae. Success with the opposite sex will be yours if you dreamed of a luscious sundae, especially if you dripped it on yourself; however, if you didn't like the flavor or something about it turned you off, the dream could be a warning against indiscriminate sex relations.

Sunday. To dream of Sunday when it isn't is a sign of coming changes in both living conditions and business interests.

Sundial. Pleasant social times are in store for you if your dream featured a sundial, and if, by chance, you were able to tell the time by it, you are soon likely to realize your deepest wish.

Sunflower. Sunflowers portend danger in regard to social activities; guard against impulsive behavior, unless you are with tried and true companions. To dream of eating sunflower seeds indicates the return of an old friend.

Sunk. See *Sink*.

Sunstroke. You are likely to have to struggle with an unexpected new family responsibility if sunstroke was featured in your dream; however, you will soon adjust and find it ultimately rewarding.

Supper. See *Dinner, Eating*, etc.

Surf. A modest but encouraging advance in either— or both—your love and business affairs is the message in a dream of the surf breaking on the shore.

Surgeon. A change of occupation is forecast in a dream of being a surgeon. Otherwise, see *Operation*.

Survey. However it featured in your dream, this activity is a warning that you are on the verge of losing something you want through being either overcautious or downright stingy. Think it over.

Suspender. For a woman, this dream signifies that she has misplaced her affections; for a man, it predicts an unexpected gain, especially if he lost his suspenders in his dream.

Swallow. See *Birds*.

Swamp. A warning not to stretch your credit is contained in a dream of being lost in a swamp; but to dream of walking in one suggests that you should take the initiative in breaking off a relationship which has become a hazard to your welfare.

Swan(s). The omen here depends on the details of the action and color. Black swans portend business problems in the offing; white swans predict happiness in love or domestic affairs if they were floating, and business or financial success if they were flying or walking. To see swans gliding in a small pond predicts great wealth through your own diligent efforts.

Swastika. This ancient symbol of luck has, in modern times, become a sign of domination by force and is a warning against allowing yourself to be too easily influenced by the opinion of others. Stand firm when you know you're right.

Swear. See *Profanity*.

Sweat. See *Perspiration*.

Sweater. See *Clothes* or *Knit*, also *Colors*.

Sweep. Whatever your troubles are they will be swept away on a happy wave of money luck if your dream featured this menial task.

Swim. For an accurate interpretation of a swimming dream, all the details of water, weather, and other conditions, such as loca-tion, etc., should be correlated to the action, but as a general guide: if you dreamed of swimming in the nude, it predicts good luck in all that concerns you; to dream of swimming in a suit suggests an upcoming social embarrassment or disappointment; and to teach someone to swim forecasts an increase in material wealth. To dream of swimming toward the shore prophesies security but only through diligent effort. To swim in a pool is a warning of hidden hostility around you; a dream of observing others swimming is a sign of good luck in love if they were females, and good luck in business if they were males, and mixed fortunes if you saw both.

Swing. This dream is a suggestion that issues hanging in the balance can be made to swing in your favor if you exercise patience and caution. Don't push.

Switchboard. A telephone switchboard in a dream is an omen of a wide expansion in your social circle.

Sword. See *Duel, Uniform, Steel, Blade,* etc.

Synagogue. See *Church*.

Syphilis. See *Sexual Organs*.

Syringe. A symbol of renewed sexual vigor or alternatively new energy and ideas which should give you pleasure and satisfaction.

Syrup. Joy and happiness in the achievements of young friends is the prophecy in a dream featuring syrup; and if you spilled it or got it on you, some benefit will accrue to you personally.

T

Tabasco. An exciting new romance, or if you're not eligible for that, an interesting new friend is predicted if you dreamed of the use or taste of this hot condiment.

Table. The meaning depends on the details and the action which must be correlated to get an accurate interpretation, but as a general guide: a kitchen table suggests a season of hard work ahead; a card table predicts a chance to increase your income; a dining table indicates an upturn in social activities; and a library table forecasts an improved status due to intellectual achievements.

Tablecloth. A soiled or messy cloth portends family quarrels, but a clean cloth augurs smooth sailing in both business and domestic affairs.

Tack(s). If you dreamed of hammering tacks, you are likely to have to help a friend over a rough patch; pulling out tacks in a dream is a warning against hasty speech which could cause a regrettable rift—guard your tongue. Driving a tack with a shoe predicts a new romantic interest.

Tail. The tails of domestic animals indicate domestic happiness; wild animal tails suggest profit after adversity; and fish tails signify successful speculation.

Tailor. Unexpected travel is the omen in a dream of seeing a tailor at work; to dream of being a tailor is a warning to be careful in whom you confide.

Talisman. See *Amulet*.

Tamale. If your dream featured this Mexican food,

353

you are likely to make a new and useful acquaintance.

Tambourine. A tambourine in your dream is a sign of a pleasant surprise, unless you were trying to play it, in which case you are likely to hear a disturbing rumor which you would do well to follow up and/or act on.

Tangerine. Convivial good times are indicated in a dream of eating tangerines. Otherwise, see *Fruit*.

Tangle. This dream is telling you that now is the time to sort out the confusion in your affairs if you want to avoid a serious embarrassment.

Tar. To dream of it in large quantities suggests that you are bogged down in an unsatisfactory personal relationship which you must take positive action to sever; stop drifting and propel yourself. If your dream concerned having tar on your person or on your clothing, it is a warning not to repeat gossip lest it rebound on you.

Tarantula. This venomous creature in your dream is a strong warning to guard your health, and if it bit you, a medical checkup would be advisable. See also *Spider(s)*.

Tassels. A dream of tassels on anything is a sign of a season of hard work without much joy, but don't despair—the best way to kill time is to work it to death.

Taxes. The omen contained in a tax dream is pretty straightforward. If you were worried by them in your dream, you are likely to have to pay the piper in some manner; otherwise, they predict prosperous times ahead.

Taxi. See *Cab*.

Tea. Whether it was iced or hot, drinking tea in your dream indicates an increase in social popularity. If you poured it from the pot, it predicts a happy surprise.

Teacher. A dream of being a teacher is telling you that, if you want to avoid unpleasant repercussions, you must control your tendency to "hunt with the hounds and run with the hare." Otherwise, see under *Learn*.

Tear(s). See *Cry*.

Tear Gas. To dream of the

use of tear gas predicts distressing news concerning a friend.

Tease. If you were doing the teasing, you can expect some happy social times to follow; but if you were being teased, you are likely to hear some pleasant financial news shortly. To dream of observing others being teased indicates the revelation and attainment of a secret ambition.

Teeth. One must, of course, correlate the action and other details of the dream, but as a general guide: false teeth signify unexpected help out of a difficult situation; broken or unusually worn-down teeth are a sign of the deterioration of an important relationship; aching teeth portend family quarrels; a dream of having teeth filled promises good news; having teeth pulled forecasts favorable business or investment opportunities; loose teeth are a warning of untrustworthy friends; if they fell out or you spit them out, it is a sign of a season of financial reverses; decayed teeth mean health problems—see your doctor; even and/or very white and beautiful teeth forecast happiness and prosperity; very long teeth predict legal action; one tooth longer than the others portends sad news; buckteeth augur unexpected travel; bridgework is a suggestion that you should be more meticulous in meeting your obligations; a dream featuring the roots of your teeth is a warning against lending money or gambling; to dream of having a nerve removed predicts a season of good luck; brushing your teeth indicates the clearance of obstacles which have been holding you back, unless one or more bristles get stuck between your teeth, in which case you will still overcome the obstacles but only after continued patient effort; picking your teeth is a warning of false friends in your close circle.

Telegram. If the message was pleasant, the dream augurs money luck; otherwise, it is a sign that you must curb your extravagance or suffer difficulties as a consequence.

Telepathy. Exciting good news, probably by mail, is forecast in a dream featuring mental telepathy.

Telephone. To dream of using a telephone is a warning that you have rivalry where you least expect it. If your dream featured a telephone which was out of order, it portends sad news.

Telescope. A dream involving the use of a telescope is telling you that you need to take a longer view in order to get a proper focus on your general activities. Reassess your aims and then adjust your sights.

Television. The meaning depends on what you saw. If you were pleased or impressed, the dream suggests that you are proceeding along the right lines; otherwise, it carries a warning that you need to resist a tendency to be too easily influenced by others. Make your own judgments.

Temper. See *Rage*.

Tent. Whatever your personal or financial worries may be, you will soon be relieved of them if you dreamed of pitching a tent; however, if your dream featured the collapse of a tent or other difficulty with it, the dream is warning you that you may have to revise your ideas as to where your future security lies.

Test. See *Examination*.

Testicle(s). See *Sexual Organs*.

Theater. A dark theater portends a season of boredom, but if a performance was going on, it predicts a period of increased social pleasures. See also *Acting,* etc.

Thermometer. If your dream featured a thermometer, it predicts that the winds of change will soon be blowing your way.

Thief. See *Robber*.

Thimble. A happy love affair is predicted for a man who dreams of a thimble; for a woman, it prophesies a happy homelife, and the omen is intensified if the thimble was lost.

Thirst. An obstacle dream which suggests that you are an aggressive leader. The meaning depends on whether or not you quenched your thirst. If you did so at a well or a spring, your success will be beyond your highest expectations.

Thorn(s). To catch your clothes or body on a thorn is a warning that your reputation is being jeopardized by unsavory companions. A little tactful

disentanglement seems to be in order. See also *Scratch*.

Thread. If you dreamed of tangling it, you will learn a secret of an embarrassing nature; if you picked it off your own or someone else's clothing, it's a warning against idle gossip. See also *Spool*.

Threat. You are being strongly warned against gambling or speculation if your dream featured any form of threat or threatening atmosphere.

Threshing. Comfort and prosperity are forecast in a dream of grain being threshed. See also *Harvest*.

Throat. If you dreamed of the throat of someone of the opposite sex, it is a suggestion to be more meticulous about your personal grooming; if you dreamed of having a sore throat. see your doctor. Otherwise, see *Neck*.

Throne. A peculiar omen of contrary predicated on your own evaluation of where you stand on the social ladder; if you consider yourself well up, the dream predicts a loss of status; but if you think of

yourself as middle to low, it indicates a rise.

Thrush. Peace and contentment will be yours if you heard the lovely song of a thrush in your dream. See also *Birds*.

Thud. An inconsequential but pleasant surprise is heralded by a dull thud in your dream.

Thumb. See *Fingers*.

Thunder. The message in the dream depends on the quality of the sound. If it muttered and rolled, it was warning you that your suspicions of false friends are well-founded; if it boomed and crashed, it was telling you that your most urgent problem will soon be solved. See also under *Lightning*.

Ticket(s). You can expect delayed news which is likely to put you on the track of something you want if your dream featured tickets of any kind.

Tickle. Whether you dreamed of being tickled or of tickling someone else, the dream is warning you against indiscreet relations with the opposite sex. This may be on either the romantic level or simply in

357

the area of giving confidences.

Tide(s). Promising opportunities are predicted in a dream featuring a high tide; an incoming tide forecasts increased resources; a low tide suggests a reluctance to alter your established way of life. Don't be overcautious—that way lies stagnation. An ebbing tide indicates that a pressing problem will soon be ended.

Tiger. See *Animals*.

Tiger Lily. See *Flowers* and *Colors*.

Tiles. To dream of handling broken tiles is a warning against taking any unnecessary risks for the time being. Otherwise, see under *Roof, Colors, Repair(s)*, etc.

Timber. Timber in a dream signifies faithful friends and/or associates, unless the timber was rotting, in which case you'd better look out for a rotter somewhere in your circle.

Time Clock. See *Clock*.

Tin. See under *Metal*.

Tinsel. If your dream featured tinsel in any form, it is reminding you that all is not gold that glitters, so don't put too much confidence in smooth-talking new acquaintances, or fast buck deals.

Tire. A dream of changing a tire is a warning to conserve your resources against an unexpected demand; buying a new tire predicts a sudden release from worry; a blowout portends problems caused by hidden jealousy—try being tactful for a while; to dream of losing a tire suggests that you would benefit from a season of stricter self-control. If you dreamed of being excessively tired, it is a straightfoward warning that you are overtaxing yourself—slow down, or see your doctor, or both.

Toad. Whether your prime concern is business or love, these ugly creatures in your dream are an unhappy omen, unless you stepped on or killed one, in which case you will frustrate the attempt at deceit around you.

Toadstool. These dangerous "look alikes" in your dream are a sign that you will have to combat some active hostility to get what you want; however, persevere if you know you are right.

Toilet. To dream of going to the toilet yourself is a sign of litigation over money or property; if you dreamed of someone else going, you are likely to be surprised by a request for a loan. Otherwise, see under *Bowel Movement, Feces, Urine,* etc.

Tomatoes. Whether you ate them, cooked them, served them, or drank the juice, tomatoes in your dream are a happy omen of coming success and contentment.

Tomb(s). A dream of contrary signifying that fortunate influences are working in your favor, unless you dreamed of being locked in one, in which case a medical checkup would be advisable.

Torch. A flaming torch is a sign of a sudden passionate love affair or alternatively an unusual stroke of luck; relax and enjoy it while it lasts.

Totem. These Indian carvings forecast interesting new friends who will widen your horizons.

Towel(s). The message here depends on the kind and condition of the towel. If it was a clean cloth towel, it promises good health and material comfort; however, wet and/or soiled towels forecast a season of frustration, while paper towels portend a period of recession.

Tower. See *Spire.*

Toys. Pleasant new developments in all the areas of your life are predicted in a dream of toys, unless they were broken or damaged, in which case the dream is warning you that your tendency to childish, impulsive behavior could seriously impede your progress.

Traffic. Watching traffic in a dream suggests that you are trying to solve a problem alone for which you should request help or co-operation; to drive through traffic successfully forecasts an easement of family difficulties, but a traffic jam predicts obstacles that will require long and patient effort to overcome.

Trail. If you dreamed of following a trail, it is a sign that you can gain your goal if you persevere; to dream of losing a trail is a caution against wasting your time in meaningless activities and/or relationships.

Trailer(s). A complete change of circumstances is forecast in a dream featuring a trailer or trailer camp.

Train. If the train was standing in the station or on a side track, it forecasts an unexpected hitch or delay in your plans; otherwise, see *Travel*.

Tramp. The meaning of the dream depends on its action, and all the details should be carefully correlated, but as a general guide: if you dreamed of being a tramp, you are likely to find peace of mind due to improving circumstances; to dream of giving food or help of any kind to a tramp predicts a rise in social status, but if you refused to give help, you can expect to have harder work and smaller rewards than you hoped.

Trap(s). It is a fortunate sign for a man to dream of setting traps, but for a woman it signifies that she has misplaced her trust. To dream of being caught in a trap is a warning to steer clear of gossip and/or intrigue.

Trapdoor. An astounding revelation is likely to follow a dream featuring a trapdoor. Don't get panicked into a hasty decision you may later regret. Play it cool.

Travel. A sudden substantial increase in status and/or income is forecast in a dream of traveling for pleasure. Other travel dreams must be interpreted by reference to the cause, means, and other details of the dream.

Tray. A full tray in a dream is a sign of approaching good luck, unless it was dropped, in which case it portends a social embarrassment due to foolish speech or behavior.

Treasure. Early prosperity is predicted in a dream of finding treasure; digging for it is an augury of improving health; and diving for it forecasts a valuable gift or unexpected legacy.

Trees. As with a lovely garden, beautiful trees are a favorable omen in a dream, and planting trees is especially auspicious for love affairs and/or matters of friendship. Cutting down trees portends difficulties of your own making, and climbing a tree is one of the few exceptions to the "up is good" rule, as it indicates hard work for small gain. Blossoming trees predict unexpected joy, and a row or line of trees indicates extended advancement. Aspen signifies a season of loneliness; Crabapple a new experience; an Oak is a sign of faithful love; a Spruce promises good health. To dream of tree stumps signifies changes and new beginnings. Otherwise, see under individual listings, or *Forest, Landscape,* etc.

Tremble. A dream of contrary. You can expect good health and happiness to follow this dream. See also *Quiver.*

Trial. To dream of being on trial is a warning to be cautious in developing new ties and/or entering into new ventures. Stick to known paths for the time being.

Triangle. New beneficial conditions and opportunities which you would do well to exploit is the omen in a dream featuring triangular shapes or forms.

Triplets. A dream of seeing triplets predicts surprising news. See also *Baby.*

Trousers. See *Clothes.*

Truck. A comfortable life and community recognition are predicted in a dream of riding in or driving a truck.

Trumpet. Hearing or playing a trumpet in your dream is a forecast of unexpected accomplishment. See also *Music* and *Musical Instruments.*

Trunk. See *Baggage.*

Tub. The meaning depends on whether the tub was full or empty, what it contained, and what it was made of, so all these details must be correlated to the action.

Tulip. Planting the bulbs portends a minor disappointment, but seeing them in bloom or gathering the flowers is a happy omen for all that closely concerns you. See also *Flowers* and *Colors.*

Tumor(s). A strange omen of contrary signifying new and interesting responsibilities.

Tunnel. An obstacle dream if you were struggling to get through it, in which case the meaning depends on the outcome of the action. Otherwise, it represents a change, a risk, or an opportunity which is causing you some mental conflict; talk it over with a trusted friend or adviser before you commit yourself.

Turkey. This bird has various meanings depending on the action in your dream. If you saw one strutting and/or heard it gobbling, it portends a period of confusion due to instability of your friends or associates; a flock of turkeys predicts community recognition or public honors; if you killed one, you can expect a stroke of good luck; and if you dressed, cooked, or served it in your dream, it prophesies a long period of prosperity. However, if you ate it, you are likely to make a serious error of judgment, so be very careful regarding any important matters which may be pending.

Turnips. See *Vegetable(s)*.

Turtle(s). These strange creatures are a symbol of frustrated ambition due to hidden hostility; if you per-

severe, you may dispel the opposition; however, if, after a reasonable time, the obstacle remains, you should reassess the position with an eye to altering your aim or your approach to it.

Tweezers. Some new and agreeable friendships are forecast in a dream featuring tweezers.

Twilight. See *Dusk*.

Twine. See *Cord* or *String*.

Twins. Double trouble followed by double joy is the omen in a dream featuring grown-up twins. Otherwise, see *Baby* and *Children*.

Typewriter. If you dreamed of using one, it signifies a substantial step forward, unless it jammed or gave trouble, in which case it constitutes an obstacle dream, and its meaning depends on the outcome of the action. Of course, if you are in the habit of using a typewriter, the dream probably has no significance.

Ugliness. It is a lucky omen to dream of an ugly person; however, if you dreamed of being ugly yourself, it suggests that you must try to cultivate a more outgoing personality if you want to hold on to valued friends.

Ulcer. See *Sore(s)*.

Umbrella. An umbrella is a symbol of security, unless it was torn, broken, or turned inside out, in which case ultimate achievement is still indicated but delayed by minor difficulties.

Uncle. See *Relatives*.

Unconscious. If you dreamed of someone else being unconscious, you are likely to hear news of an illness; if you had the rare dream of being unconscious yourself, a physical checkup

would probably be beneficial.

Undertaker. A contrary omen signifying news of a wedding or a birth.

Undertow. To dream of getting caught in an undertow is a sign that you will soon have to comfort a sorrowing friend or relation.

Undressing. If your dream featured someone of the opposite sex undressing, it is warning you not to confide in recent acquaintances; to dream of undressing yourself suggests that you have misplaced your affections and would do well to cut the relationship before it puts you in an awkward position; a dream of seeing someone of your own sex removing his or her clothes signifies that you will soon learn the secret of a long-standing mystery.

Unfaithful. To dream that anyone is unfaithful to you is an omen of contrary; you will soon have a demonstration of sincerity and/or devotion. However, if you dreamed of being unfaihful, it signifies that you are, or will shortly be, confronted by an unusual temptation to stray off the lines. Meditate but don't vacillate or you might fall between two stools.

Unhappy. Another dream of contrary. The greater your dreamed unhappiness the greater will be your coming joy.

Unicorn. This mythical creature in your dream is telling you that you are in for a period of beneficial changes.

Uniform. For a man to dream of wearing a uniform signifies an approaching improvement in status; for a woman, it predicts happiness in love and/or domestic affairs.

University. This dream is considered especially auspicious for those engaged in any field of scientific endeavor; for others it forecasts future success commensurate with effort expended.

Unkind. A dream of contrary with a meaning similar to unfaithful.

Urine. Obviously, the details of the dream action must be correlated, but according to the ancient oracles, urine, as such, is a symbol of increasing creative power and/or strength; however, to urinate signifies a release from tension and/or worry.

Urn. An urn filled with flowers or plants predicts happiness, unless the flowers were withered, in which case it portends some minor disappointment in the offing. A funeral urn featured in your dream forecasts news of a legacy or an inheritance.

Usher. To dream of being an usher or of being ushered predicts new influential social contacts that could affect your future.

Vacation. To dream of a paid vacation signifies an increase in income, but if the dreamed vacation was at your own expense, it predicts an unexpected gain or valuable gift.

Vaccination. A warning against insincere friends is the message in a dream featuring others being vaccinated; but if you dreamed of being vaccinated yourself, see *Syringe*.

Vacuum Cleaner. The use of a vacuum cleaner in a dream forecasts success in dealing with the opposite sex, unless it broke down or gave trouble in any way, in which case it is a warning to be chary about mixing romance and business as there is a danger of being exploited.

Vagabond. See *Tramp*.

Vagina. See *Sexual Organs*.

Valentine. A sort of dream of contrary in that if you received one in your dream, it predicts some minor romantic troubles or disappointment in a friend; whereas if you sent the valentine, it signifies the opening of a pleasant new door.

Valet. To dream of a personal manservant is a sign of social or community recognition.

Valley. If the valley was verdant, green, and beautiful, it signifies that you must expect to work hard for what you want; otherwise, a valley in your dream suggests that you are under tension due to emotional conflict and you would be well advised to seek medical or psychological help.

Vampire. A vampire featured in your dream is a symbol of anxiety and sharp emotional conflict. It is likely that this dream relates to some ambition which you subconsciously feel is immoral or unethical. Talk it over with a competent friend or adviser.

Van. The meaning, of course, varies according to the action, but as a general rule a van featured in your dream is a harbinger of good news. If it was carrying household goods, it indicates a change for the better; however, if your dream involved riding in it, you are likely to have a sudden opportunity to make a sizable profit.

Vanilla. If you were aware of this pleasant taste or aroma in your dream, you can expect to have a gratifying invitation shortly.

Varnish. Using varnish yourself in a dream is a sign that you will advance and prosper through your own prudence and diligence; to dream of others using it is a warning against letting outsiders meddle in your affairs; keep your own counsel and rely on your own judgment in personal matters.

Vase. Tiresome trials and tribulations are forecast in a dream featuring a vase, but the experiences will be ultimately beneficial, so try to be philosophical for the time being.

Vat. See *Barrel*.

Vault. A money vault is a caution against putting on a front which could damage your hopes instead of advancing them. Otherwise, see *Tomb(s)*.

Veal. You'll be lucky for sure if your dream featured veal in any form. See also *Meat, Eating,* and *Cooking*.

Vegetable(s). The meaning varies to some extent according to the action and vegetable involved, and where possible—or applicable—the individual listing should be consulted; however, as a general guide: eating vegetables forecasts a season of ups and downs; growing them is a sign of happy family times ahead; cooking or serving them suggests that although success may be slow it will be sure; however, if the vegetables in your dream were spoiled or rotten, you must be prepared for a period of disappointment, but in that case you can nourish yourself on the thought that it will soon pass.

Veil. To dream of a veil, as such, suggests that you are engaged in, or contemplating, some activity which is contrary to your principles; better think it over before you go any further. To dream of a torn veil indicates the revelation of a mystery or a secret; if you saw a bridal veil in your dream, you can expect a change for the better, and if you saw a bride wearing a veil, you can expect to escape payment for some current transgression; a dream of losing a veil signifies that you will suffer only a minor embarrassment in regard to a major indiscretion, so be grateful to your lucky star. Mourning veils portend vexation and disappointment.

Vein(s). Distressing news concerning a friend is forecast in a dream featuring veins. See also *Cut* and *Blood*.

Velvet. As a general rule this luxurious fabric pertains to material wealth, but its meaning in your dream will depend on the action, its color, and other details which must be correlated.

Veneer. Any dream featuring veneer is a warning against being too quick in accepting things—or people—at face value.

Venereal Disease. See under *Sexual Organs*.

Venetian Blinds. This dream is a warning to be more circumspect in your behavior with the opposite sex, unless you are prepared to be the subject of unsavory gossip.

Venison. Social embarrassment is the message in a dream featuring this gamey meat; avoid brash behavior.

Ventriloquist. If you dreamed of listening to a ventriloquist, you are being warned to guard your tongue in social conversation, unless you are certain all ears are friendly; if your dream involved being a ventriloquist, you are being warned that some ears which purport to be friendly are not.

Vermin. Vermin in a dream pertain to current projects and hopes and prophesy setbacks and disappointments, unless you killed them or otherwise got rid of them, in which case the

dream predicts unqualified success.

Vertigo. An attack of vertigo in a dream is a warning against being exploited by the opposite sex.

Vest. Trouble of your own making is the message contained in a dream featuring a vest or waistcoat: try to avoid excesses and/or impulsive behavior. See also *Colors.*

Vicar. See *Minister* and *Clergy.*

Village. If your dream featured a seaside village, it predicts temporary difficulties; a mountain village promises unexpected gain; and a country village forecasts solid achievement.

Vine(s). One of the luckiest dream omens you could have if the vines were healthy and in leaf. and if they had blossoms. success beyond expectation will be sure to come; however, vines that are withered or dry suggest that you are on the verge of overtaxing your strength; slow down for a time and try to recharge your battery. See also *Vineyard.*

Vinegar. A season of unpleasant duties is predicted in a

dream featuring vinegar; however, they won't be entirely unrewarding.

Vineyard. If the vines were stripped of their fruit, the dream is a warning against speculation of any kind; but if the vines were bearing, it predicts happiness and prosperity in ratio to the abundance and ripeness of the fruit.

Violence. See *Horror, Killing, Fight,* etc.

Violets. To dream of gathering them signifies fame as well as fortune; otherwise, they speak to you of love. See also *Flowers* and *Colors.*

Violin. If the sound is pleasant, the dream augurs well for social and domestic affairs, but disharmony or broken strings portend petty quarrels. See also *Music* and *Musical Instruments.*

Viper. A straightforward warning that you are harboring one in your bosom and it could lead you astray; reassess those in your close circle. See also *Snake(s).*

Virgin Mary. Great happiness is forecast in a dream of the Holy Virgin, but it is also a caution to be careful as to where you place your confidences.

Vision(s). If the visions were pleasant or merely strange, they predict a happy surprise: but if they were unpleasant and/or confused, they suggest a physical origin and a medical checkup would be advisable.

Visitor. A dream of being a visitor is warning you that you are in danger of being exploited by someone who knows how to flatter you; to dream of having a visitor is a warning that you are contemplating an injustice. Think again before you act.

Volcano. An erupting volcano signifies that you have been ignoring a potentially dangerous situation which you will have to adjust: the sooner you do it, the easier it will be —stop drifting. A smoking volcano is a sign of a passionate love affair based on deceit: brake the habit before it breaks you. An inactive volcano is a warning against new ventures; don't make any important changes for a few months.

Vomit. This is one of the peculiar dreams of contrary in regard to material wealth. If you are well off, it is a sign of coming reverses: but if not, it predicts financial improvement.

Voodoo. You are in danger of being led astray by undesirable associates; if you are not capable of resisting the pressure alone, don't be too proud to ask for help.

Vote. If you dreamed of voting, it suggests that you need to cultivate more self-confidence. Try asserting yourself for a change: you might be very favorably surprised with the result.

Vow. Whether you or others took the vow in your dream, it forecasts a happy solution to any domestic or love problems you may now have.

Voyage. See *Travel, Ship,* etc.

Vulture. The meaning of this nasty bird in your dream depends on the action; if you just observed it sitting somewhere, it is a sign that you have an enemy or competitor waiting for you to make a mistake; if you saw one devouring its prey, it is a contrary omen and signifies that you will overcome your difficulties; if you killed a vulture in your dream, it forecasts a sure stroke of good luck.

369

W

Wade. A dream of wading pertains to affairs of love or friendship, and, as with all such dreams, its meaning depends mainly on the condition of the water; if it was clear and clean, it signifies happiness in love and/or pleasure with true friends; if it was muddy or murky, it portends disenchantment.

Waffles. See *Pancakes*.

Wager. See *Bet* or *Gambling*.

Wages. If you dreamed of paying wages, you are likely to have an opportunity in the near future to make an advantageous change; if your dream featured receiving wages, it is warning you to guard against loss by theft—check your locks.

Wagon. Riding or driving a wagon is a warning against making hasty purchases or investments; unless the wagon was loaded (especially with hay), in which case it predicts an unexpected increase in material wealth or a windfall of money.

Waist. The meaning of this dream depends greatly on the details which must be correlated to the action, but as a general guide, to dream of your own waist pertains to your financial resources, and a dream of someone else's waist relates to the financial situation of a friend concerning which you may be requested to help—or to celebrate.

Waiter. A dream featuring a waiter (or waitress) portends news of the illness of a friend or relative.

Walk. A form of obstacle

dream, for if you walked with ease, it signifies an easy triumph, and if you walked with difficulty, you will still overcome your obstacles but it will require determined effort.

Wall(s). These represent obstacles; therefore the meaning of the dream depends on the outcome of its action. If you dreamed of jumping over one, you will achieve success through your own determination, and if your dream featured walking along the top of a wall, your future is bright indeed.

Wallet. If you dreamed of losing your wallet, you are likely to be faced with an unexpected dilemma; to dream of finding a wallet is a sort of dream of contrary, as it signifies gain if empty but loss if full.

Wallflower(s). For a dream featuring the garden variety, see *Flowers*, but a dream of being one in the social sense is an omen of contrary and predicts an increase in popularity.

Wallpaper. Whether you hung it yourself or observed it being done, the dream pertains to an alteration in your social status, but its meaning must be determined by reference to the colors (if any) and the outcome of the exercise.

Walnuts. You won't have many luxuries, but you'll never lack the necessities if your dream featured walnuts; and if they came out of the shell unbroken, you'll be especially lucky in love.

Waltz. See under *Dance* or *Music*.

Wand. You will play a more important part in life than you expect if your dream featured a wand of any kind.

Wander. See *Confusion*.

War. See *Combat, Battle, Bombs,* etc.

Warehouse A well-stocked warehouse is a straightforward symbol of prosperity; partly full or empty, it prophesies slow but sure progress.

Wart(s). Warts on your hands signify approaching money, and the more warts the more money; however, on other parts of your body, they are a warning that your generosity is likely to land you in hot water, so try to sidestep any current requests for help. If your dream featured warts on others, they symbolize hidden hostility where you least expect it—be on guard.

Wash. All the factors, such as the temperature of the water and the articles (or persons) concerned, must be correlated, but as a general guide, washing by hand suggests that you should refrain from getting involved in the personal affairs of others at the present time; washing in a machine indicates an unexpected vacation or change of location. To dream of washing your hands and/or face predicts a pleasant new friendship in the offing.

Wasp(s). These nasty creatures in your dream signify a significant time for breaking off an unrewarding relationship which is retarding your progress.

Watch. A wristwatch featured in your dream is a sign of advancement through the help of influential friends; a pocket watch is a warning that it's later than you think in regard to looking after your own interests—stop drifting and take positive action. See also *Clocks.*

Water. The meaning, of course, depends on the details and the action, but as a general guide, clear calm water is a favorable omen, while rough or murky water signifies difficulties. A dream of drinking cold water is a sign of good luck, but throwing or spilling it on anyone indicates a need to control your temper. Hot water (unless it is appropriate to the action) portends a season of social and/or business setbacks, but running water predicts lasting happiness. A waterfall in your dream forecasts a happy rise in status and/or an imminent increase in material wealth. Gently flowing water promises contentment and peace of mind. See also *Bath, Bathing, Swim, Drown, Wash, Ocean, River, Lake,* etc.

Watercress. A warning against promiscuous sex relations or confiding in casual acquaintances is contained in a dream featuring watercress, especially if you picked it.

Water Lily. This flower in your dream is telling you that your grasp exceeds your reach and you would be wise to readjust your sights.

Watermelon. If they were on the vine, they are a warning against casual love affairs; otherwise, they forecast unexpected travel. See also *Fruit*.

Water Mill. Prosperity through intelligent application of energy is promised in a dream featuring a water mill.

Wax. See *Beeswax*.

Wealth. To dream of the wealth of others indicates that you have no need to doubt the sincerity of your friends; but to dream of possessing great wealth yourself is an odd omen of contrary, for it portends financial reverses which will in some manner have long-range benefits.

Weasel. You are being alerted to a treacherous companion or associate of the opposite sex if your dream featured this sly rodent.

Weather Vane. A good omen if your prime concern is business, but if it's romance, be prepared for stormy weather.

Weaving. If you dreamed you were doing the weaving and it went well, you can expect peace of mind and contentment to follow, but any difficulty with the threads or loom portends obstacles to be overcome; to dream of watching someone else at a loom is a forecast of solid achievement in your current endeavors.

Web. A web (except that of a spider) is a warning against getting involved in any form of intrigue. See also *Cobweb* and *Spider(s)*.

Wedding. Although there is considerable variation among the oracles in regard to the meaning of this dream, a consensus seem to agree that it is a symbol of a happy but brief interlude. Of course all the details must be correlated and the interpretation thereby modified.

Weeds. If you merely observed weeds in a garden, the dream is a warning against undesirable companions who may damage your reputation; but if you were weeding or destroying them in any way, you can be sure that all your clouds will have silver linings.

Weep. See *Cry*.

Weighing. Whether the weighing involved yourself, others, or things, the dream

373

is telling you that you are under close scrutiny by those whose judgment could affect your future, so be careful not to do anything you can't justify for the time being. See also *Fat* and *Reduce*.

Well. A well with a high water level signifies abundance; a low water level indicates a period of difficulties; to draw water from a clear well predicts happiness, from a muddy well disappointment in love; an overflowing well is a warning to be careful in giving confidences, a dry well portends frustration; discovery of a well indicates approaching wealth, but digging a well prophesies hard work for small rewards. A public well predicts the uncovering of secrets; water rising in a well is a sign that your love affairs will flourish, and if you climbed into a well, you are likely to take an unexpected trip; to fall into a well predicts news of an illness, but to drink from one promises joy and success. Other than the foregoing, the dream must be interpreted by relating the action to the condition of the water and other details.

West. A long journey is predicted in a dream featuring the west or westerly direction.

Whale. This big creature is a splendid dream omen signifying protective influences around you, and if you saw the flukes of its tail, freedom from worry will soon be yours.

Wheat. The meaning depends on the condition of the grain. If the wheat was flattened or in poor condition, it suggests difficulties which can be overcome; if it was ripe, it is a sign of abundance and prosperity; and if it was harvested or in sheaves, it forecasts solid achievement in your current endeavors.

Wheels. Slowly moving wheels predict hard work but with satisfactory results; fast-moving wheels are an omen of rapid advancement; exciting adventure is forecast in a dream of losing a wheel; old, idle, or broken wheels portend disappointment or failure through lack of effort; the wheels of an airplane signify success; of a car, a quick trip; of a bicycle, expect delays in matters now pending; of an engine, change for the better. Fair wheels or gambling wheels indicate an approaching change of conditions which may not be entirely to your satisfaction but will be to your eventual benefit.

Wheelbarrow. If you pushed a loaded one in your dream, you will soon make an exciting new friend; if you pulled a wheelbarrow, it portends sad news of a friend or acquaintance; an upside-down barrow forecasts added responsibilities but they will be edifying.

Whip. A dream featuring the whipping of an animal suggests you have some injustice on your conscience; either make amends or try to forget it. See also *Chastise.*

Whirlpool. A whirlpool in your dream suggests confusion in your current affairs; if you can't sort it out alone, get professional help.

Whirlwind. Sudden changes which will require quick decisions are forecast in a dream featuring this revolving mass of air.

Whiskers. See *Hair* or *Beard.*

Whiskey. See *Alcohol, Bar, Drink,* or *Drunk.*

Whisper(s). Whispering voices heard in your dream are a warning to control hasty outbursts if you want to avoid unpleasant repercussions; count at least to ten before you speak. It's better to repress than to repent.

Whistle. If you whistled in your dream, you are likely to have to cope with some unjust criticism; if you heard others whistling, you can expect to have to revise or delay a current plan or project.

White. A good dream omen. See *Colors.*

Whitewash. A dream featuring the use of whitewash predicts that you will be asked to help a friend who is in trouble. Assist if you can, but don't get involved.

Widow(er). An omen of contrary. To dream of being in this mateless state predicts domestic satisfaction and/or happiness in love.

Wig(s). New faces in new places is the message contained in a dream featuring a wig or wigs; however, the color of the hair and details of the action must also be considered.

Will. To dream of making your own will is an omen of contrary and signifies that your health worries are unfounded; a dream concerning the will of others forecasts unexpected family problems which will soon come to your attention.

Willow. This lovely tree featured in your dream indicates a season of sadness due to the discovery of an unworthy friend; but don't let it depress you unduly—a new link will soon be forged. See also *Trees*.

Wind. If you felt a brisk steady breeze in your dream, it is a good omen for all your current concerns; but if it came in intermittent gusts, it portends some periods of frustration and delay to be overcome. A gentle wind predicts approaching good news; a stormy gale forecasts hard work ahead; and to dream of being buffeted by a strong wind indicates that you will have to fight some tough and probably tricky competition to get what you want.

Windmill. Contentment and modest financial security are predicted in a dream featuring a windmill, unless it was damaged, in which case it is a symbol of wasted energy and suggests that you should re-

assess the direction of your efforts.

Window. The meaning varies according to the type of window and the details of the dream action, but as a general guide: broken windows forecast a change of residence; bay windows predict an increase in social activity; dormer windows are a sign of improving conditions; to open (or raise) a window indicates easy success; and to close one suggests a lucky escape from a present danger. To dream of jumping or climbing out a window predicts that whatever your troubles are you will find an unexpected way to overcome them, and to climb in a window indicates a new opportunity will soon come your way. See also *Glass*.

Windpipe. A dream of having something stuck in your windpipe is a warning to economize and guard your credit.

Wine. Health, happiness, and prosperity are predicted in a dream featuring wine, unless it was being drunk from the bottle, in which case it is a warning that you should take extra precautions to avoid revealing a secret—or having one revealed.

Wing(s). Here again the meaning depends greatly on the action and what kind of wings they were, so only the most common form of the dream can be given. To dream you have wings yourself suggests that your destiny lies ever upward; a broken wing on a bird (or an airplane) suggests that your goal may be beyond your reach and you should consider changing your aim; however, if a bird was involved, the variety should be correlated for an accurate interpretation. To hear the soft rustle of wings indicates happy news from friends, but the sound of strongly flapping wings is a warning against gambling of any kind.

Wink. If your dream featured winking, it is telling you to be more discreet in your love life unless you don't care about your reputation.

Winter. To dream of winter when it isn't is a promise of financial improvement.

Wishbone. An unexpected gift, possibly a legacy, is forecast in a dream featuring a wishbone; it also signifies a fortuitous time for

taking a risk (or a gamble), but stay well within reasonable limits.

Wishing Well. Help from influential friends is the message in a dream concerning a wishing well.

Wistaria. Happiness in love and/or domestic affairs will surely be yours if you dreamed of this lovely and interesting climber. See also *Trees, Colors,* and *Flowers.*

Witch. These haggy characters in your dream indicate gay social times ahead, but if you're involved in a love affair, they are a symbol of disenchantment.

Wizard. Hidden forces are working for you if your dream featured one of these "abracadabra" types.

Wolf. This animal is, as expected, a symbol of hard times or financial embarrassment, so pull in your belt, unless you managed, in your dream, to kill it or drive it away, in which case it predicts success in spite of all obstacles.

Women. The very ancient oracles believed that groups of women in dreams were a symbol of treachery and deceit, however the more modern ones are more in line with Women's Lib and interpret such groups as a sign of increasing prosperity, and if you observed a pregnant one (or more) in your dream, you are likely to have an embarrassment of riches.

Wood. See under individual listing, as *Oak, Mahogany,* etc., or *Forest, Trees, Timber, Lumber,* etc.

Woodpecker. To hear or see him at work forecasts family squabbles due to immoderate attitudes or behavior, so guard your tongue and watch your step; admittedly it's an uncomfortable position to maintain but try it for the time being.

Wool. See *Cloth, Thread, Yarn,* or *Sheep.*

Workman. Domestic happiness and contentment are the augury in a dream featuring a workman or a work crew.

World. Journeys long, short, and medium are predicted in a dream of the world, as such; a dream concerning the end of the world is an omen of contrary and signifies new beginnings.

Worms. To use them as bait predicts a sudden material gain; otherwise, they signify news of an illness, unless you killed them, in which case the dream is a forecast of successful efforts.

Wrap. To wrap a package carefully predicts the satisfactory conclusion of a job or project undertaken some time ago. However, the contents of the package, if known, would shed more light on the interpretation.

Wreath. See *Flowers* or *Leaf* (or *Leaves*).

Wreck. See *Crash, Accident, Car,* etc.

Wren. These little birds in your dream are considered harbingers of pleasant news. See also *Birds* and *Cage.*

Wrestle. A dream of wrestlers in action signifies a stroke of luck, but to dream of engaging in the action yourself is a reverse sign and constitutes a warning against gambling or risky ventures.

Wrinkles. Facial or skin wrinkles are an odd omen of contrast and signify a gratifying increase in social popularity. Otherwise, see *Clothes*.

Writing. If you dreamed of reading handwriting, it is a warning of deception within the circle of those you trust; if you were doing the writing, the dream is telling you that you are creating problems for yourself through impulsive behavior; think before you act. If your dream featured others writing, it suggests that you can be your own best friend by not letting others influence your judgment; don't be tempted to act contrary to your principles.

X Rays. An omen of contrary signifying good health and release from worry. If your dream featured looking at your own X-ray films, you can expect to have to answer for some past indiscretion.

Xylophone. See *Music* and *Musical Instruments*.

Yacht. A yacht in your dream is a symbol of financial improvement, and if you were being entertained on it, you are sure to realize your highest hopes. To dream of being on a yacht in a choppy sea predicts a sudden stroke of money luck.

Yam(s). These sweet potatoes in your dream are a health warning; watch your diet and have a medical checkup.

Yard. See *Lawn* or *Garden*.

Yardstick. A dream featuring a yardstick portends a challenge to your reputation, unless it was broken, in which case it predicts a season of general good luck.

Yarn. To dream of winding yarn into a ball predicts new friends; otherwise, it is a symbol of domestic happiness and/or romance, but the interpretation will be modified by the color and the details of the dream action which must be correlated. See also *Knit, Embroidery*, etc.

Yawl. See *Sail(ing)*.

Yawn. Whether you did the yawning or observed others doing it, the dream suggests that your tendency to negative thinking is holding you back; try to kick the habit by living a positive day at a time.

Yeast. Wealth from an unexpected source is the message contained in a dream featuring yeast in any form.

Yell. See *Screams*.

Yellow. See *Colors*.

Yodel. It is considered a generally lucky omen to yodel or to hear yodeling in your dream; you can expect all your affairs to flourish, particularly those of the heart.

Yoke. A yoke of oxen in your dream forecasts a change of location, but to wear a yoke of any kind suggests that you are allowing yourself to be dominated by others; try asserting yourself more—it's good for the soul as well as the personality.

Yolk. See *Eggs*.

Yucca. All the spiritual as well as material comforts of life are promised in a dream featuring this lovely desert plant in bloom.

Zebra. If you dreamed of a herd of these striped animals, they are warning you that your efforts are being expended in the wrong direction; however, if your dream featured a tame one, it predicts gain from an unexpected source. See also *Animals*.

Zephyr. The feel of this mild warm breeze in your dream suggests that you are in danger of letting your heart overrule your head in regard to business or financial affairs; it would be in your own best interests to remove the rose-colored spectacles if you can.

Zero. Naughts in your dream are an omen of wasted energy; reassess your situation with an eye to altering your objectives.

Zinc. Solid achievement in all spheres of activity is forecast in a dream featuring zinc.

Zipper. Social chagrin is the message if you dreamed of a stuck or broken zipper, but if it fastened easily, the dream predicts satisfaction in minor matters now pending.

Zircon. This stone in your dream suggests that you have misplaced your confidence and/or affections. Reexamine your close relationships and keep your private affairs to yourself for the time being.

Zither. Peace of mind and

happy social times with good friends are predicted in a dream of zither music. See also *Music* and *Musical Instruments*.

Zodiac. You are likely to have fame as well as financial success if you dreamed of seeing or studying the Zodiac.

Zoo. You'll be seeing new faces in far-off places if you dreamed of being at the zoo, and if you took a child (or children) along, your travels will be profitable as well as pleasurable. See also *Animals*.

Zucchini. See *Vegetable(s)*.